Yale Historical Publications, Miscellany, 119

Jewish Activism in Imperial Germany

The Struggle for Civil Equality

Marjorie Lamberti

New Haven and London, Yale University Press, 1978

Published under the direction of the Department
of History of Yale University with assistance from
the income of the Frederick John Kingsbury
Memorial Fund.

Designed by John O. C. McCrillis and set in
Press Roman type.
Printed in the United States of America by
The Alpine Press Inc., South Braintree, Mass.

Published in Great Britain, Europe, Africa, and
Asia (except Japan) by Yale University Press,
Ltd., London. Distributed in Latin America by
Kaiman & Polon, Inc., New York City; in Australia
and New Zealand by Book & Film Services,
Artarmon, N.S.W., Australia; and in Japan by
Harper & Row, Publishers, Tokyo Office.

Library of Congress Cataloging in Publication Data

Lamberti, Marjorie, 1937–
    Jewish activism in Imperial Germany.

    Bibliography: p.
    Includes index.
    1. Jews in Germany--Politics and government.
2. Centralverein Deutscher Staatsbürger Jüdischen
Glaubens. 3. Germany--Politics and government--
1888–1918. I. Title.
DS135.G33L25   301.45'19'24043   77-17325
ISBN 0-300-02163-1

For
my father and mother

CONTENTS

PREFACE

This book is about the politics of the Jews in Wilhelminian Germany. It relates the struggle of courageous men against injustice in a society whose sense of justice was warped by bigotry, *völkisch* nationalism, and the discrimination practiced by the government authorities in violation of the law. The activist lawyers who organized German Jewry's first defense association and political lobby waged a lonely and uphill fight for civil equality. They found allies among liberals in the Progressive parties but otherwise little active support. Many Germans looked suspiciously at the arrival of Jewish interest groups on the political scene and questioned the national loyalty of Jews who spoke out for the interests of the Jewish community. In their own lifetime the Jewish activists won no public acclaim. Neither were their achievements recognized in the historical inquiries and debates that occurred after the Nazi maelstrom. What they had accomplished was overshadowed by the catastrophe that befell the Jews.

Viewed from the hindsight of the Third Reich, the Jewish defense against anti-Semitism in Imperial Germany was easily reduced to a story of ineffectual small deeds and failures. The leaders of the movement were reproached for being politically obtuse and accommodative. Critics called their strategy utterly wrong. They did not grasp how precarious the Jewish situation was. Lacking insight into the nature of anti-Semitism in German society, they trusted in the triumph of enlightenment and liberalism and so deceived themselves. Assimilationism kept them from seeing that the relationship of the Jews to the Germans was an unreciprocated love affair and blinded them to the hypocrisy of liberals who gave hesitatingly only lukewarm support to the Jewish cause. Whenever they ventured into politics, they were overcautious and inhibited by the fear of an anti-Semitic backlash. Insecurity over their acceptance into German society made them politically timid and fearful of the disapproval by the Christian majority of whatever the Jews might do in public life. Because of their submissive respect for the state authorities, they were never militant. Their "passive" defense relied mainly on counterpropraganda and the legal prosecution of defamation.

Before I began my historical inquiry, I scarcely thought that I would be writing about the politics of Jewish activists in Imperial Germany. I did not expect to find the qualities of courage, self-confidence, sound political judgment, and political militancy in the leaders of the Jewish defense. Neither did I appreciate the extent to which liberal politicians in the Progressive parties collaborated with Jewish politicians and lobbyists and defended the rights of Jewish citizens in parliament. In the past it has been difficult for scholars to study the relations of Germans and Jews before 1914 without thinking of the Third Reich and to write about the Jewish reaction to anti-Semitism without perceiving the configurations of Jewish behavior under the extremity of the Final Solution. Today the student exploring the subject of Jews in German politics brings along conceptualizations that may impede empirical research if they are accepted without question. After examining the sources, my vision of the topic changed as the evidence I found indicated that some conceptualizations applied earlier to the history of the German Jews were misleading. Also, I widened the scope of my research. The behavior of the men who led the Jewish defense from 1893 to 1914 should not be studied in isolation from German party politics as scholars have done in the past. The logic of their political decisions can be grasped completely only in the light of what was happening in German party politics, especially in Progressive party circles and in Berlin.

My research revealed that the history of the Jews of Wilhelminian Germany was more than the story of anti-Semitism and the patient endurance of injustice. From the 1898 Reichstag election on, Jewish activists participated in German politics. Through their work German Jewry became a highly self-conscious and articulate pressure group. Behind the restrained language and legal arguments in which the activist lawyers couched their demands was a bold challenge to the state authorities. They departed from the ghetto tradition of cooperating with the government in a calculated policy of gaining some amelioration and protection. No longer did they refrain from protesting the arbitrary actions of the bureaucracy or discrimination in the army and the civil service out of prudential considerations. They demanded civil equality as a right, not as a special concession granted by the state, and they grounded their arguments upon constitutional principles and the obligation of government officials to comply with the law. They were politically astute in identifying Jewish interests independently of government policies and party platforms and cultivated contacts in parliament to uphold these interests. Far from being politically naive, they devised tactics with a tough-minded assessment of the options that the Jews had in German politics. Their decisions showed a high capacity for making sound political judgments. The perserverance with which these middle-class lawyers combated discrimination rather than use baptism as "a ticket of admission" into German society attested to their moral firmness and their determination to achieve full equality without relinquishing their loyalty to the Jewish community and their distinctiveness as Jews.

Many people and institutions assisted me in writing this book. With a fellowship from the National Endowment for the Humanities in 1968–1969, I went to Jerusalem to begin research at the archives there. The warm and generous help that I received from so many people made my stay in Jerusalem more fruitful than I had anticipated. I remember especially the kindness of Mrs. Rahel Blumenthal at the Central Archives for the History of the Jewish People, Mr. Israel Philipp at the Central Zionist Archives, and Dr. Jacob Toury of Tel-Aviv University. Summer research grants from Middlebury College enabled me to continue working in Germany and New York City. For prompt and courteous attention to my inquiries, I thank the archivists at the Bundesarchiv in Koblenz, the Geheimes Staatsarchiv in Berlin-Dahlem, the Hessisches Hauptstaatsarchiv in Wiesbaden, the Hessisches Staatsarchiv in Marburg, and the Niedersächsisches Staatsarchiv in Wolfenbüttel. I am grateful also to the Deutsches Zentralarchiv in Merseburg for making available to me files of the Prussian Ministry of Education and Religious Affairs. The librarians of the Leo Baeck Institute in New York City, the Jewish Reading Room of the New York Public Library, and the Wiener Library in London were always cooperative. I have many happy memories of studying at the Leo Baeck Institute because of the exceptional kindness of Mr. Helmut Galliner. My interest in the subject of this book was stimulated years ago in a seminar on German history taught by Professor Klemens von Klemperer of Smith College. I express my thanks to him for his encouragement over the years.

The greatest debt I owe is to Professor Werner Angress of the State University of New York, Stony Brook. He read the draft manuscript and made valuable suggestions for improvements. One of the pleasures of writing this book was finding a sincere friend in him.

1

THE LEADERSHIP ESTABLISHMENT
OF THE JEWISH COMMUNITIES

Representing the Jews in public life in Imperial Germany were two leadership elites, the first connected with the administration of the synagogue congregations and the second emerging from Jewish activist organizations and interest groups. The two groups of leaders were alike in social background, but their historical origins set them apart as different types. At the head of the communities stood the traditional and legally authorized leaders. Their offices had been constituted by edicts that the German states had issued in the first half of the nineteenth century. A second elite appeared in the 1890s, when the German Jews started to form pressure groups. The lawyers who organized the Centralverein deutscher Staatsbürger jüdischen Glaubens (Central Association of German Citizens of the Jewish Faith) and the Verband der deutschen Juden (Federation of German Jews) were a new breed of Jewish public spokesmen—political activists and lobbyists. The appearance of activist lawyers in the Jewish community filled a leadership vacuum left open by the community notables, who were loath to adopt political tactics to protect Jewish rights and interests.

The legislation that regulated Jewish life in the German states promoted the development of a corps of lay officials. In Prussia the Law of July 23, 1847, required Jewish inhabitants to belong to and support through taxes the synagogue congregation of their locality and granted to each one autonomy in the administration of its affairs.[1] The law provided for two governing bodies, an executive board ranging from three to seven members, and a council of representatives whose number could vary from nine to twenty-one. The representatives were elected for a six-year term by male members who were not in arrears in tax payments. Elections were held every three years, when half the council seats became vacant. The council alone elected the executive board. This directorate appointed the rabbis and cantors, made provisions for religious observances, set the budget, and administered funds for charitable institutions and the religious instruction of the youth. The executive board acted as the delegated spokesman for the community in public life. The law empowered it to present proposals and petitions to the appropriate state authorities and to represent the community in legal matters.

The Jewish dignitaries were not accorded the status or privileges of full-fledged public officials, but they did enjoy a certain public standing and recognition insofar as their election to the executive board required government confirmation and their duties were fixed by state law. Enhancing their authority was the absence of any clerical hierarchy. The Law of July 23, 1847, assigned to the rabbi no seat or voice in the organs of administration. The rabbi was subject to the supervision and discipline of the executive board.

In the other German states, community administration resembled conditions in Prussia. Government edicts established for every congregation an executive committee and a council of representatives. Elected lay officials directed internal affairs and represented the local Jewish population in matters requiring government action. In some states, standing above the communities were supervisory councils, the *Oberrat der Israeliten* in Baden and the *Vorsteherämter der Israeliten* in the Electorate of Hesse.

The men selected for the executive boards were socially prominent and well-to-do—merchants and bankers, sometimes lawyers and physicians. The preponderance of affluent men resulted from legal arrangements as well as social values. State laws did not permit the congregations to employ salaried administrators. Membership on the executive board was an honorary office to be held without compensation. The statutes of the communities were designed to keep affairs in the hands of the wealthy members. The Cologne community, for example, had a three-class franchise in which votes were weighted according to tax payments.[2] Communities in Bavaria distinguished members who were eligible to hold offices from those who possessed only the right to vote on the basis of tax payments, age, and length of residence.[3]

The community officials carried out their duties in the spirit of noblesse oblige. They did not see themselves as popular leaders and gave little publicity to their meetings and decisions. The deliberations of the executive board and council in Cologne, Hamburg, and elsewhere were closed to the public. When the notables in Hamburg introduced reforms in 1905, a limited number from the congregation were allowed to attend sessions of the council if they procured tickets in advance.[4] Officials in the Berlin, Breslau, Cologne, and Königsberg communities opened the council meetings to the public in the years after 1900 under the pressure of attacks on their elitism and deliberations behind closed doors.[5] Otherwise the community leaders made no accommodations to democratic ideas; they continued to be socially exclusive and to conduct affairs in a guarded and bureaucratic manner.[6]

The Jewish dignitaries, anxious to see the Jewish population integrate into German society and be accepted by the Christian majority, were disposed to repress Jewish distinctiveness rather than to strengthen Jewish consciousness. They donated generously for the care of orphans and the poor, but they were less interested in institutions promoting Jewish scholarship and culture.[7] In Berlin, community officials did not select Hebrew names for the synagogues. The city's seven synagogues were designated by street names. Some notables advocated services on Sunday morning because Sunday rather than Saturday was the day of rest and worship in Germany.

In political life the community officials did not provide German Jewry with effective leadership. In 1869 a number of communities recognized the need for an association uniting and representing Jews throughout Germany and formed the Deutsch-Israelitischer Gemeindebund (Federation of Jewish Communities in Germany).[8] Emil Lehmann, a Dresden lawyer who spearheaded this movement, intended the Gemeindebund to act as the authorized spokesman for the Jews in matters affecting their public status and rights as well as their religious interests. Most community leaders did not share Lehmann's vision and did not want the Gemeindebund to work conspicuously in public life. By the end of the 1870s social welfare and religious education became its primary concerns. A policy of abstaining from politics followed from the adoption of bylaws that prohibited any discussion of political issues at meetings. Community officials were counseled to prevent outbursts of grievances or indiscreet declarations by "self-appointed" Jewish spokesmen in the

press or at public assemblies.[9] The initial plan to combat anti-Semitism
through legal prosecution was abandoned. The notables and Lehmann
himself came to believe that it was futile to importune negligent or
bigoted state attorneys to prosecute anti-Semites for defamation and
that private lawsuits stirred up harmful publicity.[10]

By temperament and outlook, the men sitting on the executive
boards were not disposed to political activism. Their deep respect for
the authority of the state bred a passive loyalty to the government
and a disinclination to become politically engaged.[11] Uncommon was
Siegmund Meyer, the chairman of the Berlin community board, who
was active in Progressive party politics and was elected to the city
council in the 1890s.[12]

Knowing the suspicion with which so many Germans eyed the
Jews, community officials tended to be oversensitive to the reactions
of the Christian majority and reluctant to discuss Jewish grievances
in public. Because of these inhibitions, many communities decided
not to affiliate with the Gemeindebund in the 1870s and later gave
a cool reception to the activist Jewish organizations. They expressed
misgivings about the political activities of the Centralverein and the
Verband der deutschen Juden. The Hamburg community, for example, rejected the request of the two associations to hold a rally to
protest discrimination in the army in October 1910.[13] When the
Verband selected Hamburg as the location for its biennial congress
in 1913, notables in the congregation worried about the effects of
this event on the fragile relations of the Jews and the Christian population in the city. Max Warburg wanted the Verband to keep off the
agenda issues that might arouse contempt for the Jews among the
gentiles.[14]

Officials of Orthodox congregations did not promote the participation of the Jews in politics for other reasons. The leaders of Orthodox
Jewry were troubled less about discrimination than about the
absorption of the Jews in their Christian surroundings. Their appre-
hension was that the Jews would surrender the traditions of their
faith for the sake of equal rights and social integration.[15] They were
uninterested in matters of civil equality so long as the Jewish confession was left free to preserve traditional religious practices and to
maintain the institutions necessary for group solidarity.

The fragmentation of the Jews into hundreds of solitary communities also militated against collective action in politics. In the German Empire the Jewish communities were not united under a central lay authority like the Central Consistory of the Jews in France. The territories incorporated into Prussia in 1866 and the other states retained their separate laws regulating the communities. These edicts dating back to the first half of the nineteenth century did not provide a central council or synod, which would act for the Jews as a corporate body. Only in Baden, where the *Oberrat der Israeliten* was established in 1809, were the Jews recognized as a corporate community. The Prussian Law of July 23, 1847, kept the Jewish population fragmented and obstructed the creation of a unitary framework by making each congregation a separate entity and allowing it to establish independently its own religious institutions and practices.

Community leaders in Baden, Bavaria, and Württemberg declined to join the Gemeindebund and were suspicious of all attempts to create a central organization representing German Jewry.[16] They resented the influence that the large Berlin community exercised in Jewish philanthropic and cultural affairs.[17] Guarding their autonomy, communities in the Southern states preferred to deal with problems on a regional rather than a national level. They justified this particularism by asserting that in Prussia Jewish grievances were acute whereas in the Southern states the governing authorities and the people were tolerant.

Much more than assimilationism and timidity led the community leaders to maintain a low profile in political life. The disappointing experience of seeing public prosecutors and judges refuse to extend to the Jewish confession full protection of the law left them feeling that any recourse to legal justice would be futile.[18] Oversensitivity to gentile reactions and the fear of providing a provocation or excuse for anti-Semitic agitation inhibited them from resorting to political tactics to defend Jewish interests.

Before Jewish political activism could develop, the attitudes that made the old leadership establishment overcautious in public life had to change. New values had to emerge to give the leaders of German Jewry the pluck to risk an anti-Semitic backlash and a way of overcoming resignation and appraising their achievement when the fight against discrimination brought no quick victories. A new type of Jewish leader had to appear, self-confident and aggressive, intent on taking the Jewish cause into the battleground of politics and mobilizing the masses of Jews for collective political action.

2

THE BREAKTHROUGH TO POLITICAL ACTIVISM

In the 1890s dissatisfaction with the timidity of the community officials arose. A debate on whether Jewish spokesmen should protest specifically Jewish grievances in parliamentary organs was touched off by Siegmund Meyer. In the Berlin City Council on May 1, 1890, Meyer criticized a high school principal who had written to Jewish parents that their daughter could not enter the school unless she was baptized. Some Berlin Jews were upset with Meyer for bringing up Jewish matters in the city council.[1]

A Jewish newspaper, published weekly in Berlin, rallied to Meyer's defense. The *Allgemeine Zeitung des Judentums* expressed the hope that Meyer's speech would set a trend and that Jewish deputies and city councilmen would discard their habit of timorously waiting for Christian party comrades to rebut anti-Semitic remarks.[2] It contended that the delicacy of feeling with which the Jews behaved in legislative bodies did not serve legitimate Jewish interests and was not usually displayed by deputies of the Christian faith. Just as the Junkers and other economic groups did not hesitate to promote their special interests in parliament, so a Jewish politician was obliged to speak out whenever the rights of Jewish citizens were violated.

This controversy was renewed two years later, in the aftermath of a sensational ritual murder trial. In October 1891 Adolf Buschhoff, the ritual slaughterer of the Xanten community in Westphalia, was arrested along with his wife and daughter on the suspicion of murdering a five-year old Christian boy. They were released when evidence to convict them could not be found. An anti-Semitic campaign accusing Buschhoff of ritual murder led to his arrest again in December and his trial in July 1892. Although the court found him innocent, the case left the Jews feeling despondent.[3] They were shocked to discover that medieval superstitions could find credence in

7

modern times, and they were embittered because decent Germans did so little to eradicate fanatical anti-Semitism.

A summons to action came from Dr. Adolf Jellinek, a preacher in the Vienna community, who urged the officials of the large German congregations to take steps to prevent the recurrence of blood-libel trials. Jellinek proposed in August 1892 that the Berlin community ask the German government to issue a declaration rejecting the myth of ritual murder and threatening to prosecute persons who disseminated such propaganda.[4] Shortly thereafter, two members of the Berlin community's executive board drafted a petition imploring Emperor William for protection against anti-Semitism. The petition also contained gratuitous remarks repudiating disreputable elements in the Jewish population and admitting the need for the Jews to improve their character. News of the petition leaked to the press, and an unexpected outcry arose. The executive board voted against sending the address to the emperor, and the two men who drafted it resigned.[5]

Berlin Jews regarded the petition as undignified. Bernhard Breslauer, a lawyer, objected to the implication that the Jewish community was accountable for the wrongdoings of individuals.[6] Isidor Kastan, a journalist, criticized the supplication for protection. Pointing to the examples of the Pius Verein and the Gustav Adolf Verein, which watched over Catholic and Protestant interests, Kastan argued that the Jews should not let aspersions about their national loyalty inhibit them from upholding their own interests.[7]

Less restrained were the attacks on the Berlin executive board in two pamphlets, which caused a sensation and ran through several editions. The anonymous author of *Volks- oder Salonjudentum* (*Popular or Salon Judaism*) rebuked the notables for not defending the Jewish religion courageously and for having unconsciously accepted the disparaging evaluation of Jewish character that unfriendly gentiles made.[8] Raphael Löwenfeld, a theater director who published anonymously *Schutzjudentum oder Staatsbürger? (Protected Jews or Citizens?),* charged that the community leaders reacted like ghetto Jews and failed to see the distinction between the rights of citizenship and the bestowal of special favors. The Jews degraded themselves when they implored the state for protection instead of demanding their rights as citizens.[9]

Out of the commotion over the petition to the emperor came a condemnation of the timorous behavior of the community officials and the conviction that self-esteem required the Jews to defend themselves. There was less certainty and agreement about what methods they should employ to combat defamation and discrimination.

In January 1893 a committee of prominent Jews sent an appeal to community leaders for money to support defense activities.[10] The committee included men with many years of experience in politics. Paul Nathan sat on the central committee of the Progressive Union and wrote regularly for *Die Nation*, the party's weekly magazine. Edmund Friedemann and Siegmund Neumann were Progressive city councilmen in Berlin. Nonetheless, their plans were vague and not marked by any ambition to organize a Jewish political movement. Nathan took the initiative in forming the committee after consulting Progressive leaders and had given them assurances that the committee had no further political aims than the distribution of propaganda opposing anti-Semitic candidates during election campaigns.[11]

Nathan's committee was quickly overtaken by a more ambitious movement. Led by Löwenfeld, about 200 Jews assembled in Berlin on February 5, 1893, to make plans for an organization that would defend the Jews through public action as well as propaganda. Again on March 26 they convened and founded the Centralverein.[12]

At the second meeting there was a clash of opinion over whether the Jews should act as a collective group in political life. One participant proposed that the Jews form a political bloc and strive to elect Jewish deputies.[13] The discussion was not reported in the press, but it is likely that the proposal was offered by someone who had read *Volks- oder Salonjudentum*. Arguing in favor of an association that would represent Jewish interests, the pamphlet stated that reliance on the Progressives had made the Jews timid and shortsighted. The Progressives whom the Jews were "accustomed to regard as [their] indispensable and chosen defenders" were losing electoral support and the power in parliament to influence government policy.[14] They fought anti-Semitism halfheartedly and did not match the zealous anti-Semites in daring and firmness of purpose.

Most Jewish notables thought that the formation of a separate political bloc would be a grave mistake.[15] Kastan expressed their misgivings when he warned that the Jewish cause would lose moral sympathy in Germany once an exclusively Jewish interest group appeared. Combating anti-Semitism, he said, was not a question of Jewish interests but of the constitutional rights and interests of the whole nation. The Jews needed no special advocates because deputies who were devoted to the principles of justice and the rule of law would naturally represent Jewish interests.[16]

During the formation of the Centralverein, rumors spread about a Jewish party. The speculation troubled the Jews all the more because the campaign for the Reichstag election was starting. The founders of the Centralverein felt compelled to refute the "myth of a Jewish Centrum" and to disavow any ambition to imitate the Catholics by creating a separate Jewish party.[17] At the outset the Jewish defense movement had to quiet suspicions that it harbored aspirations to wield political power.

The Centralverein's first chairman, Dr. Martin Mendelsohn, and other early leaders deliberately defined aims that were modest. In speeches and in a monthly publication named *Im Deutschen Reich*, they gave assurances that the organization was not political and did not intend to campaign for any party during elections. The program, which was adopted on September 27, 1893, specifically stated that Jews as a group belonged to no single party and that questions of what stand to take on political issues were matters left up to each Jew to decide.[18] The program and the address that Mendelsohn delivered at the first general assembly in Berlin in 1894 laid down a policy of nonpartisanship. Mendelsohn said that the Centralverein represented no party ideology and maintained a neutral position toward all parties.[19]

Other reasons too led the founders of the Centralverein to adopt a policy of political neutrality. It enabled the fledgling movement to recruit a membership cutting across party lines. It coincided with their aim of keeping Jewish grievances out of party politics. They believed that it would "be beneficial for both sides, the Jews as well as the Progressives, to separate the so-called Jewish question from all that is partisan."[20] They were intent on proving that anti-Semitism was not a specifically Jewish problem but a threat to all Germans.

This strategy was mapped out in a speech that Curt Pariser, a member of the executive board, gave at a meeting in 1895. Pariser called anti-Semitic demagoguery a radical assault on property and political order and noted how anti-Semitic populists such as Hermann Ahlwardt and Otto Böckel preached class conflict, conducted anti-Junker agitation, and slandered Chancellor Caprivi.[21] He sought to demonstrate that the state authorities and all law-abiding Germans had as much a stake in the Jewish defense as the Jews themselves.

The Centralverein's early leaders also disarmed critics by dissociating the movement from pressure groups such as the Agrarian League, which bartered votes for economic advantages.[22] They made repeated assurances that the organization would never be guided by selfish interests and opportunistic considerations and did not intend to give particular Jewish interests priority over the welfare of the entire nation.

Hesitant and uncertain, the founders of the Centralverein touched on the question of collective action in defense of Jewish rights. They knew the misgivings that many Jews felt concerning a Jewish interest group. Widespread were fears that such an organization would differentiate the Jewish minority from the rest of the nation and would cause other Germans to doubt the loyalty of the Jews to the fatherland. Spokesmen for the Centralverein stated over and over that the association would not result in the separation or social ghettoization of the Jews and that defending Jewish interests did not conflict with a citizen's duty to promote national interests.[23]

During the 1890s it was not certain that the Centralverein would develop into an activist organization. Jewish notables, especially active members of the Progressive People's party and the Progressive Union, disapproved of a Jewish political movement. Jewish Progressives were deeply concerned about the possibility that the Centralverein's rallying cry, Jewish self-defense, might lead to political separation and to "attempts to form a Jewish Centrum."[24] Prominent Jewish Progressives such as Ludwig Bamberger, Charles Hallgarten, and Paul Nathan did not help to build up the Centralverein. They preferred to see an interconfessional rather than an exclusively Jewish organization combat anti-Semitism and supported the Verein zur Abwehr des Antisemitismus (Association for Defense against Anti-Semitism), which Rudolf von Gneist, Heinrich Rickert, and other gentile Progressives had founded in January 1891. These

Christian liberals were disturbed by the campaigning of the anti-Semitic parties in the Reichstag elections of 1890 and thought that the time had come for all citizens to speak out in protest against this agitation, which was poisoning public life and bringing shame to the Germans as a nation of lofty culture. Despite their good intentions, the founders of the Abwehrverein eschewed activist tactics. They relied on the distribution of a weekly newspaper and the occasional publication of pamphlets to wage what amounted to little more than a literary campaign against anti-Semitism.

Expressing the views of Jewish Progressives, Emanuel Baumgarten wrote in the *Allgemeine Zeitung des Judentums* that Jews who thought that they could achieve equal rights by resorting to political tactics were deceiving themselves.[25] A Jewish pressure group could never defend the constitutional rights of the Jews as effectively as Christians in influential positions. To attain civil equality, the Jews should collaborate with the Abwehrverein and work for the election of gentiles who sincerely professed liberal convictions. He counseled against the nomination of Jewish candidates.

On the board of directors there was no consensus as to what role the Centralverein should play in public life. In the early years the directors adopted a policy of playing down prospects for an active part in German politics and prohibited members from discussing politics at meetings. Meanwhile, the board in closed sessions was wrestling with the question. Maximilian Horwitz, who succeeded Mendelsohn as chairman, and Eugen Fuchs, the deputy chairman, favored a popular political organization. They believed that an association of prominent Jews would not be effective against anti-Semitic mass movements and that the publication of counterpropaganda was of limited value.[26] Without belittling the work of Gabriel Riesser and his generation, they regretted that the Jewish Emancipation had "not been cemented by Jewish blood and sweat" and that civil rights "fell into the laps" of the Jews as a gift of liberalism rather than as the achievement of an active struggle.[27] Because there had been "no Jewish phalanx" to fight for Emancipation, none appeared to defend it when the anti-Semitic parties grew after 1870.

Convinced that the Centralverein could exercise influence and speak authoritatively for German Jewry if it had a large membership, Horwitz proposed to the central board on June 1, 1896, that it launch a recruitment campaign, arrange public meetings in big cities, and release news about its work to the daily press.[28] Other board members did not see any need to mobilize the masses of Jews. They did not want the Centralverein to be highly visible in public life. A majority voted against a newspaper campaign to recruit members and in favor of using the contacts of confidential agents in each city. On March 1, 1897, when Horwitz recommended the employment of a staff for recruitment work, the directors voted down the proposal.[29]

It was not until the Reichstag election of 1898 that the Centralverein entered politics. Its development into an activist organization was due primarily to the leadership of Horwitz and Fuchs. When the Centralverein was established, the governing board was headed by Dr. Martin Mendelsohn, a lecturer on the faculty of medicine at the University in Berlin. At the time Horwitz, an agnostic, took no interest in Jewish community life. Fuchs, a long-time friend, coaxed him to accept an invitation to become a member of the board. Horwitz, a successful lawyer, quickly stood out as a self-confident and strong-willed personality. In December 1894 he was elected chairman, an office that he held until his death in 1917. During these years Fuchs worked at his side as deputy chairman.

Horwitz was born in Berlin in 1855. Fuchs, a year younger, came from Silesia. The two lawyers met in 1884, when Horwitz was a *Referendar*, a junior law clerk, and Fuchs an assistant judge at a civil law court.[30] Both had experienced discrimination when their applications for officer commissions in the Prussian reserves were rejected. Prejudice blocked careers for them in the judiciary. Fed up after years of waiting for promotions, they took up private law practice in Berlin.

The Centralverein had the good fortune to find two executives whose personalities and talents were complementary. Whereas Horwitz was an efficient administrator, Fuchs was a man of vision and an inspiring public speaker. Horwitz had a sarcastic wit and an impulsive temper. At meetings there were occasions when his patience wore out too soon, and his behavior was too brusque. Fuchs, on the other hand, had a more affable manner and greater sensitivity of feeling. He stepped into many disputes as a conciliator.

Between Horwitz and Fuchs there was no rivalry or jealousy. Fuchs knew that Horwitz, despite his sharp tongue, was not arrogant. He valued his colleague's capacity to discipline his own personal feelings with a strong sense of duty, to make pragmatic decisions, and to act with judiciousness.[31]

As commanding a figure as Horwitz was, it was Fuchs who made the greater contribution to the Centralverein. A courageous man of action, Fuchs infused the legal defense movement with his own passionate yearning for a just society. He saw more clearly than other Jewish notables how the conduct of politics had changed in modern times and that the Centralverein had to be a popular and activist organization. His idealism did not make him headstrong. In making decisions he knew that considerations as to what was practical and feasible in given circumstances had to be weighed along with ideal aims. Personally modest, he was unselfishly dedicated to the struggle for Jewish rights.

For Horwitz and Fuchs, proud of their German nationality and culture, it was painful to admit the tenacity of anti-Semitism, but they did not seek comfort in self-deception or naive optimism. By the mid-1890s anti-Semitic rabble-rousing had subsided. In its place they perceived a more dangerous form of anti-Semitism moving quietly through academic circles, manipulated by the governing class in the Conservative party, and sustained by the administrative chicanery of the bureaucracy.[32] They were especially alert to the danger of academic anti-Semitism because of the great esteem that professors enjoyed in German society, and they noticed how anti-Semitism, under the cover of scholarship, was radiating from the universities and penetrating social circles that found populist anti-Semitism too crude and radical. Their experiences left them with no illusions about the objectivity of the Prussian bureaucracy. They believed that high-level officials maintained a benign neutrality toward anti-Semitic agitation and privately welcomed it as a battering ram against liberalism and socialism and as a safety valve for the eruption of discontents against capitalism and modernity. The failure of the anti-Semites to enact special laws against the Jews in the Reichstag sessions from 1893 to 1898 did not lessen the vigilance of the Central-verein's leaders. They knew that instead of defying constitutional principles blatantly, Prussian officials handling Jewish matters preferred to violate the law by devious methods of administration.

Pessimistic assessments of the prospects for eradicating anti-Semitism did not cause Horwitz or Fuchs to despair. Fuchs confessed that the Centralverein had not wiped out bigotry in the Prussian civil service and officer corps and that in many lawsuits the courts generously acquitted anti-Semites accused of defamation. However, he never doubted the value of legal defense and refused to conclude that the fight for equal rights was a lost cause.[33] He did not measure the success of the Centralverein according to the number of lawsuits it won. To Fuchs the essential achievement of the defense movement was the civic education of the Jews and the German nation.[34] The Centralverein kept before the Germans the ideal of a pluralistic society and reminded them that the exigencies of national unity did not preclude the right of any minority to retain a separate identity derived from historic and religious heritage. It cultivated civic courage among the Jews. It served notice to all Germans that any violation of the rights of Jewish citizens would be protested, and it impressed upon the Germans the harm that anti-Semitism inflicted on public morality, the respect for law, and the sense of justice in society.

Fuchs and Horwitz were convinced of the need for the Jews to take political action as a collective body. As early as February 1896 Fuchs said, "Living in an age of interest groups, the Jews have discovered how necessary it is to form an interest group of all German Jews."[35] The arrival of activist pressure groups on the political scene had not escaped the attention of Horwitz and Fuchs, because the Jews were immediately affected. In the Reichstag election of 1893 the anti-Semitic parties increased their mandates from five to sixteen. Anti-Semitic candidates were so successful because the Agrarian League gave them financial and political backing. To influence legislation affecting agriculture, the league supported candidates who made a pledge to vote on future bills in accordance with its policy. Having found powerful allies among the Conservatives and the Agrarians, the anti-Semites took their battle against the Jews to the Reichstag. They submitted, without success, proposals to prohibit the kosher slaughtering of animals and to halt the immigration of Jews from Eastern Europe. They found a Reichstag majority, on the other hand, to incorporate a statement of Christian belief in the oath that witnesses swore before testifying in court.[36]

Although the executive board squelched rumors about a "Jewish

Centrum," it was never the intention of Horwitz and Fuchs to refrain from political activity. Fuchs thought that Jews who insisted on keeping the Centralverein nonpolitical confused politics with partisanship.[37] From the start he saw the organization as a Jewish lobby. In his report to the first general assembly on April 16, 1894, he said that individual Jews were powerless to combat discrimination in the government and that the best strategy was to mobilize Jewish voters and to present their case in the Reichstag and state parliaments. If influential deputies interpellated ministers, the government would have to explain discriminatory practices in the open. He was confident that once ministers were compelled to be accountable for covert unconstitutional practices in their departments, they would take steps to redress injustices.[38]

In the following years Fuchs persisted in arguing that politics was the theater where the struggle for equal rights should be waged. After the Reichstag election of 1898 he said:

> Where else but in parliament can accountability be demanded on whether actions taken at ministerial instructions are constitutional? Whoever wishes that we reach our goal, attain the civil equality of the Jews and see the constitution carried out, shall not advise us . . . to abstain from participation in parliamentary elections and thereby to forfeit the most effective weapon that is given to the citizen for the assertion and the protection of his rights and interests. . . . If we have no fighters for our rights in the legislatures, no sounding board for our complaints, then all our efforts shall be fruitless.[39]

Divisions within the Jewish community created serious difficulties for the growth of an activist organization. In handling this problem Horwitz and Fuchs demonstrated a capacity for making levelheaded decisions. Both men realized that if the Centralverein was to be recognized as the authoritative voice of German Jewry, it had to be a movement in which Jews of different religious orientations could work together. They adopted a policy of neutrality in matters of religious observances.[40] Establishing this policy was by no means easy. Raphael Löwenfeld and Fritz Auerbach, who made appeals for self-defense in 1893, were outspoken critics of Orthodox practices and advocated a reform of religious traditions. As a result,

Orthodox believers associated the Centralverein with Jews who were nonobservant and assimilationist, and the *Israelit*, an Orthodox weekly, made unfair attacks on it.[41] A permanent breach was avoided owing to the conciliatoriness of Horwitz and Fuchs. Fuchs conceded that Löwenfeld's pamphlet had "unnecessarily" offended Orthodox Jews and advised the board of directors to ignore provocations in the Orthodox press.[42]

Horwitz and Fuchs made strenuous efforts to win the confidence of the Orthodox Jews and showed sensitivity to their religious feelings. When Rheydt, a hamlet in the Rhineland, enacted an ordinance prohibiting the slaughtering of cattle according to Jewish law, Horwitz and Fuchs, who did not observe kosher dietary rules, rose quickly to oppose this infringement of the religious freedom of the Jews and provided the congregation in Rheydt with legal counsel.[43] In the controversy over Sunday synagogue services in Berlin in 1897 and 1898, they were respectful of tradition. Prominent Jews circulated a petition requesting community officials to introduce services on Sunday so that Jews whose jobs required them to work on Saturday could attend.[44] More than 5,000 signed the petition, but Horwitz and Fuchs declined. Fuchs was a representative on the community council at the time the issue was debated on February 20, 1898. After listening sympathetically to the reasons offered for Sunday services, he voted to reject the proposal. He said that to take from the Sabbath its special sanctity would be an undignified accommodation to Christianity and would be regarded as an act of Jewish self-rejection.[45]

Ideological differences grew more troublesome after a circle of Zionists in Cologne founded the Jewish-Nationalist Association in Germany in 1897, and Theodore Herzl announced plans to hold the first congress of the international Zionist movement in Munich. German Jews were incensed about the location of the congress in Munich. Rabbi Mose Cossmann Werner of Munich instigated the Allgemeiner Rabbinerverband in Deutschland (Association of German Rabbis in Germany) to issue a public declaration repudiating the Zionist program.[46] Munich community officials worked behind the scenes to have the congress shifted to a place outside Germany.[47]

When the governing board heard about the upcoming Zionist congress, it met on May 5 and again on June 10 to discuss what policy the Centralverein should adopt. Horwitz persuaded the directors not to take any stand on Zionism until the assembly was held.[48] Horwitz and Fuchs advocated a policy of neutrality. They were anxious not to provoke any quarrels with the Zionists and to deepen divisions among the Jews.

After the congress met in Basel, the two directors sought to cool down the controversy. *Im Deutschen Reich* reported that Herzl's following was strong in Russia but not in Germany and that half the 33 German delegates at the congress came originally from Russia. It predicted that the Zionist solution to the Jewish condition was so utopian that it would not find widespread support in western Europe.[49] Fuchs also minimized the dangers of Zionism in an article on the Basel program. He enumerated the obstacles to the realization of the Zionist goals of resettling Jews in Palestine and founding a Jewish state. The mistakes of Zionism were attributed to a failure to make a distinction between citizenship and religion and to realize that the modern concepts of the state and the nation had no connection with religion. Fuchs called Zionism "an excess of religious loyalty" and expressed confidence that the German followers of Herzl would learn soon that the Jews did not have to renounce their religion to become German citizens and that Jewish pride and loyalty could be revived without undermining allegiance to the German fatherland.[50]

Fervent anti-Zionists did not accept the board's decision to sidestep the Zionist question. During the next months Horwitz and Fuchs had to withstand pressure from this camp. On September 6, 1897, the directors disputed a proposal to hold a discussion on Zionism at a meeting in October. Once again Horwitz convinced the central board that, "out of considerations of expediency," the Centralverein should not take any stand against Zionism.[51]

The moderation of Horwitz and Fuchs left opponents of Zionism disgruntled. Dr. Ludwig Fuld, a physician in Mainz, argued that it was not possible for the Centralverein to ignore Zionism, because it made the task of combating anti-Semitism difficult. Zionism provided ammunition for the anti-Semites by harping on the separate nationality of the Jews. Defiantly he said, "The German Jews do not tolerate attacks on their German nationality by anti-Semites and do not expect to be silent when the Zionists do."[52] Two other headstrong anti-Zionists, Rabbi Paul Rieger of Potsdam and Dr. Curt Pariser, disregarded the board's policy and debated with three Zionists at a meeting in Berlin on November 26, 1897. At the general assembly in December, one member was persistent in proposing that the Central-verein take a position opposing Zionism at a meeting called especially to tackle this problem. Horwitz remained resolute and told the assembly that such a meeting would give occasion only to bitter wrangling.[53] He issued a stern warning that any further attempt to draw the question of Zionism into the discussion would be stopped.

The moderation of Horwitz and Fuchs allowed them to work out a modus vivendi with the Zionists. After the Basel congress, German Zionist leaders decided to drop the description "Jewish-Nationalist" from their organization's name and to call themselves the Zionist Association. They wanted to avoid giving any impression of engaging in Jewish politics in Germany and of making Jewishness and German nationality conflicting identities.[54] They revised their program so that it would not cast doubt on the German nationality and patrio-tism of the Jews.[55] Instead of a Jewish state, the Zionists now spoke of establishing "a place of refuge for those Jews who can not or do not want to remain in the land of their birth."[56] The new program declared that the consciousness of a common history that Zionism sought to develop among the Jews did not exclude true devotion to the country in which they lived as citizens, and that German Jews had duties to fellow Germans as well as to Jewish brethren abroad. The Centralverein's executive board welcomed these changes in the Zionist program, and in the course of 1898 a precise policy was laid down. The committee decided not to publish any more criticism of Zionism as long as the German branch did not revert to its original program.[57]

A relationship of mutual respect developed between the Berlin Zionist leaders Arthur Hantke and Alfred Klee and Horwitz and Fuchs. At the public celebration of the Centralverein's tenth anniver-sary in 1903, Klee praised its defense work. He noted that the two movements had a common task, overcoming indifference among the Jews toward their religious heritage and cultivating in them commu-nity loyalty and pride.[58]

Under the dynamic leadership of Horwitz and Fuchs, the Central-verein became the largest Jewish organization in Germany. Its membership grew from 1,420 by the end of the first year to 12,000 individual members and 100 affiliated communities ten years later. By 1916 it claimed to represent 200,000 German Jews.[59] A drive to recruit students at the universities was started in 1901. Horwitz and Fuchs recognized the need to train young activists to succeed the older generation now in the front lines.

In the formative years the Centralverein's strength lay in Berlin and the Prussian state. In April 1898 Horwitz persuaded the board of directors to extend the organization in Southern and Western Germany.[60] Horwitz and Fuchs engaged in negotiations with spokesmen for Jews in Baden and Bavaria in 1900. The talks led to a deadlock.[61] The Jews living there reacted warily to the Berlin-based organization. They believed that the liberal milieu in Baden and Bavaria provided more favorable conditions for the Jews than Prussia and were afraid that propagandists from Berlin would disturb the harmonious relations that they enjoyed with the Christian population.[62]

Determined to make the Centralverein representative of Jews throughout the empire, Horwitz and Fuchs reopened the negotiations and made accommodations to particularistic instincts. At a meeting in Munich on December 3, 1904, Horwitz promised Bavarian leaders that the Berlin headquarters would undertake nothing affecting Bavarian affairs without consulting them.[63] The geographical representation on the central board was broadened, and seats were offered to persons living in Essen, Hamburg, Munich, Stuttgart, and elsewhere.

The Berlin office facilitated expansion also by announcing in 1906 a policy to establish local chapters wherever the membership reached 75. The executive board conceded to the demands of the Hamburg chapter to summon an assembly of delegates, which convened for the first time in 1907 and to which yearly thereafter the chapters sent representatives. A *Landesverband*, or state association, was established for Bavaria in 1905 and for Württemberg in 1906. A regional committee was formed for the Rhine Province and Westphalia in 1905. Negotiations with the Jews in Baden dragged on until 1908, when a state association was founded.

The Centralverein expanded rapidly because Horwitz and Fuchs found in Breslau, Essen, Frankfurt, Mainz, Posen, Stettin, and other cities reliable and dedicated local representatives. These men devoted many hours away from their occupations and homes to promote the Jewish struggle for equal rights. They recruited members, collected dues and contributions for campaign funds, arranged meetings, and corresponded with the Berlin bureau about Jewish matters in their locality.

Among the local agents, lawyers were especially prominent. Rudolf Geiger and Max Mainzer, two lawyers, organized the chapter in Frankfurt and traveled to nearby towns to deliver speeches publicizing the work of the Centralverein. Two other lawyers in Essen, Max Abel and Ernst Herzfeld, were energetic recruiters in the Rhineland. Ludwig Holländer, an attorney in Munich, worked with courage and perseverance to organize meetings in Bavaria and to persuade hesitant community officials to affiliate with the defense movement.

That so many lawyers were drawn into the Centralverein's leadership proved to be a great advantage. The association benefited from their legal training, skill in public speaking, and high social standing in the communities where they lived. Above all, the lawyers were more inclined to an activist fight for civil equality than Jews in business or manufacturing. Discriminatory practices made Jewish attorneys an especially frustrated and aggrieved group. The Ministry of Justice in Prussia did not appoint Jews as public prosecutors or justices to the courts of appeal. Jewish law clerks waited seven to ten years for promotions whereas gentiles were advanced after a probationary period of four to five years.[64] In the state of Hesse the Ministry of Justice had not appointed any Jew to the judiciary for over fifty years on the grounds that people would have no confidence in a Jewish judge. Although in Bavaria the Ministry of Justice did not openly practice discrimination, Jewish lawyers here ceased to feel secure and confident after Center party deputies in the state parliament in 1901 proposed that the appointment of Jewish judicial officials should be limited to the percentage of Jews in the state's population. The minister opposed a quota policy because it violated the constitution, but the remarks he made hinted that fewer Jewish lawyers could expect offices.[65] Pressure to establish a quota system continued to come from the Center party.

Jewish physicians were not so numerous as lawyers in the Centralverein's front line, but many accepted election to the executive committees of the local chapters. After 1890 Jewish doctors found more often than in earlier years that public and private hospitals announcing positions in medical journals requested applicants to submit a baptismal record.[66] Dr. Edmund Werner, who headed the chapter in the eastern section of Berlin, complained that three-fourths of the advertisements in medical journals made the Christian faith a qualification for employment.[67] Hospital directors justified discriminatory hiring practices on the grounds that the majority of the patients were Christian and that the hospitals were staffed by Christian nursing orders.

The men who worked as local organizers for the Centralverein rejected baptism as a means of professional advancement. They believed that there was more honor and integrity in remaining loyal to the Jewish faith than in conversion.[68] Moreover, they knew that baptism did not guarantee social acceptance. Christians regarded baptized Jews as social climbers. In the records of the Prussian Ministry of Justice a separate list was kept for judges who were baptized Jews. Proud and aggrieved, many Jewish lawyers were ready to join an activist organization that fought for equality of rights and opportunity.

3

ALIGNMENT WITH THE PROGRESSIVES

Up to 1897 the Centralverein's defense was confined to court litigation and propaganda. On September 6, 1897, the central board met to discuss whether it should be active in the elections for the Reichstag and the Prussian parliament in 1898.[1] Horwitz and Fuchs thought that the organization should coordinate the campaign activities of the German Jews and promote the election of Jewish deputies. The board members were not in accord so the discussion ended without any definite decisions.

Early in 1898 reports circulated about the Centralverein's plan to exert pressure on the Progressive parties for the nomination of Jewish candidates. In the left-liberal press a hue and cry was raised about a "Jewish Centrum." Jewish activists were incensed at the party leaders, who disapproved of the Centralverein's entry into politics and raised unwarranted objections. The *Allgemeine Zeitung des Judentums* published an article to set the record straight. It contained a blistering rebuttal to the insinuations that the Jews were making arrogant demands for "confessional candidates" and were aggressively asserting exclusively Jewish interests.[2] It stated emphatically that Jews elected to parliament would safeguard the constitutional rights of all German citizens.

Criticism from the Progressives did not inhibit Horwitz and Fuchs. At an April meeting the executive board voted to sponsor Edmund Friedemann, a lawyer, as a candidate for the Diet in Berlin and to ask the Progressives to nominate Jews in other districts.[3] Some board members continued to voice reservations. The rumors about a "Jewish Centrum" seemed to confirm their opinion that it would be more prudent if the Centralverein kept out of politics.

During the Reichstag election campaign Horwitz and Fuchs walked a tightrope. In April *Im Deutschen Reich* stated that it was "right" that the participation of the Jews in the election "does not appear very conspicuous because they act not in a collective mass, not as Jews but as Germans."[4] Only in one respect, in opposition to anti-Semitic candidates, "should and shall the election campaign find the German Jews united in political life." The Progressives were assured that "least of all do the Jews want to be a bloc within any one political party." In May *Im Deutschen Reich* qualified earlier assurances that the Centralverein had no ambitions to form a political bloc by adding that this policy did not prevent it from engaging in politics whenever the rights of the Jews or the equality of Judaism with the Christian confessions was at issue.[5]

The decision to promote the election of Jewish deputies was not an overnight shift in policy. The Centralverein's leaders had come to see that the Jews needed representatives who were fervently committed to the Jewish cause. The defense of Jewish rights that the Progressive *Fraktion* had made in the last legislative session seemed to them too perfunctory.[6] They thought that the speeches of the Progressives had lacked fire and moral indignation and regretted that the deputies had not attacked the devious methods by which government officials rendered illusory the constitution's guarantee of equality of rights. In upcoming legislative sessions they anticipated that the anti-Semites would try hard to turn these arbitrary administrative practices into laws making the Jews second-class citizens. The Jews needed "a defense that can only be made by a man who knows in his heart what it is like to be oppressed because of his religion."[7]

In 1898 it seemed to Horwitz and Fuchs especially urgent that several Jews sit in the Prussian Diet. Speculation in political circles led them to expect that in the next session the government would introduce a bill reforming the Law of July 23, 1847.[8] It was a vital matter to the Jews that the government put their religious community on an equal footing with the Catholic and Protestant churches, which enjoyed the legal status of religious associations accepted by the state with the rights of privileged corporations. In the deliberations on this bill the Jews needed spokesmen who were acquainted with conditions in the synagogue congregations "through birth and education."

It was to the Progressive parties that the Centralverein's directors went with entreaties for the nomination of Jewish candidates. They were eager to see Jews in the Reichstag who were affiliated with bourgeois liberal parties. Jewish liberals had long deplored the fact that Jewish deputies sat only in the *Fraktion* of the Social Democratic party.[9] This situation drew frequent notice in the right-wing press and caused embarrassment to the Jews. Jewish newspapers felt obliged to discount the prominence of the Jews in the Socialist ranks and to deny that Judaism nurtured Marxist ideas.[10] When Social Democrats took the floor of the Reichstag to defend Jewish rights, the Jewish liberals thought that the speeches did political harm to their community. In 1898, after August Bebel attacked discrimination against Jewish doctors in the army, the *Allgemeine Zeitung des Judentums* remarked "how very justified and timely" was the demand for Jewish deputies. "The fact that in recent sessions Social Democratic deputies have again and again intervened in [Jewish] questions does not benefit our cause under present circumstances."[11]

Horwitz and Fuchs found among the Progressives no sympathy for their demands. Party officials were afraid that liberal voters would turn to other parties rather than support a Progressive candidate who was Jewish. In the private talks that took place before the Reichstag election, the Progressives muddled the issue, first by describing Jewish nominees as "confessional candidates" whom the Jews regarded as qualified solely because of their religion, and then by arguing that "confessional candidates" offended the spirit of liberalism.[12] Party leaders replied pointedly that in many districts the Jews themselves objected to the nomination of fellow Jews out of fear of stirring up anti-Semitism.

Before the election for the Diet, once again the Centralverein appealed to the Progressives to select Jewish candidates. Speaking at a meeting in Berlin on September 28, Horwitz challenged the Progressives to live up to their liberal principles.[13] He reproached party leaders for thinking that political expediency obliged them to make accommodations to the anti-Jewish instincts of voters, and he called such tactics "unworthy" of a liberal party. The Progressives responded to pressure from the Centralverein this time by nominating several Jews. Two of the candidates, Max Hirsch and Martin Peltasohn, were elected to the Diet.

In 1898 the Centralverein became the first Jewish interest group to take part in national elections. In May and June the executive board approved the distribution of campaign funds to districts where the Progressives were contesting anti-Semitic candidates in the Reichstag election.[14] It set up a subcommittee to plan activities for the election to the Diet and approved a campaign fund of 5,000 marks.[15] The subcommittee included Horwitz, Leopold Kalisch, a Berlin journalist, and Martin Lövinson, a Berlin lawyer who had many contacts inside the Progressive People's party.

Through *Im Deutschen Reich* and thousands of leaflets the Central-verein appealed to Jewish citizens to vote. It implored them not to underestimate the influence of irrational propaganda, and it cited the fact that anti-Semites in the Social Reform party had polled more than 260,000 votes in 1893 as a warning that many people could be persuaded to make hatred of the Jews their prime political passion.[16] Jews who made contributions to party funds were urged to use their influence to prevent the selection of candidates who were unsympathetic to the Jews.

Voter were put on guard against candidates whom the Central-verein suspected of favoring *Ausnahmegesetze*, laws that violated the principle of equality before the law and would subject the Jewish population alone to discriminatory treatment. On June 17 the central board addressed a letter to all candidates in the run-off election. The candidates were asked to sign a statement pledging that if they were elected, they would vote against any bill that imposed restrictions on German-born or unnaturalized Jews.[17] The Berlin bureau forwarded the replies to the Centralverein's local representatives in the districts where the candidates were running.

Many members were unhappy over the Centralverein's involvement in the elections, and in October the muttering grew into a loud protest. The central board gave financial backing to Edmund Friedemann, a Progressive People's party candidate in Berlin. At a Centralverein meeting on September 28 Friedemann delivered a campaign speech. In October the Centralverein circulated broadsheets praising his defense of Jewish interests in the Berlin City Council. Overnight, letters of protest poured into the Berlin headquarters. The letter writers complained that it was not prudent for the Jews as a group to be highly visible in politics and also expressed the fear that the Centralverein's appearance in campaign politics would provoke an anti-Semitic backlash.[18] Some correspondents accused the board members of partisanship.

In the city of Posen another controversy arose in which charges of partisanship were hurled against the executive board. The Progressive People's party nominated a Christian. A coalition of parties ranging from the Conservatives to the Progressive Union pulled out a trump card and picked Lewinsky, a Jewish lawyer, as their candidate. The Progressive Union to which Lewinsky belonged asked the Centralverein to endorse him. The central board sent a commission to study the situation in Posen. It reported that the majority of Jews living in the city were followers of the Progressive People's party and that officials of the congregation had decided to back publicly Kindler, the party's contender. The board members agreed that, given these circumstances, it would not be proper to urge Jewish voters in Posen to discard party loyalty.[19] They adopted a policy of neutrality. After Kindler won, Lewinsky and his supporters denounced the executive board for taking a neutral stand in an election in which there was a Jewish candidate.

To respond to the avalanche of criticism, the central committee summoned a general meeting in Berlin on November 9 and assigned the job to Fuchs. Fuchs felt that the accusations leveled against the Centralverein were unfair and that many critics had applied a double standard in judging the political behavior of the Jews and the Christian population.[20] He was especially angry with the Progressives, who had blown up out of proportion what the Centralverein wished to do in politics and who had stirred up dormant Jewish apprehensions. The speech that he delivered was a rousing justification for Jewish political activism.

Fuchs took up point by point all the objections raised against the Centralverein's entry into politics. He contended that the Jews who had reproached Horwitz and him misunderstood the association's purposes. Although at first the defense movement stood outside politics, it could not continue to restrict its choice of weapons to judicial litigation. To protect the rights of Jewish citizens, it had to be political. It had to lobby in the Reichstag and state parliaments, where deputies debated legislative proposals affecting the Jews and

could compel government officials by means of interpellation to be
publicly accountable for discrimination in the army, the civil administration, and the school system.[21]

Fuchs did not skirt the charges of partisanship that loyalists of
the Progressive Union had raised. He denied that the Centralverein
had any special ties with the Progressive People's party. In the
Posen election, he stated, neutrality was the only sound policy. It
would not benefit the defense movement to alienate either one of
the left-liberal parties by urging Jewish voters to switch sides.[22] The
differences dividing the two parties were of no concern to the
Centralverein. It had set its own political priorities, and above any
of the matters about which the party politicians bickered were the
principle of equal rights and the goal of electing Jewish deputies.

When Fuchs rebutted the charges that the Centralverein was promoting "confessional candidates" and conducting "Jewish politics,"
he gave vent to his indignation. He asserted that these smear words
had been used by both "would-be friends" and outright enemies.
The Centralverein was not intent on electing deputies who represented Jewish interests exclusively. Only because qualified Jews had
been denied the opportunity to run in elections did the central
board feel morally and politically compelled to make demands for
the nomination of Jewish candidates. Ironically, he asked why no
Germans cried out against "confessional candidates" when the Jews
had been excluded from the Diet and only Protestant and Catholic
deputies held seats.[23] He argued that it was unjust to impugn the
effort of the Centralverein to elect Jewish deputies when over the
years the two Christian churches and economic pressure groups had
asserted their special interests in parliament without being subjected
to malicious allegations of being "un-German" and putting class or
confessional interests above the nation's welfare. In a sharp rejoin-
der to the liberals, he declared that striving for the equality of rights
of all citizens and the scrupulous execution of the constitution was
not the pursuit of special Jewish interests.

Turning to the community leaders who had counseled that organized Jewish activity in elections would arouse hostility, Fuchs
declared that these warnings would not cower the Centralverein. His
message was clear. The admonition not to add grist to the mills
grinding out anti-Semitic propaganda had "lost its power to frighten

the Centralverein."[24] With defiant pride he concluded, "We want
to determine our own destiny by our own power, and since we know
what we want and may demand, [we want]to defend our legitimate
interests uninhibited by the warnings of our would-be friends, uninhibited by the slogans of our enemies and their accusations."[25]

In a more sensational way than Fuchs could have imagined in 1898,
his stand that the Jewish defense had to be political was vindicated
in 1901, when an interpellation addressed to Minister of Justice
Schönstedt in the Diet ignited the biggest protest movement that the
Jews had ever mobilized against discrimination. On January 31, in a
reading on the ministry's budget, Martin Peltasohn demanded an
explanation of how decisions on appointments in the judiciary were
made. He noted that suspicions of a deliberate policy of discrimination had arisen from the experiences of Jewish lawyers.[26]

In what was clearly a gesture of disrespect, Karl von Schönstedt
replied sarcastically that he did not believe that Deputy Peltasohn
intended to roll out "the Jewish question." Haughtily, he said that he
was not obliged to give the House of Deputies an accounting of how
judicial appointments were made.[27] Then in a cocky spirit, he went
on to say that large numbers of Christians did not have confidence
in Jewish notaries and preferred to entrust legal transactions to men
of their own faith. The ministry had to take into account the feelings
of these people. He felt that his department did not deserve Peltasohn's reproach and, to prove his point, he told the deputies that the
Ministry of Justice was the only branch of the Prussian government
that gave offices to at least some Jews. Unintentionally, he blurted
out that the rest of the civil service excluded Jews.

Criticizing Schönstedt's answer, Theodor Barth broadened what
might have remained a Jewish remonstrance into a full-scale constitutional debate. Like Peltasohn, Barth belonged to the Progressive
Union, but he was more radical and, as a gentile, spoke with more
self-assurance than Peltasohn. He was revolted by the lack of scruple
with which the minister justified official practices that were in
flagrant violation of the law and was incensed at his contemptuous
attitude toward the House of Deputies. He assailed Schönstedt's
assertion that he was not obliged to be accountable in parliament
for his department's policies. The practice of allowing the sentiments
and prejudices of the local population to determine official decisions,

he remarked, made the Prussian constitution a worthless scrap of paper.[28] Whereas Peltasohn touched upon and then sidestepped the issue of the government's violation of the Federal Law of July 3, 1869, Barth boldly indicted the state authorities for breaking it. The law abolished all restrictions on the political and civil rights of citizens based on religion and made eligibility to hold public office independent of religious confession. It established for the German Empire what the Prussian constitution of January 31, 1850, already guaranteed in articles 4 and 12, which stated that all citizens were equal before the law and enjoyed the full exercise of political and civil rights regardless of their religion.

Overnight the debate set off shock waves in political circles and the press.[29] A high state official confessed in public for the first time the practice of discrimination against Jews in the Prussian civil service. In a clumsy manner Schönstedt displayed the bureaucracy's contempt for the rule of law and insensitivity to any concept of justice.

The Peltasohn–Barth offensive had been planned at a meeting of the Abwehrverein's board of directors on January 27.[30] The Central-verein seized quickly the opportunity that the debate and the massive newspaper publicity offered. Meeting on February 4, the executive board decided to mobilize a Jewish protest movement.[31] Three board members, Fuchs, Horwitz, and Eugen Landau, were to request an audience with Chancellor Bülow.

Hugo Sonnenfeld, a member of the central board, organized a protest demonstration of Berlin lawyers on February 6. The meeting was sponsored by the Waldeck-Verein, a Berlin club of the Progressive People's party, which Sonnenfeld headed. Giving the keynote speech, Sonnenfeld averred that public opinion must be rallied to force the government to observe the Law of July 3, 1869. He proposed that protests be sent to Bülow. As the official responsible for making the states comply with imperial laws, the chancellor should be called upon to intervene.[32] Within a few days the executive boards of the Jewish communities in Berlin, Frankfurt am Main, Königsberg, Posen, Stettin, and elsewhere addressed petitions to Bülow.

The Centralverein convened a public assembly in Berlin on February 10. Besides Fuchs, Paul Nathan and Oskar Cassel gave speeches.[33] The demonstrators, identifying themselves as a body of Jewish citizens, lodged a protest against the statements that Schönstedt had made in the Diet. Also in Posen the Centralverein organized a rally at which a crowd of more than 700 heard three Jewish councilmen arraign the minister.

The public outcry took state officials by surprise. Schönstedt himself was embarrassed by charges of violating the constitution and was annoyed over the petitions urging Bülow to intervene and to compel him to observe the law. In the Diet on February 8 he attempted to vindicate himself and to intimidate the Jews into ending the protest movement. Visibly nervous, he conceded that his speech on January 31 could be misunderstood, but he hotly denied that he was anti-Semitic.[34] He argued that the government required a certain degree of administrative discretion and that the constitution could not be the decisive or binding legal authority. There were times when officials had to depart from the letter of the law out of consideration for the needs and interests of the people. Turning to Peltasohn, he said:

> I do not understand the commotion, and I believe that Deputy Peltasohn perhaps realizes that he would have done better if he had not allowed himself to be forced into addressing his question but had remembered the principle: quieta non movere! What I am saying is said to make Deputy Peltasohn aware that his attack on the judicial administration was completely inappropriate and to make him further aware that it is really impossible in the judicial administration alone to absorb the excessive growth of Jewish applicants in the way they desire.[35]

A Center party deputy made the minister's vague threat more explicit. Felix Porsch said that Catholics had more justified grievances than the Jews and hinted that in heavily Catholic-populated cities such as Kattowitz there was already an overabundance of Jewish notaries and lawyers. He pointed out that the number of Catholics in public office fell far below the percentage of Catholics in the Prussian population and demanded a system of parity according to which the number of appointed officials would be proportional to each confession in the state's population. Knowing that a *numerus clausus* would work to the disadvantage of the Jews, he advised the Berlin Jews that it would be more prudent to make modest claims.

He counseled them to stop attacking the government and not to put special Jewish demands within a framework of constitutional principles and liberal ideas.[36] Porsch's advice was an indirect acknowledgment that the opposition had been effective in demonstrating to the educated public that at stake in what many Germans contemptuously referred to as "the Jewish question" were the principles of constitutional government and the rule of law.

For Jewish activists the affair demonstrated the value of waging the Jewish struggle for equal rights in parliament.[37] Peltasohn's speech set a precedent for demanding that ministers be accountable for policies that violated the constitutional rights of Jewish citizens. The activists were confident that embarrassing disclosures and criticisms in parliament and the press would sooner or later compel government officials to observe the law scrupulously in dealing with the Jews.

Barth's treatment of "the Jewish question" as a problem of constitutional government suited the purposes of the Centralverein, whose leaders had contended for years that anti-Semitism was not a specifically Jewish problem. The speeches that Barth and other Progressive deputies made demonstrated that the defense of Jewish rights was essentially the task of upholding the constitution, a responsibility incumbent on all German citizens. At the protest meetings Fuchs, Nathan, and other Jewish speakers harped on the dangers to the rule of law that were implicit in Schönstedt's arguments. They said that if the minister's reasoning was followed, the bigoted sentiments of the populace or demagogic movements would determine whether the government carried out the law or not.[38]

At the Centralverein's meeting in February, loud applause broke out when Fuchs rebuffed Schönstedt's admonitions and gave an impassioned defense of Peltasohn's interpellation. In the following months, however, the central board did not continue to use the tactics of interpellation. In April 1901 the Centralverein started to compile data on the exclusion of Jews from juries, and on November 4 the board discussed whether Peltasohn should open a debate on this grievance in the Diet. The majority decided that Peltasohn should not present the Centralverein's evidence or question Schönstedt about the refusal of judges to call Jewish citizens to serve on juries.[39] On March 3, 1902, the board members pondered whether to ask Progressive deputies to compel Schönstedt by means of an interpellation to answer charges of discrimination in the appointment of judges. Sonnenfeld, who was himself a lawyer, persuaded them against initiating the attack.[40]

What prompted Sonnenfeld and other committee members to reject a parliamentary offensive was not recorded. It seems that the directors differed over the advisability of antagonizing state officials with embarrassing interpellations. As Horwitz confessed, they had "reservations about creating the impression that the impetus for these interpellations is to be traced back to the Centralverein."[41] It is also likely that Porsch's speech and events in the Bavarian parliament convinced them that a highly publicized Jewish fight to abolish discrimination in the judiciary would provoke a militant Catholic campaign for a numerus clausus.

In 1901 the Center party in the Bavarian parliament introduced a proposal calling upon the government to limit the appointment of judicial officials of the Jewish faith to the proportion of Jews in the Bavarian population, slightly under 1 percent.[42] At the time in Bavaria, 51 Jews were judges, prosecuting attorneys, and notaries, constituting 2 percent of the judicial administration. The resolution was debated on November 14 and 29, 1901, and passed by 77 to 51 votes. The minister of justice pointed out that the proposal could not be carried out as it was worded, because it violated the Law of July 3, 1869. Nonetheless, he gave the party a pledge that he would bear in mind the popular sentiments from which the proposal came.

Im Deutschen Reich denounced the bigotry of the Bavarian Center party and called the demand for a system of parity "anti-Semitism practiced slyly under the mask of justice."[43] In the judgment of the Centralverein's lawyers, the Center's concept of parity did not accord with the principle of equal rights. They contended that the legal guarantees of civil equality required the state to appoint citizens to public office without regard to religion and should not be interpreted so that the state allotted public offices to each confession equal to its percentage of the population.

The Centralverein did not venture into German politics again until the Reichstag election of 1903. At a meeting on February 9, 1903, the governing board started planning for the election in June. It voted to spend up to 3,000 marks to campaign against anti-Semitic candidates and appointed a subcommittee to disperse campaign funds.[44] Spokesmen for the Centralverein lobbied for the nomination of Jewish candidates in confidential talks with leaders of the Progressive People's party. At a closed meeting with representatives from the chapters on February 19, the central board solicited their approval for its political activities. They agreed to submit to the Berlin office reports on the campaign in their districts and to support parties that opposed anti-Semitic candidates. The Centralverein printed and sent campaign propaganda to constituencies where the anti-Semitic parties agitated. Board members made arrangements with leading figures in the Progressive People's party, Julius Kopsch, Hermann Müller, and Eugen Richter, to write a brochure entitled "Anti-Semites in the Reichstag." The Centralverein financed the publication of 1,000 copies and prevailed upon Müller to have the Progressives circulate them.[45]

Throughout the spring and summer of 1903 the central committee gave no publicity to its political activities. In April it rejected a proposal from Hamburg that the Centralverein make public appeals for contributions to a Jewish election fund.[46] The Berlin bureau collected campaign funds and made a public acknowledgment of the fund raising only after the election. The Centralverein operated in the background because many of its members continued to believe that the Jews, as a collective group, should not act too conspicuously in election politics. At a meeting in Berlin on April 27 Horwitz assured the members that the executive board saw no reason for the association to be identified with any partisan campaign work except opposition to the anti-Semitic parties.[47] Notwithstanding this remark, the leadership was by no means unpartisan. The subcommittee directing campaign activities included Martin Lövinson and Hugo Sonnenfeld, prominent figures in the Berlin club of the Progressive People's party.

Board members who pressed the Progressives to nominate Jewish candidates found them unsympathetic to the desire of Jewish activists to have deputies of their own faith sit in the Reichstag.[48] Left liberals such as Barth held the idealistic view that parliamentarians should represent the interests of the entire nation and be responsible only to their consciences. Barth lamented that deputies serving interest groups were turning the Reichstag into a political stock exchange.[49]

Adding to the difficulties of the Centralverein's negotiations with the Progressives was the decentralized structure of the two parties. In the Progressive Union Barth, Rickert, and Schrader were not too concerned about matters of organization and did not create a centralized party machine.[50] Local committees enjoyed considerable autonomy. Insisting on their right to make decisions on election strategy, they did not hesitate to ignore instructions from the central committee. Discipline in the Progressive People's party was no better even though Eugen Richter, the chairman, had a reputation for being domineering. The local clubs regarded their independence as sacred and frequently acted contrary to the directives of the central leaders.[51] In 1903 several district committees refused to sponsor Jewish candidates. The central committee took into account the mild anti-Jewish feeling among liberal voters and deferred to the wishes of the local party notables.[52]

The Progressive parties made a token concession to the Jews. Some candidacies were offered, and finally nine Jews ran for election. According to the *Allgemeine Zeitung des Judentums*, the Jewish Progressives were "stand-in candidates."[53] They were sponsored just to make a political showing in districts where defeat was expected. The defeat of all nine contenders in the first balloting seemed to confirm the suspicion that party officials reserved for Christian candidates the constituencies where the odds favored the Progressives and selected Jewish nominees for places where the chances of winning were nil. Unimpressed by the honor of being "stand-in candidates," Horwitz and Fuchs quietly turned down the offers of nomination that the Progressive People's party made to them.

During the campaign the Social Democrats took credit for nominating Jews to run in "safe districts" and fired charges of anti-Semitism against the Progressives in order to discredit them in sections of Berlin where large numbers of Jewish voters resided. In the Berlin district where the Progressive Hermann Zwick, a school supervisor, ran, the Socialists circulated broadsheets associating him with the discriminatory policies against Jewish teachers in the city's school administration.[54] The Social Democrats made sensational disclosures about the nomination of two baptized Jews by the Progressive People's party and accused the party of favoring converts over steadfast Jews in picking candidates. Julius Moses, a Jewish journalist, appealed to the Jews to vote for the Social Democrats as the only party free of bigotry and willing to support Jewish candidates.[55] These noisy attacks on the Progressives were an embarrassing experience for Jewish left liberals in Berlin. They were irate at the Social Democrats for using the Jews as a political football in their campaign against the Progressives.[56]

Although the anti-Semites had been divided since the schism of the German Social Reform party in 1900, they conducted an ambitious campaign extending over 107 districts. About 50 candidates belonging to four anti-Semitic parties ran for election. The popular vote that they polled on June 16 dropped from 284,250 in 1898 to 244,543. Yet 15 anti-Semites, not counting fellow travelers in the other parties, survived the first balloting to enter the runoff election set for June 25.

Pointing out that party officials had declared that in no district should the Progressives align with the Conservatives, the *Allgemeine Zeitung des Judentums* expressed confidence that liberal voters would not support the anti-Semites. This news item gave no hint of how complicated was the question of Progressive tactics in the runoffs. In many places the left liberals were in a pivotal position to determine the outcome of the elections. It was estimated that in 40 districts the Progressives could help the Social Democrats defeat reactionary candidates, and in 13 districts the Socialists could rescue Reichstag seats for the Progressives.[57]

Barth advocated a strategy of choosing the "lesser evil," voting for the Social Democrats in order to defeat the reactionary Right. His proposal led to a sharp controversy among the Progressives.[58] Within Barth's own party, other strategists rejected his analysis that the immediate task of the Progressives was to collaborate with the Social Democrats in elections and in parliament in order to attain political reforms. Within the Progressive People's party, objections to the tactics of supporting the "lesser evil" were more vehement. The election in Berlin on June 16 had been a battle between the Progressive People's party and the Social Democrats, and the city, once a left-liberal stronghold, had been captured by the Socialists. The intense rivalry of the two parties made Eugen Richter and other party notables unwilling to negotiate any vote-trading agreements with the Social Democrats. Moreover the Progressive leaders believed that any collaboration with the Socialists would cost them the votes of bourgeois Germans. Many left liberals had a deeper aversion for social democracy than for the conservative Agrarians, and the local Progressive committees took these feelings into account in making decisions on tactics in the runoff elections.

In six districts the Social Democrats fought anti-Semites. To the dismay of the Jews, the Progressives seemed to be more anxious to defeat the Socialists than the anti-Semites. Local committees declined to make any public declarations opposing the anti-Semites. Rather than vote for Socialists, large numbers of Progressives decided to abstain, and in some places they voted for the anti-Semites.[59] In the constituency of Arnswalde-Friedeberg, left-liberal voters helped the anti-Semite Wilhelm Bruhn defeat his Socialist opponent.

The Progressive People's party was battered in the Berlin districts, and squabbles broke out after the election. Dissident left liberals attributed the defeat to the party's loss of idealism and to the exclusiveness of the oligarchic district committees.[60] They criticized Richter and other party officials for refusing to rally liberal voters against the forces of reaction in the runoffs between the Social Democrats and the Conservatives. Calling for rejuvenation, they exhorted the party to rededicate itself to liberal political goals and to bridge the chasm that cut it off from the working class.

The Centralverein's leadership did not participate in the post-election infighting. Jewish newspapers of left-liberal opinion were restrained in their criticism of the Progressives and stood loyally behind Richter. The *Israelitisches Familienblatt* rebuked Julius Moses for making wild and impolitic attacks on the left-liberal parties and especially for charging that they lived on Jewish money but failed to defend Jewish interests vigorously. The Hamburg newspaper said, "The Jews would make a mistake if they hurt those parties whose programs call for what they demand—civil equality."[61] The *Allgemeine Zeitung des Judentums* called the allegations of discrimination that the Socialists leveled against Zwick false. After admitting that other criticism of the Progressives was justified, it implored the Jews to be guided by political reason and not to be too touchy. The Progressives should be judged not according to the number of Jewish candidates they nominated but by their performance in parliament. Expressing regret over the loss of Progressive mandates to the Socialists, it remarked, "The German Jews know very well that it would be a misfortune for them if the Progressive parties were gradually extinguished in the fight between the Right and the Left."[62]

The editor of *Im Deutschen Reich*, Alphonse Levy, reported that 12 anti-Semites were elected and that "followers of other parties" had voted for them out of fear of social democracy.[63] After making a vague reference to Progressive voters, Levy's article went on to blame the political opportunism of the Socialists for the victory of two anti-Semites in runoff elections. He wrote that, in their chase for Reichstag seats, the Socialists had no scruples about making political deals with the anti-Semites and supported Ernst Fröhlich and Karl Krösell in return for anti-Semitic votes cast for Socialist candidates in runoffs in Berlin and Stettin.

Although Levy laundered out of his reporting details on the Progressives, some board members were dissatisfied with the conduct of the party leaders. At a meeting on September 10 they decided to meet privately with party officials to air their complaints.[64] The leaders of the Progressive People's party gave to spokesmen for the Centralverein assurances that in the upcoming election for the Diet the party would nominate Jewish candidates.[65] The central board delegated Martin Lövinson and Dr. Otto Wiesenthal to hold confidential talks with notables of the Progressive Union in Arnswalde and Landsberg for the purpose of preventing Bruhn's reelection. Both men conferred with Barth too. In the negotiations they proposed that the party establish a district club so that in the next election it could nominate a candidate early and conduct an aggressive campaign against Bruhn.[66] The party agreed to hire a district secretary to organize voters and to direct election campaigns, and the central board offered to contribute funds for his salary.[67]

When the election campaign for the Prussian parliament started in the fall of 1903, Horwitz and Fuchs had reason to believe that through quiet diplomacy the Centralverein had succeeded in gaining candidacies for Jews in constituencies where their prospects of winning were good. The Progressive People's party nominated Oskar Cassel, Max Hirsch, and Leopold Rosenow in Berlin, Louis Aronsohn in Bromberg, and Hugo Gerschel in Jüterbog-Luckenwalde. The Progressive Union nominated Martin Peltasohn and Eduard Wolff, whose elections in districts in the province of Posen were assured through agreements that the party had made with the National Liberals.[68] In November all were elected except Gerschel.

The nomination of these candidates did not bury suspicions that leaders of the Progressive People's party took popular anti-Semitic sentiments into account in the selection of candidates and regarded Jewish nominees as a liability for the party. The party's central committee maneuvered to block the nomination of Dr. Artur Bernstein in favor of the candidacy of Hermann Müller for a Berlin suburban district. Disregarding the fact that Bernstein's Jewish parents had their infant son baptized, the party's organ, the *Freisinnige Zeitung*, alleged that he had converted to Christianity to advance his career as a physician and was now hustling for a seat in the Diet.[69] Bernstein was infuriated by these derogatory remarks and, in an act of vengeance, made a disclosure about the prejudice of Julius Kopsch, a member of the party's Reichstag *Fraktion*, who was running now for election to the Prussian parliament.

At a Progressive club meeting on October 5, Bernstein revealed that in 1899 Kopsch had come to the district of Torgau-Liebenwerda to advise the Progressives against nominating Bernstein for the by-election. The objection he made was that Bernstein was a Jew. Bernstein contended that the remark was made to discredit him because Kopsch knew that among many left liberals it was a "notorious reproach."[70] When local party members pointed out that Bernstein attended a Protestant church, Kopsch replied, "That may be so, but he still remains a baptized Jew." Ewald Conrad, the party's district secretary who had heard the remark, confirmed the veracity of Bernstein's account in a letter published in the daily press.[71] Banner headlines gave sensational publicity to the revelations of Bernstein and Conrad.

Conrad's letter embarrassed the party leaders and forced them to make a public disclaimer. Quickly the Waldeck-Verein convened a meeting on October 7. In his speech Kopsch denied that he was anti-Semitic and argued that Bernstein's accusations were based on a malicious interpretation of what happened. According to Kopsch's version of the incident, the question of Bernstein's Jewish parents was raised in a confidential discussion of his prospects for election. Kopsch mentioned that the district was located close to Saxony,

where anti-Semitism was rampant, and he inquired whether Bernstein's Jewish background "could seem somewhat reprehensible."[72]
When Conrad expressed the opinion that it would not hurt Bernstein's chances of winning, Kopsch insisted that he immediately gave
his approval to the nomination.

The affair aroused intense bitterness among Berlin Jews. Kopsch's
account was an interpretative presentation of what happened and
not a rebuttal of Bernstein's charges. Asserting that Kopsch's denial
of anti-Semitism proved nothing, the *Allgemeine Zeitung des Judentums* challenged him to clear up the affair by suing Bernstein for
libel and offering testimony under oath.[73] Among Jewish liberals
confidence in Kopsch and the party was shaken. The scandal gave
rise to doubts about the value of favoring the Progressives with Jewish financial backing. Kopsch's explanation was implicitly a confession that party officials saw Jewish parentage as a negative factor in
appraising a candidate's prospects of winning an election and were
unwilling to risk losing votes by putting up Jewish candidates.

Jews actively involved in the Progressive People's party did not
welcome Bernstein's exposé and exploit the embarrassment that it
caused the party's officials. Reacting as loyal party men, they kept
in mind the damaging effects that the publicity was having on the
party in the midst of an election campaign and sought to mollify
the resentment that the affair aroused within the Jewish community. At a political assembly in Berlin Leopold Rosenow advised the
Jews not to be swayed by injured pride or to turn against the party
because of the Kopsch incident.[74] Hugo Sonnenfeld prevailed upon
the Centralverein's governing board to hold a big public meeting on
October 15, at which he argued the party's case. The Progressive
deputy Hermann Müller was allowed to attend as an invited guest in
order to vindicate the party's record on the nomination of Jewish
candidates.

Horwitz and Fuchs agreed to convene the meeting and to place
on the agenda the Centralverein's election activities because they believed that the executive board owed the membership an explanation of why the defense organization supported the Progressives.
Besides the Kopsch affair and the unprincipled conduct of the Progressives in the Reichstag election, the merging of the National
Social party with the Progressive Union during the summer of 1903

raised questions about the presence of anti-Semitic tendencies in the Progressive ranks.

After the National Social party was founded by Friedrich Naumann in 1896, into its ranks came the radical fringe of the Christian Social movement, which repudiated the conservatism of Stöcker. Naumann took care to suppress crude racism. Nonetheless, many National Socials were opportunistic in their position on anti-Semitism. As late as the Reichstag election of 1903, National Socials who ran against anti-Semitic Agrarians in Prussian Hesse did not condemn their anti-Semitism.[75] Helmut von Gerlach, who fought a Conservative in a runoff in Marburg, made a brazen bid for the votes of anti-Semites. His campaign committee circulated leaflets denying that he was a defender of the Jews and disputing as "vulgar slander" Conservative party propaganda that he had received campaign contributions from the Jews.[76]

After the amalgamation of the two parties, there was speculation in the press that the National Socials would infect the Progressive Union with anti-Semitism. The *Vossische Zeitung*, a liberal Berlin daily, drew attention to the Christian Social background of many of Naumann's followers and to an article of the party's program which stated that Christianity stood at the center of the cultural and moral life of the German nation. Reading these press comments, members of the Centralverein called upon the central board to respond to the speculation and to clarify the political terms on which the parties merged.[77]

Delegating Sonnenfeld to defend the Centralverein's political policy was a mistake that Horwitz and Fuchs made. Sonnenfeld won public recognition as a lawyer during the celebrated trial of Moritz Levy, a Jewish youth who was accused of ritual murder in Konitz in 1901. He provided legal counsel for other Jewish residents in the town who were complainants in libel suits against anti-Semitic news-papers. Notwithstanding this service to the Jewish community, Sonnenfeld headed the Waldeck-Verein, and his speech was bound to be partisan and written from the perspective of the party rather than of the defense movement. He was known to be a political lieutenant of the party's central committee and had made enemies by sharply rebuking dissidents in the rank and file.

At the meeting on October 15 Sonnenfeld harangued against Jewish critics of the Progressive People's party. He criticized the Jewish press for sensationalist reporting on Bernstein's disclosure and contended that the ill-chosen words of Kopsch were free of any anti-Semitic overtones.[78] Singled out for harsh reproach was Julius Moses, who had appealed to Jewish left liberals to cast a protest vote for the Social Democrats in the Reichstag election.

Sonnenfeld scolded Jewish activists who had spoken out boldly for the election of Jews to the Reichstag. Here he served Horwitz and Fuchs badly. Instead of representing their point of view, he advanced a line of argument that party officials had used to fend off pressure to nominate Jewish candidates. He declaimed:

> Not to elect anyone because he is a Jew is just as bad as to elect someone because he is a Jew. Jews must be concerned that in the Reichstag and Diet sit men who will guard against any infringement of the rights of Jews. But to demand that these men should be of the Jewish religion is not our intention for the simple reason that we oppose distributing positions in the state, the administration and the legislatures, according to confession.[79]

Horwitz and Fuchs thought that just as other interest groups had done, the Jews made legitimate demands for representation in the Reichstag and state parliaments. Sonnenfeld confused the Central-verein's stand with Catholic proposals for a system of parity.

In discussing how the German parties acted in matters affecting the Jews, Sonnenfeld sought to impress upon his listeners that the Progressives were the most steadfast defenders of the Jews. He cautioned Jewish voters to be wary of candidates affiliated with the National Liberal and Center parties. The National Liberals did not consistently defend the principle of equal rights, and in their ranks were many in whom anti-Semitism could be discerned even though it was not exhibited in a vulgar fashion. He called the Center's position on the Jewish question "ambivalent." With fervor the Catholic party took up arms against any bill restricting religious freedom, but the party was split on issues of civil rights, with one segment being anti-Semitic.[80] After conceding that Jewish voters could have "complete confidence" that the Social Democrats would never support any legislation abridging the rights of citizens, he added the cutting remarks that the party's opposition to *Ausnahmegesetze* was a matter of self-interest and that its propaganda against anti-Semitism "comes to nothing."[81] In various debates on Jewish grievances in the Reichstag, Socialist deputies had "participated relatively little," and in run-off elections "the party has no scruples about allying with the anti-Semites when this appears advantageous to its tactics."

When Sonnenfeld started to talk about the Progressives, he was nervous. Reports that the Progressive People's party had declined to select Jewish candidates had led to accusations of hypocrisy and an erosion of confidence in the party. He admitted that the fact that no Jew sat in the Progressive *Fraktion* in the Reichstag gave some substance to the suspicions, but he insisted that members of the central committee were not to be blamed and that the allegations made against them "come from a lack of information."[82] He said that he was in close contact with party officials and could testify from his own experience that they "have expended great effort" to nominate Jewish candidates. In many districts the Jews themselves raised objections on the grounds that it was more pragmatic to promote the election of a gentile than a fellow Jew, who could not hope to win wide public support. In some instances, after the central committee had persuaded Jewish left liberals to run, the district clubs had declined to sponsor them. To restore trust in the Progressives, he stated that the party leaders deeply regretted that the Jews had received the impression that they had refused to nominate Jewish candidates, and gave him assurances that in future elections the central committee would put more pressure on the local clubs which had rejected Jewish candidates.

Discussing the fusion of the National Socials with the Progressive Union, Sonnenfeld sought to impress upon the Jews that their apprehensions were unwarranted. At first, he conceded that National Social propaganda contained a dose of anti-Semitism and that since the merger there was "present the danger that sympathy for the Jews in the ranks of the Progressive Union could weaken somewhat."[83] Then with ardor he vowed that the National Socials would never be able to impose their tradition of anti-Semitism on the Progressives. He said:

Don't let yourselves be filled with mistrust toward the Progressive Union. In my opinion, abhorrence of anti-Semitism is so firmly rooted in the ranks of the Progressive Union that the influx of National Socials will be unable to change this feeling. We can say now as before: whoever belongs to the Progressive Union is to us a man who loves justice, a man who wants to see all citizens in the German nation treated equally and speaks out for us just as for all Christian citizens in the German Empire.[84]

Sonnenfeld's pugnacious remarks provoked an uproar. Outbursts of dissent interrupted his speech, and afterward a vehement discussion, which lasted past midnight, took place. Critics of the Progressives thought that Sonnenfeld whitewashed the unprincipled behavior of the party's bigwigs and distorted their own objections. Rather than flinging the charge of anti-Semitism at Kopsch, they had argued that Progressive leaders made accommodations to the bigotry of voters out of political expediency.[85] Sonnenfeld skirted this point. Karl Lewin, a Zionist radical, retorted that party officials who refused to nominate Jewish candidates out of consideration for popular sentiment followed the same policy that the Ministry of Justice practiced when it excluded Jews from judicial offices.

Hermann Müller was stung by the comparison and rose angrily to rebut Lewin. What the Progressive deputy said, however, gave some substance to Lewin's criticism. He declared that the party was obliged to take into account certain tendencies in public opinion in order to win elections.[86] Defending Kopsch, Müller contended that the central committee had sent him to the district of Torgau-Liebenwerda to survey local public opinion. In his confidential talks with party members about Bernstein, Kopsch was not expressing his own views but reporting on what he sensed were local objections to a Jewish deputy.

Horwitz and other board members were upset over the reactions to Sonnenfeld's speech and stepped into the debate to stop the attack on the Progressives. Wiesenthal said reproachfully that any group which had to fight for its rights could not afford to alienate its few friends by expressing mistrust. Fuchs entreated Jewish liberals not to exaggerate the significance of Kopsch's remarks and not to let the incident cause a breach between the Jews and the Progressives. In deciding how to vote in the Prussian parliamentary election, he urged them to give more attention to the goals that the Jews shared with the Progressives than to the occasional disagreements.[87]

The commotion over Kopsch's indiscretion passed away, and in the November election six Jews whom the Progressives nominated won seats in the Diet. The election of these deputies tightened the bonds between the Jewish activists and the Progressives but did not end the problems that strained the relationship. The election tactics which Progressive politicians thought that party interests and political expediency required continued to create friction.

In February 1904 a by-election was held for the Reichstag seat of Eschwege-Schmalkalden in Prussian Hesse. In the last general election the Progressive People's party had won, but now its candidate was eliminated from the runoff by the Socialist Wilhelm Hugo and the German Social Reformer Wilhelm Raab. In the runoff, which was to be held on March 1, the Progressives were in a position to tip the scale in favor of Hugo or his anti-Semitic challenger.

In the district an opposition movement against Raab was organized with funds provided by the Centralverein.[88] In Berlin Jewish Progressives pressed the party's central leaders to take a stand against Raab. Paul Nathan called upon them to assert their influence on the district club and to issue an announcement urging liberals not to abstain or to vote for Raab.[89] Speaking at the Centralverein's annual congress on February 22, Horwitz declared that the election held out to the Progressives an opportunity to sweep away accusations of moral indifference to anti-Semitism. He urged the Progressives to set aside their political rivalry with the Social Democrats and to give priority to Raab's defeat.[90]

Jewish Progressives raised the question of the party's tactics in the runoff at a meeting of the Waldeck-Verein on February 24. One party member took the floor to rebuke the central committee for not mobilizing left liberals in Eschwege-Schmalkalden in opposition to Raab. He contended that the party would betray its principles if it followed a noncommittal policy. After a second fervent speech favoring an alignment with the Social Democrats to defeat Raab, two party members cautioned the excited crowd that it was unrealistic to hope that the central committee could be persuaded to change its stand. The majority agreed that Richter could not be

pressured into supporting Hugo and decided "to dissociate themselves as far as possible from the sin of omission of the party leaders."[91] A resolution was passed appealing to the left liberals in the
district to defeat Raab by casting their votes for Hugo.

The central committee adamantly declined to release any statement
opposing Raab. The Progressive chiefs attributed the party's loss of
votes in recent elections to the Social Democrats and were not
disposed to collaborate with their archrivals. Their policy affected
the decision that the district club made. Georg Hauck, the club
chairman in Eschwege, issued a declaration telling the party's followers to act according to their own point of view in the runoff.[92]
On the eve of the election, when moral scruples prompted some Progressives to circulate a leaflet urging left-liberal voters to support
Hugo, Hauck objected to its distribution and publicly disavowed
it. The intent of this strategy was made plain by Marten, the party's
defeated candidate, who helped to make Raab an acceptable choice
by saying repeatedly in public that in runoffs all patriotic parties
must stand together against the Socialists.[93]

Raab made a bid for Progressive votes and won. The morning after
the election, a front-page article in the *Berliner Tageblatt* vehemently
denounced the central committee of the Progressive People's party,
whose tactics were held responsible for Raab's victory. Through an
analysis of the election returns, the newspaper demonstrated that
the margin of votes enabling Raab to win came from the Progressives.[94] It dismissed as a lame excuse the argument, offered in the
party's press, that party bylaws obliged the central committee to
respect the autonomy of the local clubs in deciding on election
tactics. It revealed how party officials followed a covert policy
favoring Raab.

The amoral behavior of the party leaders, who were so intent on
preventing their principal competitors from winning control over the
district that they abetted the election of an anti-Semite, shocked
many Progressives. At party meetings resolutions were introduced
censuring the central committee and demanding that it announce
the party's opposition to anti-Semites in future elections.[95] The
Progressive wing behind Theodor Barth attacked Richter. Writing in
Die Nation, Paul Nathan conceded that the Progressive rank and file
did not have the discipline of other parties and did not always follow

directives from the central committee, but he argued that this reason did not justify Richter's refusal to take a public stand against Raab.[96] The reticence of the central committee enabled those left liberals who could not summon the moral courage to oppose anti-Semitism to persist in believing that Raab's election was preferable to that of a Social Democrat. Nathan warned the party leaders that they were losing the confidence of earnest liberals because of their opportunism and readiness to compromise principles. Even members of the Party's *Fraktion* seemed stricken with shame. Richard Eickhoff tried to make amends by taking up the Centralverein's case on the denial of reserve officer commissions to Jews in a Reichstag debate on March 5.[97]

The tactics of the party officials in the by-election were a blow to the Centralverein's policy of aligning the Jews with the Progressives. Disillusioned by the opportunism and hypocrisy of the Progressive politicians, some Jews started to talk about withdrawing from politics and questioned critically the support that the Centralverein gave the party. Julius Moses seized upon the by-election to discredit the Progressive-oriented leadership of the Centralverein. In the newspaper that he edited, he baited members of the central board for not condemning the "pseudo-liberalism" of the Progressives and posed the question of what lessons they would learn from Eschwege-Schmalkalden. Tartly he replied, "If they are not blind and stupid, they must see this election as the betrayal of liberalism and the interests of the German Jews by the Progressive People's party."[98]

At a meeting on March 7 the central board decided to speak out publicly against the party's tactics in the runoff. Fuchs presented a draft article for *Im Deutschen Reich*, which Sonnenfeld insisted on revising before publication.[99] He watered down Fuchs's criticism so that the final version represented a compromise between the arguments of those members who thought that the time had come to draw a sharp line against policies which the party followed without any regard for Jewish interests and sensibilities and other members, who were anxious to maintain amicable relations with Progressive leaders.

In the March issue *Im Deutschen Reich* expressed disappointment with the decision of the central committee not to intervene in the runoff and, instead, to leave the question of tactics to the district club. It stated emphatically that suspicions of anti-Semitism were unfounded and that "tactical considerations" led the central committee to adopt a noncommittal stance.[100] After attributing the dubious conduct of the party leaders to "only questions of strategy," *Im Deutschen Reich* called the party's tactics wrong from the standpoint of the Jews and all Germans who wanted to safeguard liberalism. It reproached the central committee for shifting the responsibility for decisions on matters of fundamental policy and principles onto the local clubs. For the future it recommended that the central committee assert authoritative direction over the district organizations and exert greater influence on the opinions of left-liberal voters.

Jews disaffected with the Progressives were not easily reconciled. At a Centralverein meeting in Berlin on March 28 Horwitz tried to placate critics of the Progressive People's party. He admitted that the central board was unhappy about the refusal of the Progressives to campaign against Raab, but he saw no reason for members of the Centralverein to quit the party. After he spoke, several members sharply attacked the party. Curt Rosenberg, a lawyer who worked in the Centralverein's legal defense bureau, announced that he was withdrawing a resolution censuring the party leaders, which he had intended to introduce. All the same, he insisted that a strong protest against their opportunistic tactics was necessary.[101] Karl Lewin was so irate at the efforts of Horwitz to mollify the indignation of Jewish critics of the Progressives that he sarcastically snapped that "no sedative is needed."[102] After expressing his disillusionment with the Progressives, Robert Wohlberg added that the Jews should withdraw from party activities.

The meeting ended without voting on a resolution threatening the party with a massive Jewish defection. Horwitz closed the debate by affirming his confidence in the Progressives. He was reported to have said, "If the leaders of the Progressive People's party make mistakes, their Jewish followers must strive to bring them back on to the right course and should not renounce them and make it hard for them to return to a genuine liberal position."[103]

Between 1898 and 1903 the Centralverein moved step by step into an active role in German politics. By 1903 Horwitz and Fuchs had succeeded in persuading the Jewish community of the legitimacy of a Jewish interest group and of the necessity for making the defense against anti-Semitism politically activist. Instead of forming a separate Jewish bloc, they aligned the defense movement with the Progressives. After Sonnenfeld was coopted to sit on the governing board in 1900, identification especially with the Progressive People's party became more and more open.

From the start the Centralverein and the Progressive parties had a relationship full of ups and downs. The priorities of the Jewish activists and the Progressives were not set alike. On one side, the Progressive politicians did not welcome the intrusion of a Jewish pressure group in party affairs. The Centralverein made Jewish left liberals more conscious of their particular interests and more assertive. The Progressives did not see the anti-Semites elected to the Reichstag as a great menace. A tiny *Fraktion*, the anti-Semites did not engage in obstructionist tactics in parliament, and all their legislative motions to resolve "the Jewish question" ended in failure.[104] The increase in the Social Democratic vote and the loss of Progressive strongholds to the Social Democrats were matters more urgent to the party officials than the demagogic oratory of the do-nothing anti-Semitic parties. On the other side, Jewish activists thought that the party leaders were insensitive to the feelings of the Jews and did not see opposition to the anti-Semitic candidates as a matter of moral principle. In elections in which anti-Semites campaigned, party officials insisted on making decisions on tactics exclusively from the vantage point of party interests and expediency and were annoyed at Jewish criticism of their unprincipled behavior.

Nevertheless, the Progressives found loyal supporters among the Centralverein's leaders. From the speech that Fuchs made after the election of 1898, it is clear why he and Horwitz insisted on politicizing the Jewish defense. Less evident is why they discarded the policy of nonpartisanship and aligned the organization with the Progressives.

The decision to align the Centralverein with the Progressives came out of the debate that Peltasohn's interpellation set off in 1901. Jewish activists discovered that only among the Progressives could they expect to find allies for their fight against discrimination. At the time, Fuchs complained that the Center and National Liberal parties were indifferent to the violation of the rights of Jewish citizens and, in effect, gave a vote of confidence to the arbitrary and unconstitutional practices of the Ministry of Justice.[105] He deplored that the Center party no longer followed the course charted by Ludwig Windhorst, who had spoken out against the anti-Semites in the 1890s, and that the National Liberals had forgotten their liberal traditions and now left the defense of the constitution up to the Progressives. Referring to the bold speeches that Barth and other left-liberal deputies had made, he said, "Since our fate is tied up with the victory of constitutional government, I have no fear of the future even though now we have apparently few friends, and in the debates in parliament only the Progressives have spoken out for our rights."[106]

Convinced that the achievement of civil equality depended upon the survival of the true remnants of liberalism, Horwitz and Fuchs thought that the Jews had a stake in maintaining the Progressive parties. Caught in the middle between the Social Democrats and the parties on the Right, the Progressives came out of the two elections in 1903 weakened and demoralized. The loss of votes that the Progressive People's party suffered produced factionalism and dissidence. The Centralverein's two directors believed that Jewish interests were better served by working within the party for change instead of pillorying it.[107]

Horwitz and Fuchs were well-informed on the affairs of the Progressive parties. Frequent communication with Martin Philippson, Hugo Sonnenfeld, David Waldstein, and other Jews who were in close touch with the inner circles of the two parties enabled them to make astute judgments. They declined to join Bernstein's agitation against Kopsch not because of an obsequious respect for the party officials as Julius Moses and other critics thought. Horwitz and Fuchs knew that Kopsch's explanation was not truthful. As pragmatic men of the world, they had a sense of what was excusable and what was not, and they did not allow emotional feelings to affect their view of the affair. They concluded that the belated disclosure of anti-Jewish remarks that Kopsch had made four years ago was the result of intraparty squabbling. At a meeting in Posen Fuchs warned the Jews against "false friends" who leveled charges of anti-Semitism against Kopsch.[108] Bernstein's conscience was not troubled about the inconsistencies in the party's policies toward the Jews. He feuded with the central committee for personal reasons. In league with Bernstein were other dissident party members, who resented Richter's autocratic way of running the party and the rigidity with which he stuck to his opinions on certain issues. Horwitz and Fuchs saw no political advantage for the Jews in blowing up the scandal and in antagonizing the party establishment.

After the fusion of the National Socials with the Progressive Union, the Centralverein's leadership had good reason to assure the Jews that the suspicions of anti-Semitic influences in the party were unwarranted. In the agreement that Barth and Roesicke negotiated with Gerlach, Naumann, and Weinhausen on July 11, 1903, the National Social leaders accepted the two conditions of dissolving their party and adopting the Progressive Union's program.[109] Furthermore, Gerlach made a forthright reply to the speculation that anti-Semitic influences were penetrating the Progressive Union. In a statement that he asked the editor of the *Berliner Tageblatt* to publish, he wrote that it was wrong to identify Naumann's party with Stöcker's movement. He confessed that before 1896 he had been an anti-Semite and a follower of Stöcker. When he saw the political sterility of anti-Semitism and its connection with the reactionary Agrarians, he turned his back on the movement. He made an emotional plea to Jewish liberals not to condemn the National Socials for what they were in the past and not to deny any politician the chance to correct the mistakes of his youth.[110]

In judging the behavior of the leaders of the Progressive People's party, Horwitz and Fuchs grasped the complexity of the party's situation in runoff elections. Party officials were not concerned with anti-Semitism when they decided the question of tactics in the race between Raab and Hugo. Looking at the runoff from the perspective of how the Progressives could recapture the district in the next election, they saw the Social Democratic party as the tougher enemy. Quite sensibly, *Im Deutschen Reich* chose to discount the hearsay about latent anti-Semitism in the party and to focus its criticism on the tactical reasoning that determined the decision not to oppose Raab.

Unfortunately for the relations between the Jews and the Progressive People's party, the by-election was connected with the controversy over Barth's proposal for an election cartel with the Social

Democrats. The outcome of the two elections in 1903 made party leaders less inclined in February 1904 to listen sympathetically to the argument that they back Hugo as the "lesser evil." In the Reichstag election of 1903 the Progressives lost Berlin and the suburbs to the Socialists, and only by slight margins did Progressive candidates defeat Socialist contenders in the election for the Diet. In former years the Social Democrats boycotted the Prussian parliamentary elections out of protest against the three-class suffrage. In 1903 they participated actively and were tough competitors to the left liberals in Berlin and other cities.[111]

In the runoff elections for the Diet the Progressive People's party rejected an offer that the Social Democrats made for mutual support in the districts where their candidates faced right-wing challengers.[112] The Progressives found themselves fighting the Social Democrats more frequently than candidates of the Right in the second round of voting. Party leaders were afraid that collaboration with the Socialists in some districts would cost them the votes of National Liberals and Free Conservatives, which they needed in cities such as Danzig and Stettin to defeat their biggest competitor for popular votes.

In the debate on election strategy, Barth was opposed not only by gentile party leaders, Max Bromel, Hermann Pachnicke, and Eugen Richter, but also by prominent Jewish Progressives, Oskar Cassel, Martin Philippson, and David Waldstein. At the congress of the Progressive Union on October 11, 1903, when Barth's proposal was on the floor for a vote, neither Philippson, who was the chairman of the Gemeindebund, nor Waldstein, who helped to organize the Central-verein chapter in Hamburg, backed him.[113] They thought that priority should be given to the fusion of the splintered Progressive parties with the National Liberals and that the possibility of such a merger would be killed if the Progressive Union entered an election coalition with the Social Democrats.

In the winter of 1903-04 the Centralverein leaders were all the more anxious to win the good will of the Progressive *Fraktion.* They were adopting an offensive posture and wanted to use parliamentary interpellations and debates to draw national attention to Jewish grievances and to put pressure on the government to comply with the Law of July 3, 1869. Since 1901 the board members had not been in full accord on the expediency of this strategy, but in October 1903 they started to discuss the possibility of a parliamentary debate on Jewish grievances. After six Jewish Progressives were elected to the Diet, *Im Deutschen Reich* called upon them to interpellate top state officials and to attack discrimination in the army and civil administration.[114] Horwitz and Fuchs were willing to risk incurring the displeasure of the state authorities. They were convinced that ministers whose aides had given evasive replies to their private complaints could be compelled through interpellations to confront the evidence of discrimination in public and to be accountable for unconstitutional policies.[115]

The central board submitted evidence that it had compiled to deputies of the Progressive People's party and requested them to censure the government in forthcoming budget hearings.[116] Richard Eickhoff agreed to attack the army's policy of denying officer commissions to Jewish doctors in the Reichstag on March 5, 1904.[117] Robert Gyssling reopened the campaign against the Ministry of Justice when the Diet was examining the budget on January 30, 1905. The Progressives kept up the pressure on Schönstedt, and Cassel sharply criticized him again on March 18.[118]

The Centralverein followed the debates closely. *Im Deutschen Reich* wrote that Cassel documented the practice of discrimination in the judiciary and exposed the unconstitutionality of Schönstedt's assertions in such an unimpeachable manner that the minister was embarrassed and at a loss for words, and none of the deputies took the floor to defend him.[119] It praised the Progressive *Fraktion* for having the courage to speak out against injustice and pointed out that the Center party and the National Liberals stood by silently.[120]

In the years after 1904 the leaders of the defense movement relied increasingly on the Progressive deputies. After several years of frustrating efforts to establish a Jewish political union with a mandate to act for German Jewry, the Verband der deutschen Juden was founded in 1904.[121] A position of considerable influence was granted to Horwitz and Fuchs because the Centralverein financed the organization of the Verband and provided it with clerical personnel before it could afford to hire its own staff.[122] Horwitz and Fuchs sat on the board of directors, and Horwitz was elected to succeed the first chairman in 1909. The Verband functioned as a Jewish lobby, setting out to exert influence on government policy-making and legislation.

Instrumental to the political work that Jewish activists undertook were cordial relations with the Progressive *Fraktion.* Frequently, they solicited the help of left-liberal deputies. Cassel and Peltasohn were asked to sponsor specific legislative proposals and amendments to bills affecting Jewish interests. A close rapport was established also with Christian deputies: Richard Eickhoff, who regularly confronted the Army Ministry with cases of discrimination; Hermann Müller, who succeeded Richter as party chairman in 1906; Georg Gothein, who headed the Abwehrverein after Barth's death in 1908; and Franz von Liszt, a Berlin professor of law, who was elected to the Diet in 1908 and the Reichstag in 1912.

4

THE DILEMMA OF THE JEWISH LEFT LIBERALS:
THE YEARS OF THE BÜLOW BLOC

Between 1898 and 1906, when the defense movement entered German politics, the difficulties of acting as a collective group in political life were not altogether evident. There was considerable political agreement among the German Jews, who were generally identified with the Progressive parties. At times the opposition that the Progressives put up against government anti-Semitism seemed weak, but, despite disappointments, Jewish liberals continued to believe that the principles which the Progressives upheld provided the best shield for the rights of the Jewish minority.

In 1907 and 1908 this consensus broke down. The Reichstag election of 1907 and the entrance of the Progressives into the coalition of parties that Chancellor Bülow promoted sowed uncertainty and confusion in Jewish political circles. The Progressive *Fraktion* ignored Jewish grievances in order to avoid attacking government anti-Semitism. Party officials followed election tactics that confronted Jewish left liberals with a conflict of conscience, the problem of choosing party politics or Jewish interests, party allegiance or loyalty to the Jewish community. Disillusionment with the "bloc politics" of the Progressive People's party deepened, and some Jews searched for political options other than alignment with the Progressives. Disaffection with the Progressives and criticism of the Centralverein's association with the party were expressed by young radicals in the Zionist movement. Hitherto, Zionist leaders Max Bodenheimer and David Wolffsohn, seeing the solution of the Jewish situation outside Germany, kept the movement apart from domestic politics. After 1906 young Zionists who advocated a consciously Jewish stance in German politics clamored that the Jews should stop depending on the Progressive parties. Finally, dissension broke out within the left-liberal camp, and Theodor Barth and his followers seceded from the Progressive Union. Notwithstanding the determination of Horwtiz and Fuchs to keep out of party squabbles, the Centralverein found itself dragged into the conflicts.

On December 13, 1906, after months of denouncing abuses and exposing scandals in the colonial administration, the Center and Social Democratic parties defeated two government bills for appropriations to construct railways in Southwest Africa and to send a military expedition to quell a native revolt in the colony. Chancellor Bülow immediately dissolved the Reichstag and called new elections. To create a progovernment majority and to defeat the "antinational" opposition of the Socialists and the Center, Bülow advanced the formation of a coalition of progovernment *bürgerlich* parties, the Conservatives, the anti-Semitic Economic Union and German Reform party, the National Liberals, and the Progressives. His calculation that the Progressives would join such a cartel weighed heavily in his decision to dissolve the Reichstag.[1] In the Chancellery the opportunism of the Progressive People's party had not gone unnoticed. Bülow had observed how the party had toned down its attacks on imperialism and militarism and had voted for the navy and colonial bills in 1905 and 1906.

Left-wing Progressives viewed the election campaign and the prospect of becoming political bedfellows with Agrarians and anti-Semites with disquietude. The *Berliner Tageblatt* expressed distrust of Bülow's intentions and warned the Progressives that the chancellor planned to use them in a political game of maneuvering and did not intend to pilot the government on to a liberal course.[2] Barth believed that the Progressives would compromise their integrity and liberal principles if they allied with the Conservatives. He argued that the reactionary Right remained the main enemy of liberalism and that party officials who thought that political advantages could be gained from a chauvinistic campaign against the Socialists were deluding themselves.[3]

Within the Progressive parties these grim warnings were ignored. Party leaders were confident that campaigning on the government side and as defenders of national honor against the red–black bloc would enable the Progressives to win many seats in the Reichstag.[4] On December 15 the Progressive People's party joined negotiations for an election coalition. Representatives of the parties made a deal to support joint candidates in several districts. Reluctant to make any public announcement of an alliance with the Conservatives, the party's central committee decided not to sign a joint election manifesto that the negotiators had drafted.[5] The Progressives concluded an agreement only with the National Liberals to support a single candidate in districts where a big vote for the Center or the Social Democrats was expected.

At the start of the campaign the *Allgemeine Zeitung des Judentums* expressed enthusiasm about the formation of the Bülow bloc and thought that now the Progressives would have an opportunity to exert a beneficial influence on the government and the National Liberals.[6] Jewish left liberals soon became distrustful of Bülow's strategy. A letter that the chancellor addressed to the Imperial Union Against Social Democracy on New Year's Eve scored the Progressives for overemphasizing principles and contended that negative doctrinairism prevented them from playing a constructive role in politics.[7] The letter contained no hint of reforms; it made clear that Bülow expected the Progressives to compromise. Speaking at a campaign rally on January 6, 1907, Cassel appeared to be troubled by Bülow's remarks. In response he said, "In the present campaign, it is our solemn obligation to uphold our traditional party principles without wheeling and dealing for any kind of patronage."[8] He stressed that the Progressives would demand domestic reforms as a quid pro quo for joining the progovernment majority in the Reichstag. In campaign speeches on January 18 and 22, Cassel made hard-hitting attacks on government policies, especially the new school law, which the Ministry of Education had proposed to put the primary schools on a Christian confessional foundation. He denounced the New Year's Eve letter as a lullaby of vague promises and expressed doubt that the Progressives would be able to pry liberal concessions from the government.[9]

Cassel's skepticism was echoed in the columns of *Im Deutschen Reich*. Alphonse Levy, the editor, wrote that Bülow's campaign against the Center party was a temporary maneuver and signaled no shift in governmental policy. The chancellor's friendly overtures to the Progressive party leaders would not lead to any liberal changes in the government administration. Bülow regarded the Progressives in the bloc "only as an alloy" and intended to be reconciled with the

Center party as soon as it stopped agitating for reforms and retrench-
ment in the colonial administration.[10]

In deliberating on what election tactics to adopt, the Centralverein's leaders took account of the new party alignments and the
conflict of loyalties that would arise for Jewish liberals from the
decision of the Progressive clubs in many districts to collaborate
with parties on the Right. The Progressives were formally aligned
with the National Liberals, who had shown no scruples about
backing anti-Semitic candidates in previous elections or approving
government practices that excluded Jews from public offices and the
officer corps. The Jewish activists observed also how chauvinism and
antisocialism in the election propaganda of the government and the
Bülow bloc parties gave a new lease of life to the anti-Semites.[11]
They were apprehensive that liberal voters, swayed by nationalist
slogans, would not always judge candidates on the basis of their
commitment to protect the rights of all citizens.

The Centralverein did not heed Bülow's appeal to rally behind the
nationalistic progovernment parties and, in respect to the Progressives, adopted a more independent posture than it had taken in
1903. The *Allgemeine Zeitung des Judentums* announced that if the
Progressive parties wanted the votes of the Jewish liberals, they
would have to endorse candidates whom all Germans, including the
Jews, could trust. For Jewish voters considerations of whether a
candidate stood in official grace "must take second place to considerations of Jewish self-respect and rights."[12]

Party affiliation and loyalty were played down in the election
manifesto that the Centralverein issued. The Jews were warned that
"never was the danger greater than at present that, under the cloak
of lofty phrases, disguised anti-Semites will solicit our votes."[13]
The manifesto urged Jewish voters not to let party affiliation determine their attitude to any candidate but to examine his heart and
mind. It instructed the Jewish liberals not to be influenced by the
changing political banners and alignments of the Progressives.
Irrespective of the pronouncements of the Progressives, the Jews
should not vote for National Liberal candidates "whose outlook
could offer only a weak guarantee" that they would defend civil
equality for the Jewish minority.

The Centralverein's executives thought that the Jews had to

confront, independently of the Progressives, the question of which party to support as the "lesser evil" when left-liberal candidates were not in the race. Both *Im Deutschen Reich* and the *Allgemeine Zeitung des Judentums* emphatically stated that self-respect obliged the Jews to vote for the Polish and the Center parties in districts where the other candidates were Conservatives and National Liberals who supported government policies violating the rights of Jewish citizens.[14] Defending the choice of the Catholic party as the "lesser evil," both newspapers pointed out that respect for the equality of all confessions was more deeply rooted in the conscience of the Center than the Conservatives and that many National Liberals had anti-Semitic feelings.

The Centralverein stood apart from the campaign that the Progressives conducted against the Center party. In many instances Progressive politicians, who were envious of the Center's strength in the Reichstag, joined Bülow's fight against it with more verve than the Conservatives, who were reluctant to attack a party that shared their views on school policy and tariff measures.[15] The Progressives posed as defenders of freedom of learning against clericalism and obscurantism and criticized the Center party for supporting confessional public schools and compulsory religious instruction for schoolchildren. Overzealous Progressive campaigners hinted that the Center's subservience to the Roman Curia kept it from being patriotic.

This agitation fanned Catholic hostility toward the Jews. The Center complained about a *Kulturkampf* and blamed the "Jewish" liberal press. The Centralverein firmly disavowed the campaign against the Center party and insisted that the Jews as a collective group were not responsible for those newspapers that opposed the party.[16] *Im Deutschen Reich* stated that in the provinces of Posen and Silesia the Jews enjoyed harmonious relations with the Catholic population and recognized gratefully that the Center party championed the rights of all Germans in matters of religious worship. It added that Jewish left liberals differed with the Center over school policy but would never attack the Catholic church because the Jews, as a confessional minority like the Catholics, had to stand guard against anyone who would treat them as second-class citizens.[17]

In deciding not to rally to the government's call for a united front against the red–black bloc, Horwitz and Fuchs knew that the Central-verein would be criticized for lacking national loyalty. To Germans who reproached the organization, *Im Deutschen Reich* had a bold reply: "It is not our fault if we adopt a separate position in political elections inasmuch as we not only profess a political creed as voters of other religions do when we cast our votes, but we also must put up a defense which our honor and self-respect command of us."[18]

Another decision that the central board made was not to lobby aggressively for the nomination of Jewish candidates. Twelve Jews ran as Progressive candidates, and the Centralverein expressed the desire to see "several Jews who are not Social Democrats" sitting in the Reichstag.[19] However, the board decided "for well-considered reasons" not to promote Jewish candidates conspicuously. Other than this cryptic remark, it made no public statement about the election of Jewish deputies.

A probable explanation is that Horwitz and Fuchs were deliberately reserved because early in December the Centralverein had been approached by Zionists who wanted the Jews to take a specifically Jewish stance in German politics. Dr. Carl Kassel, a Zionist in the city of Posen, conferred with two local agents of the Centralverein. Little is known about the discussions, which were kept secret, apart from Kassel's reports to Arthur Hantke at the Zionist office in Berlin.[20] Kassel made a plea for the two organizations to end their rivalry. He said that, despite ideological differences, the Central-verein's members and the Zionists had many common interests and could cooperate without abandoning their goals. The Zionists would concede German domestic politics as the Centralverein's sphere of influence if it recognized, in return, the validity of Zionism's aims for Jewry as a whole.

Kassel advanced proposals for a Jewish political platform and a caucus of Jewish deputies. For the Reichstag election he recommended the nomination of Alfred Klee, a Berlin Zionist, Eugen Fuchs, and Paul Nathan. He thought that the Centralverein should break its connections with the Progressive People's party and that it was not advantageous for the Jews to adhere to a party from which the masses of voters were turning away. From his observation of the political situation in the province of Posen, he concluded that the Jews incurred the hostility of the Polish Catholic population by aligning with the German-speaking Progressives, whose "anti-Catholic policies" provoked the Polish ethnic minority. "Political abstention" was the only other honorable course he saw open to the Jews in Germany if they could not succeed in electing deputies to represent their special interests.[21]

Kassel was not the first Zionist to argue for a new political orientation. At the convention of the German Zionist Organization in June 1906, Hans Mühsam, a quick-tempered militant, presented a proposal for a Jewish party. Publicizing his ideas later in the Zionist newspaper *Die Welt*, Mühsam wrote that discrimination and social ostracism stamped the Jews as a distinct class and gave them separate interests from the rest of the German nation.[22] He wisecracked about the Centralverein's relationship with the Progressives and remarked that the Jews should elect deputies who affirmed their Jewishness and "not patronizing Aryans who will let an anti-anti-Semitic rocket fly out the window as a favor to the Progressive party and its 'Mosaic' friends." He was confident that once the Jews were mobilized as an independent political bloc, they would be able to negotiate agreements with other parties and would elect their own candidates or use their bloc of votes as bargaining chips in districts where they were heavily concentrated.

Living in Posen, Kassel was easily attracted to the idea of a Jewish political bloc. He had before him the example of the party that the Polish-speaking Catholics of the province had organized alongside the Center party. In the Reichstag election of 1903 the Polish party won 16 seats. Its deputies concentrated on the defense of the rights of the Polish minority and opposed the anti-Polish school and land settlement policies of the Prussian authorities.

Furthermore, the Jews living in Posen were treated as a national group, different from the German Christian population. Around the turn of the century anti-Semitism entered the conflict between the Germans and the Poles. The Deutscher Ostmark Verein, a powerful lobby of militant nationalists whose chief aim was the germanization of the Eastern provinces, spread propaganda disputing the German nationality of the Jews and inciting Christians to boycott Jewish businessmen, doctors, and lawyers.[23] For years the Jews had taken pride in upholding German culture in Posen and had helped the German Protestants to maintain ascendancy over the Poles. In some places the Jews and the Germans had reached agreements on the distribution of seats in the city councils. Now the Jews were shocked to see the Germans excluding them from local election committees and voting for anti-Semites.[24] While the Pan-Germans ostracized the Jews, the Poles resented them as tools of the *Hakatisten*, as the fanatical German nationalists in the league were nicknamed. Polish newspapers incited the Poles to boycott Jewish merchants and tradesmen. Suffering business losses or seeing no prospects for professional success, many Jews emigrated.[25] Trapped in the middle of the struggle between the Germans and the Poles, the Jews became aware of themselves as a third and separate group in political life.

In his talks with the Centralverein's agents Kassel could not persuade them to accept his proposal. At first he blamed the failure of the negotiations on the personal antipathy that Kirschner and Pincus felt toward the Zionists. Later he gave as the main reason that "the men of the Centralverein regard Jewish matters as something entirely secondary and that the affairs of the Progressive People's party are their foremost concern."[26]

Kassel's reports may account for the responses of Kirschner and Pincus but do not explain why Horwitz and Fuchs did not participate in the negotiations.[27] *Im Deutschen Reich* denied a press leak that connected Kassel's scheme with the Centralverein.[28] Apart from their ideological differences with the Zionists and their affiliation with the Progressives, Horwitz and Fuchs had many reasons for being unreceptive to Kassel's overture. They were convinced that activists in the movement for civil equality had to work with the German parties. The Jewish population was too scattered and numerically too weak to be able to elect deputies on an exclusively Jewish platform. They did not believe that the Jews in Germany had "Jewish-national" political goals. German Jews were striving for social integration with the rest of the nation. They felt themselves to be German and regarded themselves as a religious rather than a separate ethnic community.[29]

From his experience in the East Kassel generalized a political strategy for all German Jews. Horwitz and Fuchs, who lived in Berlin and traveled throughout the country, saw Posen as a peculiar situation, which offered no guidelines for the political conduct of the Jews elsewhere. Even for the Jews remaining in Posen, the Centralverein saw no remedy in a separate Jewish party or political platform. It advised them not to become bitter or to emigrate but to maintain solidarity with the rest of the German population.[30] Held out to them was the hope that sooner or later government officials would see that the emigration of the Jews was a loss for the German nationality in the province and would suppress anti-Semitic agitation.

Horwitz and Fuchs knew that top figures in the Zionist movement were not promoting Kassel's or Mühsam's schemes. Zionist leaders adopted an attitude of reserve toward Kassel's discreet undertaking, but they were irked at Mühsam, whom they regarded as a trouble-maker. In Cologne Max Bodenheimer, the chairman of the central committee of the German Zionist Organization, felt obliged to make public assurances that Mühsam's ideas were not official policy and that the Zionists fulfilled their civic duties with loyalty.[31] In Berlin Adolf Friedemann and Arthur Hantke deplored the articles on "Jew-ish-national politics" in *Die Welt*.[32] In a sharp rebuttal to Mühsam, Friedemann wrote that the situation of the German Jews was differ-ent from that of the Jews in Austria-Hungary and Russia, where each nationality densely inhabited certain regions and maintained its own culture. The Jews in Germany had the same interests as the Christian population, and their culture was German.[33] Operating behind the scenes, Friedemann put pressure on the editor of *Die Welt* to squelch further discussion of these proposals.[34] He thought that it was not advisable for the Zionist press to publicize ideas which, besides being impractical, alienated non-Jewish Germans.

Horwitz and Fuchs were not likely to respond warmly to any Zionist proposal for common political action because the Central-verein found among the Zionists no enthusiastic support for its work. In November 1906, just before the Posen talks, the Cologne chapter invited Bodenheimer to become a member. As he had done once before, the Zionist official declined and told Hermann Jonas, who headed the chapter, that he could not recommend membership to fellow Zionists.[35] He objected to the Centralverein's emphasis on the German nationality of the Jews and its characterization of the Jews as simply a religious community. Articles in the Zionist press jeered at the Centralverein. The *Jüdische Rundschau* called its defense tactics ineffective and berated its leaders for the folly of defining the solution to the Jewish condition in terms of civil equality and religious tolerance. The Zionists said over and over that in Germany the Jews would never achieve equal rights except through baptism and "absorption," the renunciation of their group distinctiveness.[36] To substantiate this pessimistic appraisal, the Zionist press published, with a feeling of satisfaction, reports on the lawsuits that the Centralverein's legal defense department lost.

During the election campaign the Centralverein was very active but gave no publicity to its work. At a meeting on January 29 Julius Brodnitz reported what the organization was doing "so far as the discretion required by the circumstances of political elections permits."[37] The Berlin office solicited campaign contributions and supplied funds to contest anti-Semitic candidates in 32 constituencies.[38] The money was funneled to district election committees through the Centralverein's local agents. The Centralverein printed thousands of leaflets disclosing the record of criminal convictions for slander, libel, embezzlement, extortion, and other offenses that the anti-Semitic candidates had committed to prove their moral unfitness to sit in the Reichstag.

The Progressive Union fulfilled its obligations to the Jewish defense movement more conscientiously than the Progressive People's party did. The central committee of the Progressive People's party decided on a noncommittal policy, leaving left liberals free to vote as they wished in the runoff elections.[39] After a meeting on January 27, officials of the Progressive Union issued a manifesto, which warned that the parties threatening the achievements of liberalism, universal suffrage, civil equality, and the right of association for the working class, had advanced far in the first balloting on January 25. It called upon left liberals to vote for candidates whose character and program offered a solid guarantee that they would not serve the cause of reaction.[40] In a guideline on campaign speeches the Progressive Union recommended that candidates should demand that the government observe scrupulously legal guarantees of equal rights and end discrimination against the Jews.[41]

When the runoffs were over on February 5, the Centralverein estimated that among the elected deputies were 30 anti-Semites. Anti-Semitic party candidates were defeated in 13 of the 32 districts in which the Centralverein gave financial backing to the challengers.[42] The report added that 4 anti-Semites owed their Reichstag seats to Progressive voters. Left-liberal votes were decisive for the election of Friedrich Bindewald in Alsfeld-Lauterbach, Gustav Gäbel in Meissen-Grossenhain, Walter Gräf in Weimar-Apolda, and Friedrich Raab in Eschwege-Schmalkalden.[43] Ernst Müller-Meiningen, a Progressive People's party deputy running for reelection, helped an anti-Semitic National Liberal to victory in Jena with his endorsement.[44] Party leaders in Weimar backed Gräf after making an agreement with the Agrarian League whereby its defeated candidate in Erlangen asked his followers to vote for the Progressive in the runoff.[45] Progressives in Eschwege-Schmalkalden, swayed by nationalist propaganda, put pressure on their defeated candidate to issue an endorsement of Raab as the *bürgerlich* candidate.[46] In Saxony the state committee of the Progressive Union, including two members of the Abwehrverein's board of directors, supported anti-Semitic candidates who were contesting Social Democrats.[47] Explaining this decision, a party newspaper stated that it would be "a terrible, irremediable mistake if we Progressives isolated ourselves from the upsurge of indignant citizens. Never may a Progressive vote be cast for a Social Demo cratic candidate. Compelled by the circumstances of the runoff election, we shall have to support even those *burgher* elements for whom we feel deep aversion."[48] It added that the defeat of socialism was the heroic task of the 1907 election and "whoever turns his back on it risks the danger of becoming completely isolated."

At the Centralverein headquarters the outcome of the election was regarded as a setback for the Jews. Despite the increase in the number of Progressive mandates, from 37 in 1903 to 49, all 12 Jewish candidates whom the left-liberal parties nominated were defeated. The anti-Semites won 9 more mandates. More disheartening to activists in the Jewish defense movement was the voting pattern of Progressives and National Liberals in the runoffs.

The election was the main item on the agenda of the Centralverein's national convention, which was held on February 24 in Berlin. More than 130 delegates representing chapters throughout Germany attended. To give the main address this time, the central board selected Dr. Joseph Lewy. Lewy, a physician by profession, had a more detached attitude toward the Progressives than Sonnenfeld.

Speaking on behalf of the governing board, Lewy deplored the upswing in anti-Semitic votes, from 244,543 in 1903 to 448,809, and the likelihood that it would create the impression that hostility to the Jews was spreading. He urged the delegates not to become despondent. He attributed the big anti-Semitic turnout to the higher percentage of voters who went to the polls, 85.4 percent in 1907 in comparison with 75.8 percent in 1903, and to the government's campaign against the Socialists and appeals to national honor, which the anti-Semitic parties exploited to their political advantage.[49]

More discouraging to Lewy than the victory of so many anti-Semites was the helping hand that the Progressives and National Liberals gave them. He exclaimed that seldom before the 1907 election did the runoffs have such a "demoralizing influence" on party leaders, who made opportunistic deals and identified liberalism with the reactionary Right. As a result, "anti-Semites entered the Reichstag to a large extent on the crutches of the parties on the Left."[50] He announced that four anti-Semites owed their election to the Progressives, four to the National Liberals, and one to the Social Democrats. Unable to hold back his own angry bitterness, he sputtered: "What has been so deeply painful and the most discouraging sight in this campaign is that the followers of the [liberal] Left see the anti-Semites as the lesser evil in comparison with the Social Democrats—the anti-Semites who want to undermine the foundations of constitutional government and force our civilization back decades and who have conducted demagogic agitation of the most incredible kind and reveal themselves to be in reality the embryo of anarchism."

Lewy criticized the central committee of the Progressive People's party for not instructing the district clubs to oppose anti-Semitic candidates. He blamed the party's noncommittal stand for the fact that many liberals who disliked the Social Democrats had voted for anti-Semites or had abstained as the Jews in the district of Eschwege-Schmalkalden had done. Looking to the future, he made several recommendations. The Centralverein must act more vigorously before the runoffs and apply pressure on the Progressive party leaders to take Jewish interests into account when they made decisions on tactics. It must interview candidates to get a clarification of their political views and then advise Jewish voters on which candidates to support. The Centralverein's local agents must increase their influence in the Progressive district committees in order to "prevent some unfortunate incidents."[51]

After Lewy's address, the delegates gave expression to their anger with the Progressive People's party. Dr. Benno Wilhelm Badt, a high school teacher representing the chapter in Breslau, proposed what was intended to be a motion of censure against the party. He asked the convention to pass a resolution declaring that it was "inconsistent with the honor of a Jew to belong to a political organization which makes agreements with anti-Semites or sympathizers of anti-Semites for the purpose of winning elections."[52] Ludwig Wertheimer, a lawyer who headed the Frankfurt chapter, argued that party officials should be admonished that if they continued to adopt opportunistic tactics, they would lose campaign contributions from the Jews and would alienate the Jewish intelligentsia.[53] Rabbi Kopfstein criticized the performance of the Progressive *Fraktion* in the recent parliamentary deliberations on the Prussian school law.

Rising to defend the party, Sonnenfeld asserted that Jewish attacks on the Progressives could be more dangerous than the increasing number of anti-Semites elected to the Reichstag. Sonnenfeld was disturbed by the possibility that the Jewish left liberals would leave the party and form a separate political union. He assured the delegates that the Progressives did not slight the importance of Jewish interests, but they saw the Social Democratic party, with its tight bureaucratic organization and disciplined mass following, as a greater challenge to liberalism than the disreputable and intellectually barren anti-Semitic splinter groupings. He appealed to the delegates to understand the tactical reasoning that determined the party's policies and to hold no grudges.[54]

The wrath of the delegates fell also upon Jewish voters who abstained in the runoffs between anti-Semites and Social Democrats. In the district of Hofgeismar-Rinteln, where many Jews declined to support the Socialist candidate, victory went to the anti-Semite Richard Herzog.[55] In the district of Meseritz the Jews voted for the German candidate, a Conservative Junker, in preference to the Polish candidate.[56] The delegates severely reproached these voters for allowing themselves to be intimidated by the upsurge of chauvinism and insisted that under all circumstances the Jews must vote against anti-Semites.[57] Underscoring this dictum, Lewy contended that besides upholding the honor of Germany, the Jews must defend their personal honor and the dignity of Judaism. If the Jewish liberals found Progressive policies conflicting with the imperatives of loyalty to their religious community, party leaders who created the predicament must be blamed.[58]

What alarmed the Centralverein's leaders about Badt's resolution was the feeling of disillusionment out of which it came. They moved swiftly to prevent any defection from the Progressive People's party. Addressing a meeting in Königsberg two weeks before the convention, Horwitz impressed upon his listeners that the Jews would commit a blunder if they boycotted the German parties.[59] He said that the Jews should remain affiliated with the Progressives and should work harder to influence their policies. At the convention Horwitz repeated these views and refuted Rabbi Kopfstein's criticism of the Progressive deputies by calling attention to the amendments that they had introduced to improve provisions of the school bill affecting the Jews.[60]

To counter Badt's motion, Hermann Cohn, a Progressive deputy in the Diet, proposed another resolution, which called upon the Jews to work more energetically in whatever party they joined.[61] He sought to convince the delegates that if the Jewish left liberals proved to be loyal party workers and contributors, the Progressives would recognize the value of the Jewish members and would give more consideration to Jewish interests in making decisions on policy and tactics. Before the convention adjourned, Badt withdrew his motion, and the delegates passed Cohn's resolution.

Cohn's toothless resolution left the unrelenting critics of the Progressives dissatisfied. They were disappointed that the convention did not vote a motion of censure against the party's central committee for refusing to instruct the district leaders to oppose anti-Semitic candidates.[62] They wanted the Centralverein to threaten the Progressives with the loss of campaign funds unless the party made a pledge to oppose all anti-Semitic candidates in upcoming elections and disavowed publicly the tactics of those local party leaders who had abetted the election of anti-Semites in runoffs against Socialist candidates.

Strident attacks were made on the Centralverein from militant Zionists, who sought to exploit Jewish disaffection with the Progressives in order to discredit the defense organization as the political spokesman for German Jewry. *Die Welt* pronounced the election a blow to the "fawning" followers of the Progressives in the Central-verein and a vindication of the Zionists, who had foreseen the futility of the defense movement and had warned against its self-deceptive optimism and assimilationist policies.[63] With unconcealed relish, the newspaper observed that the election must be a bitter experience and humiliation for the central board, which campaigned for the Progressives, poured money into their treasury, and was rewarded by the spectacle of Progressives helping anti-Semites win Reichstag seats. In an article on the Centralverein's convention *Die Welt* criticized the governing board for not taking a tough stand against the Progressives and chided the delegates for swallowing the pet phrases of *Schutzjudentum.*

From Lewy's speech at the convention it is clear that, unlike Sonnenfeld, some board members were critical of the Progressive People's party for treating the Jews as a negligible factor in making decisions on election tactics and for giving their election rivalry with the Social Democrats priority over the obligation of liberalism to withstand anti-Semitic attacks on the rights of Jewish citizens. Nonetheless, they reacted with a restraint that sneering critics did not understand. Horwitz and Fuchs were too conscious of their responsibility as recognized spokesmen of the Jewish defense move-ment to make grandstand protests threatening party officials with the loss of Jewish votes and financial backing.

Horwitz, Fuchs, and other Jewish activists believed that the defection of the Jews from the Progressives would be a disastrous mistake.[64] In their opinion the political separation of the Jews from the German left liberals would accomplish what the anti-Semites wished. The Jews would eventually find themselves isolated in German society, severed from the rest of the nation in social and cultural life as well as in politics. Political separatism would put the Jewish struggle for equal rights in jeopardy. From experience the leaders of the defense movement knew that arguments for equality of opportunity based on legal guarantees would win assent in German society only if the Jews insisted on being, and were regarded by other citizens as, part of the German nation. If the Jews walked out of the Progressive parties, many Germans would see this act of protest as a sign that the Jews had given up their fight against discrimination.

Horwitz and Fuchs were convinced that the Jews could achieve more by striving for an influential voice inside party circles than by shooting off defiant threats. In this conviction they were supported by the mature and politically informed Zionists in Berlin. Arthur Hantke disapproved of the articles in *Die Welt* and sent a letter of protest to the editor.[65] He wrote that the Centralverein's campaign strategy was the "only sensible one" and regretted that cordial relations with its directors might have been damaged.

Hans Gideon Heymann publicly rebuked the radicals of *Die Welt* for their intemperate attacks on the Centralverein and the Progressives. "Those Jews who support the Progressives through work and money," he declared, "have served the cause of the Jews better than those who compromise Zionism by promoting unconstructive and crypto-anti-Semitic crankiness."[66] He stated that the party's central committee was making a conscientious effort to promote the election of Jews to the Reichstag. As evidence, he mentioned Jewish left liberals who were not "stand-in candidates" in the 1907 election, Cassel and Rosenow in Berlin and Weil in Karlsruhe for the Progressive People's party and Braband in Hamburg and Preuss in Czarnikau-Filehne for the Progressive Union. Pointing out that the Progressive Union had taken a stand against anti-Semitism, he argued that it was not the fault of the central leaders that Progressives in many districts ignored the directive and persisted in seeing the Social Democrats as a greater danger than the anti-Semites or the Conservatives. He attributed these incidents to the weak organization and discipline of the Progressive parties and said that this situation would not be remedied "by throwing in the towel and condemning liberalism wholesale." After rejecting the idea of a Jewish party, he proposed that the left-liberal voters be better organized and trained in party discipline and that the Jews create out of the Centralverein and the Verband more effective political instruments.

The fluidity of the political situation was probably another reason for the determination of the central board to head off any precipitant break with the Progressives. At this time it was not clear what direction Bülow would follow, but some board members believed that the government would take a liberal course. This optimistic view was conveyed to delegates at the convention in a speech that Martin Lövinson delivered on how the newly elected Reichstag would deal with Jewish matters and whether the government would make concessions to liberal demands.[67]

To Lövinson and other leading figures in the Centralverein the Progressives appeared to be in a more favorable political position than they had been for years. The Progressives had supported the chancellor's campaign against the red-black bloc, and in the coming Reichstag sessions the government needed their votes.[68] Jewish activists expected the Progressive *Fraktion* to insist on reforms as a condition for joining the progovernment coalition. In December there was speculation about the resignation of Minister of Education Konrad Studt in political circles.[69] Jewish liberals, who opposed Studt's policy of giving the primary schools a Christian confessional teaching staff and curriculum, were hoping that Bülow would cashier him and introduce reforms in the Ministry of Education as a concession to the Progressives.

The Centralverein's directors could not ignore the mood of the Jews after the election—the resentment toward the Progressive politicians and a feeling of pessimism about the attainment of equal rights and social acceptance in Germany. The convention left the central board with a strong impression of how widespread this mood of despondency was. From March on, chapter meetings were arranged at which the Jewish deputies Cassel and Cohn delivered speeches that were intended to squelch the idea of boycotting the Progressive parties. At such a meeting on April 17, Cohn contended that a separate party or exclusively Jewish political platform was not a practical alternative. He appealed to the Jews not to be moved by emotions of despair but to increase their social contacts with Christian citizens and to keep on striving for civil equality.[70]

The Centralverein sought to rekindle the commitment of the Jews to a politically activist defense strategy. Speeches delivered at chapter meetings harped on the theme that instead of succumbing to pessimism, the Jews should learn from the election how necessary it was to engage in politics more actively than before.[71] Members in the chapters were urged to join local party clubs. They were told that because the Progressives had neither the rigid discipline nor the tight centralized organization of the Social Democrats, the Centralverein could influence their election tactics more effectively if it engaged in negotiations directly with the party's district clubs rather than working through the central committee. The chapters were encouraged to help the Berlin headquarters by establishing contacts with party officials on the district level.

The Centralverein made a great effort to restore confidence in the Progressives. The April issue of *Im Deutschen Reich* gave extensive coverage to the convention of the Abwehrverein on March 2, at which Barth delivered the keynote address, entitled "Our Position on Anti-Semitism during and after the Reichstag Election." Barth was commended for talking frankly about the opportunism of the Progresssives in the election and the inroads that anti-Semitism was making in government and society.[72] To show that the Progressives were still trustworthy and, in matters affecting the Jews, would make no accommodations to Conservatives and anti-Semites in the progovernment coalition, the article quoted Barth's stern warning that the Progressives would lose integrity and suffer a political decline if they compromised the principle of equal rights or accepted token concessions that offered less than what the constitution guaranteed.

The Centralverein impressed upon the Jews the important part that gentile left liberals played in combating anti-Semitism. *Im Deutschen Reich* pointed out that the organizers of the Centralverein had always recognized the value of the Abwehrverein, whose members regarded opposition to discrimination as "the logical consequence of genuine liberal principles" and felt that "it is a shame for the entire German nation if the majority of the population misuses its power to deny justice to a small minority."[73] The Centralverein's founders created an exclusively Jewish defense organization because only such a movement could perform the task of stengthening the self-esteem and community loyalty of the Jews. In fighting discrimination, on the other hand, the Jews "must welcome allies" who shared with them a sense of justice and did not look to baptism as the way of eliminating anti-Semitism.

When the Progressive People's party held its congress in September, the Centralverein gave wide publicity to the resolution that was introduced by Hermann Müller, the party chairman after Richter's death in 1906. The resolution stated that full equality of rights should be speedily implemented and that qualified persons should not be denied appointment to public offices or officer commissions because of class or religious differences.[74] *Im Deutschen Reich* informed its readers that in passing this resolution the Progressives intended to refute criticism coming from the Jews. Müller's declaration was one that left-liberal politicians routinely uttered, but the Centralverein's leaders sought to give it practical and immediate application. *Im Deutschen Reich* concluded its news report on the party congress by stating that the prospect of winning a seat in parliament must not weigh heavily in the party's decisions on election tactics if the principle of equal rights was betrayed through political compacts with opponents of this liberal tenet. Having passed the resolution, the party must now persuade the Bülow government that "the bloc strategy is worthless and untenable without the enforcement of the Law of July 3, 1869."[75]

Jewish trust in the Progressives was not easily restored. After the election the Progressive *Fraktion* joined the Bülow bloc, the progovernment majority in the Reichstag. Whereas the chancellor saw the bloc as an expedient political combination and never intended to swing over to liberalism, the Progressives mistook his tactical maneuvers as the dawn of a new era. They were confident that Bülow, who remained at odds with the Center party, needed their votes and would make concessions. Barth disapproved of the coalition with the right-wing parties, but other Progressive deputies were eager to participate in the bloc. They were fed up with the political impotence of opposition, and participation in the progovernment majority seemed to be a chance to exercise some influence on legislation.[76]

The alignment of the Progressives with the Bülow bloc put the leadership of the Centralverein to a severe test. During the election Horwitz and Fuchs were skeptical of Bülow's intentions. Afterward they set aside their doubts and adopted a wait-and-see policy. In private talks with officials in the Chancellery, party spokesmen did not set any conditions for supporting the government and extracted no specific concessions or promises of reform. Instead, they contented themselves with two ministeral changes, the dismissal of Studt and the appointment of the reputedly enlightened Bethmann Hollweg to the Ministry of the Interior. They interpreted the chancellor's vague remarks about applying bloc politics to Prussia as a promise to reform the three-class suffrage.

Eager to cooperate with the government and anxious to avoid friction with the other bloc parties, the Progressive *Fraktion* was reluctant to attack injustices done to the Jews in parliamentary debates. In the readings of the budget in 1907, Progressive deputies refrained from annoying the war minister or the minister of justice with interpellations about government discrimination. In the Diet on February 19, when Cassel and Peltasohn raised questions about the forcible expulsion of Russian immigrants, they sidestepped the fact that most of the victims of the police authorities were Jews. Apologetically, Cassel assured the legislators that he did not intend to discuss the matter at length.[77]

When some Jews murmured that the Progressive *Fraktion* was avoiding Jewish questions, the Centralverein counseled them to be patient. *Im Deutschen Reich* explained that the Progressives were waiting with their demands for reforms because they did not want to split the bloc by raising too hastily issues over which the parties disagreed. Once the coalition was stabilized, there was "all the more hope for concessions from the Conservatives and the government."[78]

By the end of 1907 the patience of Horwitz and Fuchs with the conduct of the Progressive *Fraktion* was wearing thin. In November *Im Deutschen Reich* demanded that Bülow give proof of his professed desire to strengthen the government with liberal support by introducing reform legislation and appointing liberals to administrative positions.[79] The Centralverein served notice to Progressive party officials that there were limits to the distance which the Jews would go in supporting their coalition with the bloc parties. After vouching for the readiness of the Jews to make sacrifices for the sake of the fatherland, *Im Deutschen Reich* declared gravely that the Progressives should not ask the Jews to make the sacrifice of supporting men in political power who denied their claim to equality of rights and did not respect their religion. It added, in respect to speculation that the Progressive *Fraktion* was dodging Jewish matters, "The Jews may offer no sacrifice for the continuation of the bloc if the central [party] leaders should conclude, behind the backs of their Jewish comrades, compromises with enemies of the Jews," which allowed them to determine what issues should be taken up in parliament.[80]

On December 4 the Progressive People's party held a caucus and voted to adhere to the Bülow bloc. Once again Horwitz and Fuchs kept their reservations silent and stood loyally behind the party. Justifying the party's decision, *Im Deutschen Reich* said that the bloc was "highly desirable for progress in the step-by-step realization of equal rights for the German Jews" and that it would be "impossible to achieve progress in this field without the continuation of the Progressives in the bloc at least for the time being."[81]

It was not until February 1908 that the Centralverein's leaders admitted that the bloc politics of the Progressives had failed. Bülow's rejection of any reform of the Prussian three-class suffrage convinced them that the government was not willing to alienate the Conservatives.[82] What finally shattered their hopes for moderate reforms was the discovery that the new minister of education intended to follow rather than to change Studt's school policy. Speaking in the Diet on February 13, Minister of Education Ludwig Holle remarked that school teachers should combine "a warm heart for the Protestant church" with intellectual competence and were expected not only to give academic instruction but also to "develop a Christian character in the youth."[83] He made clear that this point of view would be official policy. From Holle's speech and the continued presence of Philipp Schwartzkopff and other men known to be unsympathetic to the Jews in senior positions in the ministry, Horwitz and Fuchs concluded that a more liberal administration of school affairs could not be expected from Studt's dismissal.[84]

The Centralverein's justification of the decision of the Progressive People's party to remain in the progovernment coalition dismayed critics of this policy. Barth and his followers, who lamented the demoralizing effect that the bloc had on the Progressives, could not comprehend how Jews in the defense movement could close their eyes to the fact that the Bülow government had made no concessions to Jewish demands.[85] The Abwehrverein, whose executive committee Barth headed, missed no opportunity to remind Jewish liberals that among the bloc partners of the Progressives were anti-Semites and Agrarians. It attacked the Progressive *Fraktion* for retreating from liberal principles in order to accommodate the bloc.[86]

Julius Moses blasted the Centralverein's directors for justifying the continuation of the Progressives in the bloc. He contended that the

Progressive *Fraktion*, obliging Bülow and the bloc parties, stopped bringing up Jewish grievances in parliament.[87] His newspaper mockingly called the Jewish deputies in the Progressive *Fraktion* "the famous silent seven." He castigated them for failing to seize the opportunity of parliamentary debates on bills for Germanizing the provinces of Posen and West Prussia to expose the injustices suffered by the Jews there. Even the politically left-liberal *Allgemeine Zeitung des Judentums* admitted in January that the Jews had not benefited from the bloc politics of the Progressives. It remarked, "While the enemies [of the Jews] do not desist in the slightest from agitating now just as before, 'good friends' keep silent in a way that makes them look downright ridiculous."[88]

The astonishing persistence with which the Centralverein's leaders justified the participation of the Progressives in the bloc sprang from the faulty assessment that they made of the political situation in 1907. At the start their decision was by no means unsound. Horwitz and Fuchs believed that the Progressives, working in the progovernment majority, would be able to do more for the Jews than they had done in opposition. Moreover, the formation of the bloc did not seem to them detrimental to Jewish interests. It meant the rupture of the Conservative–Center cartel, which they held responsible for the passing of legislation confessionalizing the primary schools in 1906. Their error was the presumption that the Progressives were in a stronger bargaining position than they actually were and that Bülow, in need of Progressive votes because of his rift with the Center party, would make some moderate concessions. Because at first they were so optimistic in discerning new winds blowing through the Chancellery, it was all the more difficult for them later to discount the possibility of reforms.

The leaders of the defense movement misjudged also the extent to which the Progressives would make accommodations to the government and the bloc parties on Jewish questions. They were too impressed by the ideological cleavage between the left liberals and the Right and were confident that the Progressives had long ago learned that the Conservatives used anti-Jewish hostility in order to strike at liberalism.[89] Accordingly, they convinced themselves that the Progressives in the bloc "can and shall not give up justified demands" and would collaborate with the Conservatives only in matters of defense and foreign policy.[90]

Making this assessment all the more credible were the repeated assurances of Jewish politicians that the Progressives, in their cooperation with the progovernment majority, would not surrender fundamental liberal principles. Martin Peltasohn made such a pledge in a widely publicized article, "Bloc Politics and the Jews," which he wrote specifically to placate Jewish liberals who suspected that the Progressive *Fraktion* was backsliding on the defense of Jewish rights in deference to the wishes of the government. In the article, which the Centralverein commended to its members, Peltasohn declared that the Jews were needlessly alarmed over the bloc. The bloc was formed to handle certain imperial questions in the Reichstag and did not extend to the state parliaments, in which matters bearing on Jewish affairs were deliberated.[91] The Jews could trust the Progressives to vote for government bills "only insofar as they are reconcilable with their principles." "The Progressives are not inclined and have not the slightest reason to abandon the defense of the rights of the Jews out of consideration for the bloc in the Reichstag," he vouched. He concluded with a remark implying that Jewish distrust of the Progressives was unwarranted: "The conduct [of the *Fraktion*] up to now gives no cause for fears that insofar as Jewish interests are represented in parliament and defended against attack, belonging to the bloc could lead to a neglect or abandonment of this duty."[92]

5

THE CONFLICT BETWEEN PARTY
AFFILIATION AND THE IMPERATIVES OF
JEWISH HONOR AND LOYALTY

Martin Peltasohn sought to sustain the faith of the Jews in the Progressives at a time when disaffection was rising. The Progressives were politically demoralized and divided. On January 10, 1908, Bülow rejected a Progressive proposal to reform Prussia's three-class suffrage. On the next day the Progressive deputies held a caucus, and after a heated debate on whether to withdraw from the Bülow bloc, the majority voted to stay in it. Several members on the central committee of the Progressive Union were upset over this decision and requested the *Fraktion* to propose a motion of no-confidence in Bülow. The deputies refused to break with the government.[1] Remaining in the progovernment majority, the Progressives retreated from their principles step by step. They helped the Conservatives and the National Liberals to pass a harsher law against lese majesty and a law on political associations, which abolished restrictions on the right of association for women but in another provision limited the exercise of the same right for the French-speaking and Polish-speaking minorities in the empire. Attacking these actions as a surrender of the party's principles and integrity, Barth proposed a motion to censure the *Fraktion* at the congress of the Progressive Union in Frankfurt in April. When the delegates voted down the motion, Barth and his followers walked out of the party.[2]

Barth's secession came at the opening of the election campaign for the Prussian parliament. Jewish left liberals were in a state of uncertainty over what course they should follow. Many Jews had lost respect for Progressive politicians. Deputies such as Otto Mugdan and Otto Wiemer, courted by Bülow with decorations and invitations to private talks in the Chancellery, now spoke evasively on the issue of suffrage reform in Prussia. The occasional criticism that Progressive deputies made about government anti-Semitism was perfunctory and couched in vague language; little pressure was put on the state authorities to comply with the law and to end discriminatory practices. Jewish left liberals found themselves in the dilemma of no longer trusting the Progressives and of not knowing what other party they could join and keep their honor as Jews uncompromised.

The year of 1908 was a time of crisis for Jewish liberals in German politics. Jewish activists started to question the expediency of the Centralverein's political strategy and to explore alternatives to the alignment of the defense movement with the Progressives. Young Zionists expounded the idea of making the Jews a respected political force in Germany by organizing them as a disciplined voting bloc and by trading off their support to whatever party offered the most favorable terms. The option chosen by other Jews was the Democratic Union, a party that Barth and other Progressive secessionists founded in May.

Early in the spring the Centralverein issued an election manifesto. In a brief paragraph Horwitz called attention to the issues affecting the Jews that the next session of the Prussian parliament would deliberate. He exhorted the members to join political parties and to start working in the campaign early enough to prevent the selection of candidates who were unsympathetic to the Jews.[3]

The central board refrained from openly endorsing the Progressives in the manifesto, but partisan sympathy was evident in an article that *Im Deutschen Reich* published just before the balloting. By implication, the Centralverein stated that other party options would not offer the Jews better political guarantees than the Progressives. The article contended that the Progressives were necessarily obliged to speak out for Jewish interests because the very existence of liberalism was at stake in the government's scrupulous observance of laws safeguarding the principle of equal rights.[4]

After praising Center leaders in the past, Lieber and Windhorst, *Im Deutschen Reich* suggested that now Center party members who spoke for religious freedom did so in their own interests. The article went on to say that the Catholic party showed less concern for the rights of other minorities when it supported government policies that put the Prussian primary school system on a Christian confessional foundation or when it cited the idea of the "Christian state" in debates on discrimination against the Jews in the civil service. Some Center newspapers were in the habit of making anti-Semitic slips. The Centralverein pointed out that attitudes toward the Jews varied in the party and advised voters to scrutinize Center candidates individually and to support them only if they gave sufficient proof of not being latently anti-Semitic.[5]

The Centralverein adopted a stand on the Social Democrats with an eye on Berlin, where four Jews nominated by the Progressive People's party (Cassel, Gerschel, Rosenow, and Weigert) were fiercely contested by Social Democratic candidates. Benefiting from the three-class franchise, the Progressives had won all of Berlin's nine seats in the Diet in 1903. In 1907 the Socialists had fought hard against the left-liberal stronghold and had captured five of the six Berlin Reichstag districts. In the upcoming election, even with the advantage of the three-class voting system, the Berlin Progressives were not very optimistic about beating their challengers from the far Left.[6] Cassel and Rosenow, like many other Progressive politicians, regarded the Social Democrats as the party's foremost threat and rejected the idea that the left liberals should vote for Social Democrats as the "lesser evil" in runoffs against candidates of the Right.[7]

Furthermore, Jewish Progressives bore a grudge against the Social Democrats because of the rough campaign that they waged in the 1907 election. Several rallies at which Rosenow gave campaign speeches were disrupted by the commotion of Socialist intruders.[8] Cassel too was the victim of mean campaign tricks. He ran for election in a constituency with a large Jewish population, and, to turn Jewish voters against him, Social Democratic agitators distributed handbills alleging that he had deserted the Jewish faith and that his children had been baptized.[9] Early on the morning of the election they circulated another leaflet urging Jews not to vote for Cassel, in order to punish his party for supporting anti-Semitic reactionaries in other districts.[10]

The enmity between the Progressives and the Social Democrats made it difficult for the Centralverein to take a public stand in districts where the big contenders were Social Democrats and rightwing candidates. The Centralverein espoused the policy that under all circumstances the Jews must act to prevent the election of anti-

Semites. The central board edged away from this rule and was reluctant to give a public endorsement to Social Democrats in runoffs against Conservatives or National Liberals.

Horwitz and Fuchs made a frank admission of this predicament on the occasion of a by-election for the Reichstag seat of Hofgeismar-Rinteln in 1906. The governing board came under fire for not promoting the election of the Social Democratic candidate, who was defeated by Richard Herzog of the German Social party. Justifying the board's inaction, *Im Deutschen Reich* asserted that any effort to campaign for the Social Democrats would have been useless because the antagonism of the Progressives to the Social Democrats was so intense. It elaborated that "there prevails in many Jewish circles deep resentment not only at the various election agreements between the Social Democrats and the anti-Semites but also at the constant anti-Semitic slips in the Social Democratic press." [11]

In view of these circumstances the Centralverein gave the Social Democrats a cold shoulder during the 1908 election. *Im Deutschen Reich* went to great lengths to show how inconstant the Socialist defense against anti-Semitism was. It remarked pointedly that the Social Democrats themselves felt threatened by any kind of *Ausnahmegesetz* and thus they opposed the anti-Semites only so far as they agitated for laws to curtail the rights of Jewish citizens. Otherwise, the Social Democrats were opportunistic and anticipated "a rich harvest wherever anti-Semitism plows the soil." [12] The Centralverein called attention to the party's ideology of historical materialism and noted that whenever matters affecting the Jewish religion arose, Social Democratic deputies were usually indifferent. No names were mentioned, but it had not gone unnoticed in the defense movement that Jewish deputies in the Social Democratic *Fraktion* in the Reichstag (Bruno Schönlank, Paul Singer, Arthur Stadthagen, and Emanuel Wurm) were uninterested in and kept aloof from any public discussion of Jewish grievances.

Young Zionists reacted to the Centralverein's election manifesto with a scorching indictment of its campaign strategy. Julius Becker, the Berlin correspondent of *Die Welt*, wrote that the generalities of the campaign message show how inadequately the Centralverein fulfilled the needs of the Jews in politics. He charged that its leaders restricted their campaign activity to "a passive defense against anti-

Semitism" instead of playing an assertive role in the elections.[13] Becker's article noted that the manifesto omitted to state what stand Jewish voters should take in runoffs between Social Democrats and candidates of the Right. He maintained that the Centralverein evaded the problem of Progressive nominees who had made anti-Jewish remarks or who were baptized Jews. The manifesto did not instruct Jewish voters to disregard party allegiance and to rebuff these Progressives at the ballot box.

Becker pounced upon the Centralverein for giving campaign funds to the Progressives on cheap terms, without demanding that party officials satisfy certain conditions. He contended that because the leaders of the defense movement kowtowed to the Progressive party bigwigs, the left-liberal politicians treated the Jews as a "negligible factor" in their deliberations on election and parliamentary tactics.[14] In 1907 the Progressives had not made the elimination of discrimination in the civil service and the army a condition for joining the progovernment majority. Becker thought that the Jews could become a political force once they engaged in political bargaining with the parties and pledged their votes and campaign funds to candidates who accepted their terms.[15] He conceded that the Jews were too small a minority to form a separate party, but he insisted that it was futile for the Jews to participate in German politics as long as they did not organize as an independent voting bloc and adopt a strategy of expediency.

Zionists believed that the Jews commanded enough votes in certain districts to tip the scale in favor of any one candidate. They drew up programs outlining demands that the Jews should use as bargaining terms in negotiations with party leaders. Max Kollenscher, a Zionist living in Posen, drafted a "minimal program" containing objectives that Zionists and non-Zionists could agree upon.[16] Adolf Friedemann and Alfred Klee proposed another platform for discussion at the Zionist congress in Breslau on June 8 and 9, 1908.[17] These programs demanded: (1) the observance of legal guarantees of equality of rights; (2) recognition of the equality of the Jewish religion with the Protestant and Catholic confessions, especially in the matter of government subsidies to provide religious instruction for schoolchildren and to assist poor small synagogue congregations; and (3) legislation protecting unnaturalized Jews from police harassment and forcible expulsion.

Becker's ideas did not impress Horwitz and Fuchs as pragmatic. Replying to his criticism, they said that he was poorly informed on what the central board did in politics.[18] They did not agree that it would be advantageous for the Centralverein to play a highly visible role in elections, and they held fast to the policy of not publicizing their contacts with party politicians. Besides, they doubted that Becker's strategy would succeed and thought that he did not consider the unfavorable circumstances in which Jewish lobbyists had to operate. From their own experiences they knew how uncomfortable the Progressives were made by antiliberal and anti-Semitic propaganda reviling them as paid mercenaries of the Jews, *Judenknechte* and *Judenschutztruppe*. They were of the opinion that if the Centralverein offered Jewish votes and funds on the condition that a candidate accept a Jewish political platform, it would provide ammunition with which the Right could assail him. It was not likely that a candidate would be willing to be publicly identified as the paid mouthpiece of any Jewish pressure group.[19] The Centralverein could exact from candidates, at the most, a pledge not to support discriminatory legislation in parliament.

Julius Moses also sniped at the Centralverein. The manifesto exhorting the Jews to join political parties and to participate in the election campaign seemed oblivious to the dilemma that the Progressive politicians had created for the Jews by fraternizing with Agrarians and anti-Semites in the Bülow bloc. Writing in his newspaper, Moses sarcastically asked the Centralverein's leaders to name a party that the Jews could join and trust.[20] He argued that the liberalism of the National Liberals was a sham and that the Progressives sold out the ideals of liberalism for the advantages of government favor. The only option left for Jewish voters was the Social Democratic party.

Apart from Moses' agitation, several disaffected Jewish left liberals sought out a new political orientation, a shift leftward into a newly created democratic party. Paul Nathan contemplated such a political move even before Barth's secession and the founding of the Democratic Union. Nathan, a protégé of Barth, sat on the central committee of the Progressive Union and was one of its biggest financial backers.[21] In 1906 Nathan vetoed proposals to bring about a fusion of the Progressives and the National Liberals and advocated that the Progressives work for closer relations with the working class and the

Social Democrats.[22] He opposed the decision of the *Fraktion* to stay in the progovernment coalition and discerned with a troubled heart the drift of the Progressives to the Right and their lukewarmness to the cause of suffrage reform. After Bülow dashed all hopes that the government would concede to reform the Prussian franchise, he proposed in January 1908 that the Progressive Union repudiate the bloc, cut off ties with the Progressive People's party, and establish an alliance with the Social Democrats.[23] Before the central committee he argued that the Progressive Union could no longer tarnish its integrity for the sake of maintaining the bloc and solidarity with the Progressive People's party. He warned that if the Progressives did not act courageously for the reform of the Prussian franchise, liberals of moral character would walk out in disgust and join the Social Democrats. The party's right-wing objected to any collaboration with the Socialists, and in March 1908 he resigned from the central committee.[24]

Nathan was among the followers of Barth who bolted the party at the Frankfurt congress in April. The secessionists in Berlin formed a new party, the Democratic Union, on May 16. Nathan joined the secessionists, and it was expected that many Jewish Progressives would switch over to the Democrats. Democratic agitators such as Helmut von Gerlach and Rudolf Breitscheid, with considerable help from Julius Moses, sought to alienate Jewish left liberals from the Progressive People's party.

Simon Bernfeld, who wrote for the *Israelitisches Gemeindeblatt* in Cologne, was the most interesting example of a Jew who joined the Democratic Union. Bernfeld was a fervent admirer of Barth and Nathan. Like his mentors, he was a left-wing Progressive and wanted the party to work wholeheartedly for democratic reforms and to establish close ties with the working classes. Whereas Nathan was hesitant to take a Jewish stance in political life, Bernfeld believed that there were occasions when Jewish Progressives had to speak out as Jews. Following the 1907 election, he upbraided Jewish liberals for not denouncing at party congresses and meetings the tactics of the Progressive leaders in runoffs between anti-Semites and Social Democrats. He disputed the objection that the Jews joined the Progressive parties as German citizens and not as members of a religious community. "There are times," he said, "when one can not divide oneself, and when my honor as a Jew is injured, then I can not feel happy as a citizen."[25] He added that Judaism was something essential, and not incidental, to one's being, so that Jewish Progressives could not say when they stopped being Jews and started to be German citizens and could not participate eagerly in party affairs when the dignity of the Jewish religion was not respected.

As early as 1907 Bernfeld advanced proposals for a new party. Probably with Nathan in mind, he wrote that "perhaps to Jewish politicians, who have been previously so innovative, shall fall now the unrewarding but great task of reconciling socialism with liberalism."[26] In March 1908, before Barth's secession at the Frankfurt congress, he published a blistering attack on the Progressive *Fraktion* and an impassioned appeal for the creation of a new democratic party around Barth and Naumann.[27] He expressed the hope that the Jews would join it to defend their special interests and, above all, to promote democracy and political morality.

Bernfeld and Nathan did not start a bandwagon. Jews who were actively involved in German politics did not cross over to the Democratic Union. None of the Jewish Progressives in the Diet approved of Barth's secession. Hermann Cohn probably expressed their views when he said at the Frankfurt congress that the squabbles of the Progressives were hurting the cause of liberalism and should cease.[28] Cohn took issue with Barth's views on election tactics and insisted that in Anhalt-Dessau the Social Democrats contested the Progressives so fiercely that he and other party leaders could not negotiate political agreements with them.

The Centralverein's executive directors admired Barth's integrity and appreciated his fight against anti-Semitism as chairman of the Abwehrverein. Renouncing the Progressives and moving leftward into the Democratic Union, however, was a course that neither Horwitz nor Fuchs would take. In public, the Centralverein never took a stand for or against Barth's party, and reports on the disputes that led to the fracture of the Progressive Union at the Frankfurt congress were kept out of *Im Deutschen Reich.*

Horwitz and Fuchs exercised sound judgment in reacting so cautiously to Barth's secession and the Democratic Union. The prospects of success for the fledgling party were slight. At the time of the election in 1908 it counted a membership of 734 in Berlin.[29]

The influx that the party's founders expected from the provinces never occurred. Social Liberals, the left-wing of the Progressive Union, met in Cassel, Magdeburg, and elsewhere in May to decide whether to join the Democrats. In most instances they voted down resolutions to secede.[30]

The reasoning that determined the decisions of most left-wing Progressives not to switch over to the Democratic Union was made clear at a party congress of forty delegates representing districts in the Rhine Province and Westphalia. Here the Progressives had a democratic outlook and were less antagonistic to the Socialists than party members in Berlin and the cities along the North and Baltic seacoast. Nevertheless, the delegates defeated a motion calling for secession. The resolution they accepted declared that from the standpoint of genuine liberalism the decision of the *Fraktion* to remain in the Bülow bloc was wrong, but it was tactically necessary for critics of this coalition to stay in the party in order to act as a counterweight to the party's right wing. The resolution underscored this argument by adding that working inside the party was the best way of ending the drift of liberalism to the Right.[31]

The decision of many unhappy Progressives to remain loyal to the party was undoubtedly influenced by the left-liberal press, which was critical of Barth's secession. The *Berliner Tageblatt,* for example, argued that Barth and his followers erred in walking out of the party at a time when it was in a state of demoralization and in need of uncompromising liberals.[32] The prestigious Berlin daily called Barth's ideas about the collaboration of all democratic elements a worthy goal but noted that, after years of bitter rivalry in elections, the Progressives and the Social Democrats were not likely to ally in the immediate future. It reproached Barth for advocating a democratic front with the Social Democrats with doctrinaire obstinacy. Looking to the future, the newspaper expressed doubt that the Democratic Union would succeed and predicted that outside the Progressive ranks Barth would become politically isolated and lose influence.

The spring of 1908, when Barth organized the Democratic Union, was not a time when Horwitz, Fuchs, and other political spokesmen for German Jewry were likely to sever their ties with the Progressives and to experiment with a new party alignment. The performance of the Progressives in the parliamentary session of 1907 had been a letdown, but early in 1908 the *Fraktion* showed a willingness to take up the Jewish cause once again.

Lobbyists for the Verband der deutschen Juden submitted to the *Fraktion* material they had compiled on the cases of Jewish one-year volunteers in the army who were denied commissions in the reserves. They asked the Progressives to bring up this grievance in a forthcoming debate on the military budget.[33] In the Reichstag on March 30 Julius Kopsch confronted the War Ministry with the Verband's evidence. He demanded measures to ensure that commanders comply with the Law of July 3, 1869, in dealing with Jewish soldiers who took the officer training course to be eligible for a commission in the reserve.[34] When General Sixt von Arnim gave the indifferent reply that War Minister von Einem would study the matter, Otto Hermes, another member of the Progressive People's party, called the answer unacceptable and demanded assurances of prompt action.[35]

Jewish lobbyists were pleased to see the Progressives raise this issue in the Reichstag. *Im Deutschen Reich* commented that "such an injustice as the unconstitutional treatment of Jewish soldiers, which could not be eliminated in spite of all the complaints made by Jews, can only be effectively attacked under the protection of parliamentary immunity." Criticism voiced in the Reichstag "finds an echo not only in the whole nation but also on the government bench where such complaints are always embarrassing." The journal concluded: "If the Progressives would often mention the harm inflicted on the army because of discrimination, then the government would find ways to abolish medieval prejudices, which are still manifestly present in the officer corps."[36] The Centralverein gave wide publicity to Kopsch's speech. It seemed eager to prove that the Progressive People's party was not abandoning the defense of Jewish rights or soft-pedaling opposition to government anti-Semitism.[37]

Although Jewish followers of Barth and young firebrands in the Zionist movement scoffed at the cautious pragmatism with which Horwitz and Fuchs eyed the political situation in 1908, other politically experienced leaders of organized German Jewry shared their point of view. Martin Philippson, the chairman of the Gemeindebund and a Progressive Union insider, did not approve of Barth's secession. He thought that Barth's quarrels with other party leaders had impaired the work of the Abwehrverein. Writing to the Progressive deputy Karl Schrader just before the board of directors of the Abwehrverein convened in 1909 to select Barth's successor, Philippson advised that a prominent figure in the Progressive *Fraktion* be elected to the chairmanship. He explained that only in this way could the Abwehrverein regain the importance which it had lost because of Barth's political weakness.[38]

Neither did the mature leaders of German Zionism advocate the rupture of the Jewish alignment with the Progressives. After Becker's criticism of the Centralverein appeared in *Die Welt*, the *Jüdische Rundschau*, the official voice of the German Zionist Organization, took care to clarify that Zionist attacks on the Progressives were "not a radical demand to break away."[39] The article, which was probably written by Hans Gideon Heymann, made emphatic that the reorientation of the Jews toward the Democratic Union or the Social Democratic party was not a politically expedient alternative. Calling appeals that the Jews should move to the far Left "dangerous," the *Jüdische Rundschau* contended that the working classes were not interested in combating the violation of the rights of Jewish citizens and that the Jews would incur the ill will of the government if they allied with radical parties. Instead of withdrawing from the Progressive parties, the Jews were advised to make the Centralverein and the Verband more effective in influencing the decisions of the party leaders.

Just before the election Heymann sought to counteract the anti-Progressive agitation conducted by Julius Moses and a string of radical young Zionists. Writing in *Die Welt* on what the Zionist position in German politics should be, Heymann contended that the Jews would make a mistake if they took a more radical stance than the Progressives and joined opposition parties on the far Left.[40] He doubted that the Democratic Union would thrive and hinted that the party was not likely to have any political weight because of the enmity between it and the state authorities. Neither was affiliation with the Social Democrats likely to benefit the Jews, he added, because the working classes were as reactionary on Jewish questions as the Conservatives were. Alignment with the Progressives remained, in his judgment, the most expedient option for the Jews. Participating in the progovernment majority, the Progressive *Fraktion* could apply more pressure on high-level officials to end the exclusion of Jews from public offices and the officer corps.

Throughout the 1908 election the Centralverein was noticeably reserved. Horwitz and Fuchs moved with extreme caution because of the possibility that the defense movement might become entangled in the feud that broke out between the Democrats and the Progressives. In May the Democratic Union issued an election manifesto branding the "bloc Progressives" flunkies of Bülow. Calling suffrage reform the key campaign issue, the manifesto urged liberal voters to set aside their differences with the Social Democratic party and to vote for it.[41] In Berlin throughout May and June the Democrats organized public rallies where they assailed their onetime political friends more aggressively than the Right. Democratic activists in league with Social Democrats invaded the meetings of the Progressive People's party, heckled candidates who were making speeches, and created disturbances.[42] Barth himself did not resort to invective, but other Democrats were not so restrained. Finding himself isolated and rebuffed by the respected political spokesmen of German Jewry, Julius Moses lashed out against Jewish Progressives with sarcasm and reckless accusations. Rudolf Breitscheid, passionate and doctrinaire by temperament, was convinced that the Progressive chieftains were morally corrupted by the desire for power and the politics of compromise.[43]

The agitation of the Democrats threatened to embroil the Jews in the campaign. Rumors were circulated that the National Liberals were supporting anti-Semitic candidates in runoffs against Social Democrats in two Berlin districts and that the Progressives, who were cosponsoring candidates in several districts with the National Liberals, had joined this agreement. Officials of the Progressive People's party denied the rumors.[44] Nevertheless, the Democrats accused the Progressives of endorsing the anti-Semite Ulrich in the Berlin-Moabit runoff and obliging Jewish party members to vote for him.[45] Moses attempted to implicate the Centralverein in the affair. He alleged that, following appeals from the party's Berlin committee, left liberals voted for Ulrich. Because Hugo Sonnenfeld sat on the committee, Moses demanded that the Centralverein be held accountable for this scandal.[46]

Another affair that Moses exploited to estrange the Jews from the Progressive People's party was the election agreement that Schepps, the party's candidate, made with the Conservatives in the district of Oberbarnim and Niederbarnim. Schepps, who was also the chairman of the local club, secretly concluded a compromise with the Conservatives whereby the two parties would support two Conservative nominees and himself. Later, through shady procedures, the agreement was ratified at a party caucus.[47] Some party members lodged a protest against Schepps, but the central committee refused to intervene and disavow the compromise.

The Democrats organized demonstrations in the district and in Berlin to capitalize on the dissension over Schepps's collusion with the Conservatives and to recruit disaffected Progressives into their own party.[48] Moses and Helmut von Gerlach delivered speeches denouncing the underhandedness of Schepps and inciting the Progressives to register their disapprobation by voting for the Social Democratic candidate or by abstaining. Moses formed the Jewish Election Committee of the District of Oberbarnim and Niederbarnim. In the committee's name he circulated propaganda exhorting the Jews to protest the agreement by defeating Schepps.[49] He reminded Jewish voters that the Conservatives' Tivoli Hall program of 1892 contained an anti-Semitic plank.

A third scandal that the Democrats blew up in order to discredit the Progressive People's party in Jewish circles was the bargain that Duns, its candidate in Flensburg, made with the Agrarian League. Bidding for right-wing votes, Duns promised the Agrarians to back their nominee in the next Reichstag election if they supported him. The cynicism of Duns shocked many left liberals. The disclosure that the Agrarian candidate, who was elected as a National Liberal in 1907, had been a member of the German Social party made Duns's conduct especially repugnant to the Jews. The party's central committee responded to public indignation by denying any prior knowledge of Duns's negotiations and refused to be held responsible for the decisions of a district committee.[50] At campaign rallies Democratic Union speakers attacked the central committee for not repudiating the Flensburg agreement and accused the Progressives of helping to elect Agrarians and anti-Semites.

Reporting on the 1908 election, *Im Deutschen Reich* passed over silently the sensational disclosures in the daily press about the Progressive politicians. Horwitz and Fuchs, knowing that Democratic Union agitators bore a personal animosity toward the Progressives, were anxious not to get entangled in the disputes. They had reason to conclude that these scandals were isolated incidents and did not reflect official party policy. Immediately after the election the Progressive party committee in Schleswig-Holstein repudiated the Flensburg agreement.[51] One member of the committee was David Waldstein, who had just won election to the Diet. Waldstein was a longtime member of the Centralverein and an organizer of the Hamburg chapter.

Jewish activists in the defense movement had many reasons to be elated over the outcome of the election. Nine non-baptized Jews were elected, seven Progressives, Aronsohn, Cassel, Gerschel, Peltasohn, Rosenow, Waldstein, and Wolff, and two Social Democrats, Heimann and Hirsch. The Centralverein welcomed the election of so many Jewish deputies. It approved the decision of the deputies not to form a "Jewish Centrum" and agreed that they were "elected not as Jews but as Prussian citizens."[52]

The Centralverein took satisfaction in the success of its own campaign against the anti-Semites. *Im Deutschen Reich* commended the opposition that the Jews had mobilized for the defeat of Wilhelm Lattmann and Ludwig Werner, a stunning setback for these two anti-Semites who had been elected to the Reichstag in the 1907 campaign. It also credited the Centralverein's campaign agitation with the defeat of two Christian Social candidates, Pastor von Bodelschwingh and Pastor Reinhard Mumm.[53]

Although the 1908 election ended without any shift of the Jews leftward into the Democratic Union, in the course of the campaign the Jewish defense movement identified itself with the democratic wing of the Progressive camp. Reform of the Prussian suffrage was a key campaign issue, and on this question the left liberals were not of one mind. The three-class franchise was advantageous to the Progressives in elections to the Diet, where they were overrepresented in comparison with the Social Democratic vote as well as in municipal elections, in which they won majorities in the city councils. Privately, many Progressives had a lukewarm attitude toward suffrage reform and feared the loss of political influence to the Social

Democrats once equal suffrage was introduced into Prussia.[54] They were willing to postpone suffrage reform and to compromise with the National Liberals on two moderate changes, a secret ballot and a redrawing of electoral districts.

In May the *Allgemeine Zeitung des Judentums* took a forthright stand for equal suffrage and called upon Jewish citizens to support this reform, which would lead to a more democratic parliament in Prussia.[55] In a second article the newspaper disputed the argument that the Jews should favor retaining the three-class suffrage because they had proportionally more high income taxpayers than either the Protestant or Catholic confessions. Rejecting this reasoning, it stated that the Jews did not follow a strategy of political expediency and would not uphold an unjust voting system. It announced that the Jews favored equal suffrage "although it is apparently less advantageous" to them. "We are Jews in our synagogues, homes, and families, but in public life, at the ballot box, we are Prussians and Germans and speak, act, and vote only as the interests of the nation require," it declared.[56]

In subsequent articles advocating a democratic suffrage, the *Allgemeine Zeitung des Judentums* argued that the advantages which the plutocratic three-class voting system offered the Jews were more apparent than real. It asserted that the increased electoral influence was politically worthless because the three-class franchise buttressed the political dominance of reactionary forces in the Prussian state, which refused to observe legal guarantees of equal rights.[57] Jewish activists in the defense movement saw clearly the connection of suffrage reform with their own struggle against discrimination.

After the Prussian parliamentary election was over, the crossfire between the Democrats and the Progressives continued, and by the end of 1908 the Democrats extended the line of combat into the Centralverein. In the winter of 1908–09, the organization found itself locked in a dispute that threatened to tear it apart. This time the controversy was graver than the dissension over the Bülow bloc because the issue, the nomination of baptized Jews as Progressive candidates, aroused heated passions. With circumspection and flexibility, the central board dealt with a matter in which the Jews expected a principled stand and bold action. In the behavior and public remarks of Jewish Progressives who sat on the board, many Centralverein members saw the obligations of party allegiance and the imperatives of Jewish loyalty and honor collide. A ticklish question that Horwitz and Fuchs had tried to avoid was now debated: How should the leaders of Jewish interest groups take a position in German politics?

Horwitz and Fuchs were slow to realize the depth of indignation felt by members who were concerned more about Jewish pride than about Berlin party politics. The association's centralized structure prevented the Berlin headquarters from gauging Jewish sentiment in the provinces. The storm over the nomination of baptized Jews brought anguish to the Centralverein's leadership. What was less apparent at the time was that the crisis revealed how effectively the defense movement had transformed the outlook of Jews in Germany. Members who criticized the directors on the central board judged their actions by new values and new expectations of what aims the Centralverein should pursue.

In September 1908 a caucus of the Progressive People's party picked Dr. Otto Mugdan, a Jewish physician who had converted to Protestantism, to run for election to the Berlin City Council in the district of Potsdamer Tor. This section of the city had a large concentration of Jews. Jews were prominent in the party's district club, and it was estimated that about half the men who attended the meeting at which the choice of Mugdan was ratified were Jewish.[58] Cassel gave a speech seconding his nomination. Among the party members endorsing him on campaign leaflets was Martin Lövinson, a Berlin lawyer who served on the governing boards of the Centralverein and the Verband. In the past no commotion flared up when the Progressives nominated baptized Jews. Several converts had been elected to the Berlin City Council in recent years, and Mugdan won election to the Reichstag in 1907 in Görlitz.

The circumstances of Mugdan's campaign in Berlin in 1908 were bound to cause a sensation. The Democratic Union nominated Paul Rickert, and the two parties fought a tough battle.[59] To improve Mugdan's chances of election, three Progressive city councilmen prevailed upon city officials to postpone the election date three weeks. The Democrats decried this maneuver and made a political issue out of Mugdan's conversion. They disclosed that earlier in a runoff he had supported the anti-Semite Stöcker instead of the Social Democratic contender. The distasteful manner in which he had paraded his Christian faith in past campaigns was publicized. At the same time, the Conservatives backed Mugdan, and the anti-Semitic press called him "a friend of Stöcker."[60] As a result of Democratic Union agitation, it became a matter of self-respect for Jewish Progressives to cross party lines and to vote for Rickert. Rickert received a margin of two votes over Mugdan in the election. Three ballots were not properly cast. Opinions about the legality of these ballots differed, but city officials ruled that a second election had to be held. The emotional excitement of the campaign mounted. In December, with a heavy turnout of voters, Mugdan was elected.[61]

After Mugdan's nomination was announced, spokesmen for the Centralverein privately complained to party notables that the nomination of baptized Jews was offensive to the Jews. In public, however, the central board was reticent and adhered to the dictum of not participating in elections except to contest anti-Semitic candidates.[62] Horwitz and Fuchs eyed the situation pragmatically. Neutrality was an expedient policy, which kept the Centralverein from impairing its relations with the Progressives. Also, Horwitz and Fuchs probably thought as Paul Nathan did that public protests against the nomination of baptized Jews would stir up a backlash and cause many Christians who would not have voted for Mugdan to be sympathetic to him.[63]

Ignoring such political considerations, Berlin Zionists joined Jewish Democrats in organizing demonstrations to protest Mugdan's nomination and to denounce Jewish Progressives who had supported him.[64] As early as September Julius Moses used Mugdan's candidacy to foment disaffection against the Progressives and to discredit the leadership establishment of organized German Jewry, which was affiliated with the party. Writing in his newspaper, Moses questioned the propriety of the endorsement of an apostate by prominent figures in the Centralverein. He maintained that their action undermined the association's struggle against discrimination and made a mockery of its moral condemnation of baptism.[65] He pressed the point that Mugdan's nomination put Jewish followers of the party in the dilemma of having to vote for a man who had abandoned their religion and that it confronted them with a conflict between the dictates of their consciences and the commands of party loyalty.

Moses kept up his attack throughout October and November, and his criticism became increasingly spiteful. Indiscriminate allegations were made about the baptism of Peltasohn's children. Moses seemed to relish baiting Jewish deputies in the Progressive *Fraktion* and to take pleasure in the embarrassment that Mugdan was causing the Centralverein's leaders.[66] Since 1904 Moses bore a grudge against Sonnenfeld and other board members who had moved to expel him from the organization because of his criticism.[67] He resented the Centralverein's efforts to head off his drive for a Jewish boycott of the Progressives and the loyalty it showed to the Progressives in dispensing campaign funds. In one harangue he said that the Centralverein acted so often as "the lackey of the Progressive party leaders that now among voters it is called the Progressive People's party translated into Yiddish."[68]

Moses and a band of radicals set out to bring pressure on the leaders of the Centralverein to cut their ties with the Progressives and intended to split the organization if this end was not attained.[69] Their strategy was to agitate against Lövinson. A Jewish Democrat sent a letter to the central board demanding Lövinson's resignation. When the committee refused, Moses circulated a petition calling for a special meeting to deal with the Lövinson case.[70]

If Horwitz and Fuchs had been in close rapport with the chapters and had known the moral outrage that the Mugdan affair had aroused among Jews who stood outside Berlin party politics, they would have frankly expressed their private opinion that Lövinson's endorsement of Mugdan was a mistake.[71] However, they suspected that the uproar was contrived by Jewish Democrats and radical Zionists who were bent on instigating trouble in the Centralverein.[72] The central board decided to shield Lövinson instead of throwing him to the lions. It stated publicly that he had not consulted his colleagues and had made his decision to vote for Mugdan as a party member. Other board members voted for Rickert, but all agreed that what Lövinson had done was a personal matter and had nothing to do with the Centralverein, whose official policy in the election was neutrality.[73]

What Horwitz and Fuchs overlooked was that this stand collided head on with the Centralverein's purpose of promoting loyalty to the Jewish religion and self-esteem among the Jews. Since 1906 it had criticized the government for putting a premium on conversion by appointing baptized Jews to public offices from which steadfast Jews were excluded. Baptism was condemned as a morally contemptible act, undertaken without faith and wholly for career ambitions and social climbing.[74] Indoctrinated by this propaganda, members of the Centralverein had come to see conversion as a betrayal. Whereas in the past Jewish liberals had been indulgent toward educated Jews who used a baptismal certificate to overcome barriers to professional advancement, now pride combined with moral integrity to condemn the convert as a renegade and a worse enemy than an anti-Semite.[75]

To justify its policy of neutrality in the Mugdan campaign and to respond to Lövinson's critics, the central board held a meeting in Berlin on December 9. Speaking in a conciliatory manner, Lövinson denied playing any part in the nomination of a man whose character he knew many Jews did not admire. He explained that he had promised to vote for Mugdan out of party discipline and that his name had been printed on campaign leaflets without his permission.[76] Horwitz discussed the Mugdan affair as a fracas between two parties. Both speakers failed to win over a restless crowd. Lövinson left unanswered the question of why he did not complain to party officials about the misuse of his name. Horwitz saw the commotion exclusively from the perspective of Berlin party politics and was not sensitive to the indignation of those Jews who thought that the Progressives slighted the dignity of the Judaism by nominating Mugdan.

In an emotionally tense discussion several members sparred with Horwitz. They contended that it was wrong for an activist Jewish organization to be neutral in an election in which a baptized Jew campaigned. They demanded that the Centralverein fight renegades who ran for elected offices and that it admonish the Progressives sternly not to force on Jewish party followers an agonizing choice between party allegiance and the honor of Judaism by nominating baptized Jews.[77] From the crowd came dissenting catcalls when one speaker said that many Jews agreed with Lövinson that religion should not determine how one voted. He added emphatically that the Centralverein was an association of German citizens and must allow its members freedom to act in religious matters as Jews but first and foremost as Germans in political life.[78]

The meeting sparked a general debate on what position a Jew should take in the party to which he belonged. Over the years the men who led the defense movement treated this question as a delicate matter. Now Jewish activists found themselves confronting the question of whether a Jew could separate his political activities as a German citizen from his association with the Jewish community, and whether party affiliation should supersede the imperatives of religious loyalty in determining how he should vote.

By February 21, 1909, when delegates from the chapters arrived in Berlin for the biennial convention, dissatisfaction with the central board was smoldering. Letters protesting the Centralverein's neutrality in the Mugdan campaign flowed into the Berlin office. Disgruntled members drafted a motion calling for Lövinson's resignation.[79]

The central board commissioned Lewy to speak on its behalf. From the outset Lewy admitted that Mugdan's nomination had produced a grave crisis and conceded that much more could have been done to prevent his candidacy.[80] He assured the delegates that the central board had started private talks with party officials in order to avoid such predicaments in the future. Prior to the convention the board members had met for long and wearisome discussions without deciding on a policy. Lewy presented the policy that they had finally voted to adopt: "We oppose baptism which is undertaken not out of religious conviction wherever and whenever we can, but we can not hide the fact that a general rule for the position of Jews on the candidacy of baptized Jews can not be established."[81]

The wording of this resolution represented a compromise. Fuchs and Julius Brodnitz, who headed the legal defense bureau, favored a clear-cut policy stating that under no condition should Jews vote for baptized Jews. On the other side were Cohn, who was coopted as a board member in 1908, Lövinson, and Sonnenfeld. Actively involved in the Progressive People's party, they did not want the Centralverein to agitate against candidates who were baptized Jews.

At the convention the speakers opposing a hard line were once again party stalwarts. Cohn argued that the Centralverein was not entitled to instruct its members on how they should vote beyond the directive to defeat anti-Semites.[82] Hinrichsen, a Progressive from

Hamburg, contended that the Centralverein could not announce a blanket policy opposing the election of baptized Jews because the question must be "judged only according to political and local considerations."[83]

Underlying the arguments of the Jewish politicians were apprehensions about the consequences of such a policy. They were worried that the Centralverein's politics would complicate their own position in the party. Cohn stated plainly that the association must "not bind the hands of Jewish politicians."[84] He warned the delegates that if this happened, it would "compel Jews who are politically active in important positions to turn their backs on the activities of the Centralverein" because they could not work in any major political party "following a dictated marching line." Repeating this admonition in a second speech, Cohn said that the defense movement needed Jewish politicians and "should not let the impression arise in the parties that among us is anyone whose hand in making political decisions is bound by the Centralverein."[85]

Jewish politicians were troubled also about the reactions of the Christian majority. Apparent in Sonnenfeld's speech was the fear that the Jews would call attention to their exclusiveness by agitating against candidates who had converted to Christianity. Sonnenfeld chided the delegates for forgetting that they were German citizens of the Jewish faith and not German Jews. He counseled the Jews not to incur the reproach that they gave priority to narrow-minded confessional concerns over the good of the nation. The Jews were not an exclusive group and must promote their special interests only so far as they stood in harmony with the general interests of the state.[86]

The Progressives launched a counterattack on the Democrats. Imberg, a city councilman in Berlin, told the delegates that no objections were raised about Mugdan's baptism until the Democrats tried to make political capital out of it.[87] Hinrichsen deplored the fact that the Jews had been caught in the feud between the two parties and accused Barth's followers of causing dissension in the Centralverein. In a defiant posture Lövinson exclaimed that he had no regrets about what he had done and would side with his party again if he was in the same situation.[88] He argued that sitting on the Centralverein's board of directors did not restrict his actions in politics and that Jews should vote for the candidates of whatever party represented their political point of view and should not let religious matters affect their political decisions. These speeches raised the emotional level of the debate. Dissenting remarks were shouted, tempers flared, and a quarrel broke out between Horwitz and a Democrat when the chairman cut his speaking time.[89]

The offensive that the Progressives waged against the Democrats exasperated delegates from the chapters. They came to the convention expecting from the central board a militant stand against candidates who were baptized Jews. They were distressed to hear the Berlin leaders talk about the Mugdan affair as if it were nothing more than a squabble between two parties. The failure of the board members to see the moral issue raised by his nomination and the ground swell of outrage in the provinces shocked them. Moreover, the delegates were annoyed with the Berlin executives for not keeping the chapters informed about what they had done to dissuade the Progressives from nominating Mugdan and what preventive steps they intended to take in the future.

The delegates found the mild and equivocal wording of the board's resolution a letdown. Rabbi Felix Goldmann of Oppeln contended that the Jewish left liberals should warn party officials that they would withhold contributions and would cease to work for the party unless it stopped nominating baptized Jews.[90] Karl Lewin exclaimed that if the Centralverein did not want to lapse into political opportunism, it had to act according to the ideals it professed. He pointed out to the central board that among the members of the Centralverein there was a growing conviction that certain issues in politics required the defense movement to take an absolute stand on principles. Amid loud applause he declared fervently that baptized Jews were morally unscrupulous and that the Jews must tell party leaders flatly that under no circumstances would they support such candidates.[91] Delegates from Aachen and Cologne also rose to condemn baptized Jews. They were critical of the board for taking a weak stand out of political expediency and demanded a declaration categorically obliging members not to vote for baptized Jews.

The convention ended without a split. The governing board crushed a motion for Lövinson's removal.[92] It blocked the adoption of a policy binding the Centralverein to oppose candidates who were baptized Jews in all elections. The Berlin leaders had not cajoled the angry delegates. What saved the Centralverein from any lasting divisions was the sense of responsibility displayed by regional leaders such as Ernst Herzfeld.

At the convention Herzfeld, a lawyer in Essen who headed the regional committee for the Rhineland, pointed out to the contingent of Berlin Progressives that whereas some Jews exploited Mugdan's nomination for partisan purposes, others looked at it "from a strictly Jewish perspective."[93] Herzfeld thought that something positive could come out of the incident, which had caused so much anguish. The Mugdan campaign had stirred the consciences and had awakened the pride of the Jews so that they would no longer complacently allow the Progressives to humiliate them. He told the delegates that whether the obligation to vote against baptized Jews should be stated in categorical or flexible terms was not worth destroying the unity of the Centralverein. Working within the party to prevent the nomination of baptized Jews would have greater practical value than disputes over the wording of a formula.

After the convention the Centralverein spoke out more bluntly against baptized Jews in the Progressive People's party than it had done before. In the winter of 1910-11, expecting the government to dissolve the Reichstag and call new elections, Horwitz and Fuchs served notice to the Progressives not to nominate baptized Jews. *Im Deutschen Reich* asserted that the Jews would back the party "only on the condition that it does not make such support impossible by nominating candidates whose defection from the Jewish religion confirms anti-Semitic accusations about the inferiority of the Jews and offends the religious feelings of the Jews."[94] This question was brought up by delegates who attended the convention in February 1911. Discussing preparation for the coming election, Max Mainzer and Rudolf Geiger of Frankfurt am Main urged the delegates to make emphatically clear to party committees in their districts that the Jews would not support a candidate who spurned his Jewish origins.[95]

Applying pressure on the Progressive People's party not to honor baptized Jews with seats in parliament proved to be more frustrating than Jewish activists had thought. Early in 1911 the Progressives named Julius Lippmann as their candidate for Stettin in the next

Reichstag election. Lippmann had been elected to the Diet in Stettin in 1908. His conversion to Christianity was made known during the campaign, and no flurry arose.[96] In 1911, with a heightened sense of pride, the Jews raised objections. Party notables in the city replied with a public appeal for the Jews to be tolerant.[97] Still hoping to influence party nominations by quiet lobbying, the central board reacted to this setback with restraint. With Lippmann's nomination in view, *Im Deutschen Reich* voiced regret that the Progressives encouraged insincere conversion by putting pressure on Jews who sought elective political offices to be baptized.[98] It commended the Social Democrats for allowing Jews such as Paul Singer to sit in the party's Reichstag *Fraktion* without disavowing their religion.

The Progressives were annoyed at the criticism of the Jewish left liberals and the threats to withhold campaign funds. The *Weser-Zeitung,* a Progressive organ in Bremen, published an article reproaching the Centralverein for obstructing the party's preparations for the election and for exhorting the Jews not to vote for baptized Jews. The newspaper loftily declared that the Progressives had sound reasons for resisting "such fanaticism" firmly and mentioned that the party's ideological and moral principles did not permit them to mix religion with party politics. In a remark intended plainly for Cohn and other Jewish deputies, the party organ expressed the hope that "authoritative figures among the Jewish people shall succeed in asserting their influence in the Centralverein so that it does not put obstacles in the pathway of the politics of the Progressives and in this way provide assistance to the anti-Semites indirectly."[99]

Horwitz and Fuchs were incensed by the condescension with which the Progressive newspaper treated the Centralverein and were dismayed by the failure of party officials to understand sympathetically the point of view of the Jews. The rebuttal that Ludwig Holländer wrote was unusually sharp. The Centralverein's secretary-general agreed with the Progressives that nominees should not be judged according to creed, but he insisted that baptized Jews converted for opportunistic reasons and lacked the integrity which was needed for public office. He stated that if the Progressives earnestly desired to have moral principles guide their politics, they must reject baptized Jews as unqualified to sit in parliament.[100]

Disregarding Jewish remonstrances, the Progressives continued to honor Mugdan. He ran for reelection to the Reichstag in January 1912. After he was defeated, party leaders agreed to nominate him for a by-election in the summer of 1912, when a safe Progressive seat in Berlin became vacant. The district, which included the Tiergartenviertel and parts of Friedrichstadt and Schöneberg, had a large Jewish population. When Horwitz and Fuchs heard rumors that Mugdan sought the nomination, they entreated the party's central committee not to force Jewish left liberals to choose between party allegiance and the dignity of the Jewish religious community.[101] The Progressives replied to Horwitz that, in accordance with its liberal character, the party could not discriminate against baptized Jews. This answer struck Horwitz and Fuchs as insolent, and they were disheartened. Convinced that they had done everything in their power to prevent Mugdan's candidacy, they let the matter drop. At the time Horwitz became ill and left Berlin for a health spa.[102]

In the meantime Jewish activists who were not constrained by the necessities of practical politics registered the outrage felt by many Berlin Jews. Most outspoken was Fabius Schach, the editor of the *Israelitisches Gemeindeblatt*, who denounced the party's reply to Horwitz as a flagrant exhibition of disrespect. Schach wrote that party officials had insulted the Centralverein by misrepresenting its objections to baptized Jewish candidates as intolerance and discrimination. He accused of hypocrisy those Progressives who loftily invoked the principle of tolerance to defend Mugdan's nomination. As evidence he noted that the Progressives justified their refusal to nominate Jewish candidates in some localities out of consideration for popular sentiments but turned a deaf ear to the demands of the Berlin Jews, whose loyalty to Judaism and self-respect obliged them not to vote for a baptized Jew.[103]

The Centralverein was widely criticized for failing to block the nomination of Lippmann and Mugdan. The circumstances of Mugdan's nomination led close observers of the Berlin political scene to believe that members of the central board could have prevented it if they had acted energetically. Mugdan was not popular with the party's left wing. Before the caucus met on October 2, 1912, there was much opposition to his nomination. The party's central committee discussed at length whether to recommend Mugdan alone or to present other names. Finally, it proposed Mugdan and ruled that the caucus could consider other persons if they received 30 votes. From the floor Friedrich Naumann and Hugo Preuss were proposed but neither received 30 ballots. Except for two dissenting votes, the party members ratified the choice of Mugdan.[104] As Heymann related at a meeting of Zionist leaders, Mugdan's political ambitions could have been dashed if the Centralverein had taken the initiative early to rally a protest movement among Jews and gentiles in the party who disliked him.[105] The Jewish press chided the central board for not using the threat of withholding campaign funds as a leverage of influence on party officials.[106]

The Zionists moved quickly to capitalize on the Centralverein's setback. Already on October 1, 1912, the Zionist executive committee made plans for demonstrations to protest Mugdan's nomination. The intention of the Berlin Zionists was clearly to exploit the incident to undermine confidence in the defense movement.[107] The Zionists held protest rallies in Berlin, Hamburg, and other cities.[108] The speeches of the agitators followed an article published in the *Jüdische Rundschau* under the headline of "The Bankruptcy of the Centralverein." The newspaper asserted that the Centralverein's failure to stop the Progressives from nominating renegades "should open the eyes of German Jews to how futile and impotent the official Jewish politics of defense is."[109] It reproached the central board for refusing to mobilize the Jews for an election boycott against the Progressives and cited this fact to prove that the Centralverein was not bold or aggressive in the defense of Jewish interests.

Horwitz and Fuchs thought that the critics of the Centralverein did not consider the difficult conditions under which Jewish lobbyists and deputies worked and held unrealistic expectations of what they could accomplish.[110] They were especially angry at the agitation of the Zionists. On December 18 Horwitz, Fuchs, and Holländer met with the Zionist executive committee and complained about attacks in the Zionist press and at public meetings.[111] Fuchs and Horwitz contended that they had done "everything in their power" to prevent Mugdan's nomination.

The perversity with which the Progressives ran Mugdan for election in districts heavily populated with Jews left many activists in the defense movement perplexed. Some Jews saw evidence of a disrespect for the Jewish community in the behavior of party officials. It is more likely that reasons other than prejudice made the Progressives insensitive to Jewish objections to the nomination of candidates who had been baptized. The Progressives disapproved of what they regarded as the effort of Jewish spokesmen to drag confessional matters into politics. In this respect they were reflecting life in Berlin, which became an a-religious city during the Imperial era.[112] Fewer and fewer Protestant couples had their marriages sanctified in the church, and increasing numbers of Jews married spouses of a different confession. Party leaders did not grasp fully how the consciousness of Jewish liberals had changed since the turn of the century, how their sense of pride had deepened, and why so suddenly they were raising a hue and cry about baptism. Christian left liberals did not entertain the idea of a mass conversion to Christianity as a solution to "the Jewish question," but they did assume that Jewish exclusiveness was an obstacle to the complete integration of the Jews into German society.[113] Unconcerned about the survival of Jewry as a unique community, they saw no reason to discourage baptism and intermarriage.

6

A NEW GENERATION AND THE REORIENTATION
OF THE DEFENSE MOVEMENT

The crisis arising from Lövinson's endorsement of Mugdan marked a turning point for the Centralverein. To the chapter leaders, who came as delegates to the 1909 convention, the affair was a vindication of their complaints that decision-making was too concentrated in the Berlin bureau, which did not consult or keep the chapters informed. It was their long-awaited chance to press hard for the decentralization of the Centralverein and for the delegation of more responsibilities to the chapters. What the regional leaders wanted was essentially a more popular and activist defense movement.

The delegates who raised demands for reforms were a generation younger than the men who had established the defense association in the 1890s. The younger activists shared with the older notables fervent pride in belonging to the German nation, but in other respects their outlook was different. The younger men participated actively in Jewish community life. Instead of harboring ambivalent feelings about their background, they proclaimed their Jewishness boldly and were acutely sensitive about their honor as Jews. They had fewer illusions in regard to the social relations of Jews and Christians and spoke frankly of the frustrations of striving to overcome prejudice in professional and social life. They joined Jewish fraternities, literary societies, and other organizations more readily than educated Jews had done in the past. Neither accusations of exclusiveness nor apprehensions of self-imposed segregation inhibited them psychologically.[1]

The outlook of the younger activists was shaped by their experience at the universities. Entering the universities in the 1890s, they found anti-Semitism more rife than ever before. Discrimination prevented Jewish scholars from attaining the rank of full professorship. The fraternities excluded students of Jewish background. Only in the *Finkenschaft*, the association of independent students, did the Jewish students find open doors. The *Finkenschaft* was created in the 1880s by liberals reacting against the anti-Semitism of the traditional fraternities, but it was not a successful experiment. Jewish students discovered that few Christians had the liberal idealism to join the independents, and after the turn of the century chauvinism infected these students too.[2] Invoking the principle of academic freedom, the independents declined to combat anti-Semitism in the universities.

Insecure and uncomfortable in their relations with Christians, Jewish students sought out each other for comradeship. Those who were pessimistic about finding a solution to the Jewish condition in Germany were attracted to Zionism. Others who would not let anti-Semitism deny them the right to be and feel German joined Jewish fraternities—Spevia which was founded in Berlin in 1894, Licaria in Munich in 1895, Rheno-Silesia in Bonn in 1899, and Badenia in Heidelberg in 1902.[3] By 1910 there were seven Jewish fraternities united in a federation called the Kartell-Konvent.

The Jewish fraternities conceived of themselves as a "comradeship in arms" and a "league of protesters."[4] They set out to fight anti-Semitism at the universities and to educate their members to be self-confident Jews who would "strive in public life for the complete civil equality of German Jewry."[5] Grooming future leaders, the fraternities provided their members with the moral and psychological character that was needed in the struggle for equal rights. They were determined to dispel popular notions about Jewish physical weakness and timidity and encouraged their members to become adept in gymnastics, fencing, and swimming. From the German fraternities the Jewish students adopted the custom of dueling to defend personal honor. When some Jews asserted that by dueling the Jewish youth was stooping to the low level of the anti-Semites, fraternity members retorted that some Germans were not impressed by dignified reserve and that dueling proved that the Jew was as brave as the Christian.[6]

The Jewish fraternities provided many recruits for the Centralverein and were recognized quickly as a "training school" for its work.[7] Ludwig Holländer was the most notable example of a young Jew whose disposition to political activism and sense of Jewish identity were enhanced in a fraternity. Holländer joined Licaria at the university of Munich. Remaining in Munich after his studies were finished, he practiced law. He did not conform to the pattern of behavior that was expected of a young, ambitious attorney. Among colleagues in the profession he acquired a reputation as a radical because he brought suit against an anti-Semitic newspaper in Munich and gave legal counsel to Jews in libel lawsuits. Criticism from other lawyers did not dim his idealism. He took pride in being an activist lawyer representing Jews as a community and as individual clients.[8] He agreed to work as an agent of the Centralverein in Bavaria. In 1907 the governing board appointed him to the newly created office of secretary-general, and he moved to Berlin. Heading the executive committee of the Kartell-Konvent at the same time, he was instrumental in strengthening ties between the Centralverein and the Jewish fraternities. Speaking tours brought him in touch with the chapters so that at the Berlin bureau he conveyed the point of view of the regional leaders.

Salinger, who practiced law in Oppeln and helped to organize the chapter there, was another activist trained in a Jewish fraternity. Emotionally intense and outspoken by nature, Salinger was impatient with the cautious leadership of the older notables. He wanted the Centralverein to be a movement of dedicated and militant activists who were aroused to indignation when the rights and the dignity of the Jews were violated and who were willing to make sacrifices in the fight for justice and equal opportunity.[9] He deplored the fact that most Centralverein members paid annual dues and were otherwise inactive.

Salinger attributed this apathy to the bureaucratic manner in which the central board directed the movement. He mocked the tendency of the Jewish notables to make guarded and circuitous statements and to be fearful of how the government and the Christian majority would react to what the Jews did in public life. He admitted that Jews fighting for their rights ran the risk of encountering disapproval and insults, but he refused to wait patiently.[10] To Jews in Hamburg and other cities who complained that mass assemblies and public protests would disrupt the quiet state of coexistence between the Jews and the Christians, Salinger pointed out that such harmonious relations were based on an acceptance of injustice. He urged the Centralverein members to be zealous activists and declared that if their ideas won over masses of people, "the government and the legislatures would very soon have to yield to such a storm."[11]

Although the men who built up the Centralverein were committed to a policy of public defense, they did not put into practice the implications of this tactical concept. Lawyers by profession, they preferred the methods of judicial litigation, professional lobbying, and private negotiations with government officials and party leaders. The Centralverein was not envisioned by its founders as a mass movement of confrontation politics, protest demonstrations, and free-wheeling meetings.

Born and educated in a country with an authoritarian political system, the founders of the defense movement had no understanding of the requirements of political life in an age of democratic aspirations. They recognized no need to be democratically accountable to the membership at large. The directors coopted persons to fill vacant seats on the central board. At the biennial assembly a slate listing the names of board members was presented for acceptance by an acclamation vote rather than by ballot. When the Berlin executives promoted the organization of chapters after 1905, they did not strive to stimulate grass-roots initiative. It was the custom of the Berlin bureau to call upon one or two prominent Jews in a city to set up a local committee and to establish a chapter.

Preparations for the founding of a chapter in Danzig shed some light on the administrative practices of Horwitz. In December 1906 Horwitz sent a letter to Philipp Simson investing him with the chairmanship of a branch to be established in Danzig and authorizing him to fill the other executive positions. Simson demurred and questioned the propriety of forming an executive committee by appointment and without assemblying all the local members. To answer Simson's objection that such procedures violated democratic principles, the Berlin bureau informed him that in many places it was not possible to summon chapter meetings for the purpose of electing a committee because it "would cause too many delays."[12]

Another reason, which the reply to Simson omitted to mention, was the unwillingness of the central board to grant autonomy to the branches in administering their affairs. A proposal from the Hamburg chapter for more independence in the selection of its executive committee was rejected in 1905. The Berlin directors voted to retain the principle of centralization on the grounds that "the central board can not turn over the election of the chapter's chairman to an accidental majority at a meeting of the local members."[13] They insisted on making the final choice from recommendations that the chapters submitted.

The regional leaders believed that the operation of the Centralverein was too centralized and undemocratic. They complained that the Berlin bureau withheld from the chapters the freedom to manage their own affairs.[14] It kept a close watch on arrangements for meetings, including the choice of speakers and the topics of discussion. The statutes drafted for the chapters reserved to the central board the right to be represented at all local meetings through a deputy, who was entitled to vote and to speak at any time.[15] The Berlin executives handled all political matters and left to the chapters little initiative and responsibility in political affairs.

Communications between the Berlin headquarters and the branches was another rankling grievance. The central board made all important decisions at closed meetings and disclosed little about its work. Activists in the provinces thought that more responsibilities should be delegated to them. Some outspoken critics disliked the overbearing manner in which Horwitz and other board members acted at the conventions and reproached the chairman for interfering in and cutting off debate on controversial questions. They complained that too often the delegates were expected to rubber-stamp decisions that the central board had already made.

The young activists wished to widen the autonomy and the responsibilities of the chapters. At the convention in 1909 Salinger proposed the revision of the statute requiring the chapters to submit to the central board for prior approval the subjects of speeches that were to be delivered at meetings.[16] The chapters wanted to discuss matters that vitally concerned the local community rather than listening to canned speeches. The Berlin directors fought to retain the regulation as a safeguard to prevent the members from discussing touchy political issues. At the convention in 1911 Ernst Herzfeld introduced a motion to allow the chapters to increase dues so that they could engage in local political activities without being dependent on the Berlin bureau.[17] Herzfeld spoke for chapters in the Rhineland which were eager to participate in city council elections. The delegates voted down the proposal after hearing the argument that it would create invidious distinctions between rich and poor chapters.

Jewish newspaper editors, who were not partisans of Zionism or unsympathetic to the goals of the defense movement, expressed disapproval of the oligarchic leadership of the Centralverein and the Verband. In the *Jüdisches Volksblatt*, Louis Neustadt of Breslau criticized the preponderance of lawyers on the executive boards of the two organizations and accused the notables of conducting affairs in a bureaucratic manner and of eliminating the common people from any active participation.[18] In 1906 he tried to organize a Jewish political association in Breslau to remedy what he openly declared was the principal fault of the Centralverein—its failure to mobilize lower-class Jews.[19]

Two years later Fabius Schach in Cologne took up Neustadt's attack against the elite of lawyers who stood at the head of Jewish defense and welfare organizations. When Fuchs, Horwitz, and Nathan convened a "conference of notables" on September 20, 1908, to deal with the problem of settling Jews emigrating from Russia, Schach assailed the secrecy of their deliberations and the very idea of such a summit meeting as contrary to the democratic trends of the time. In the *Israelitisches Gemeindeblatt* he wrote:

> In the age of democracy our Jewish leaders should finally learn to take into consideration the most fundamental concepts of democratic thinking. If one demands the enthusiastic participation of the public in a big relief undertaking, then one must also give it some insight into the real conditions. We Jews are the most radical democrats in outside affairs, but in our own institutions we are hardly modern and democratic. . . . Even the phrase "assembly of notables", derived from the Biedermeier era, we have not yet outgrown.[20]

Because many of the chapter organizers were in the legal profession, they were not so outspoken as Neustadt and Schach in criticizing the exclusiveness of the leadership of organized Jewry. Yet they felt uneasy about the fact that the defense movement was run mainly by Jews in the professions. Holländer deplored that too much attention was devoted to the grievances of university-educated

Jews, especially to discrimination in the reserve officer corps.[21] He thought that priority should be given to problems affecting the common people, such as the anti-Semitic boycott against Jewish shopkeepers in the Eastern provinces and the unfair treatment of Jewish pupils in the primary school system.

Delegates to the conventions in 1909 and 1911 attempted to broaden the social composition of the Centralverein's leadership and to make the conventions more representative of all social classes by increasing the attendance of Jews of modest means. In 1909 the Frankfurt chapter proposed that compensation for travel expenses to Berlin be given to delegates "in order to prevent [the Centralverein] from acquiring a plutocratic character."[22] Demands for the election of businessmen to the central board were raised at the convention in 1908. Three years later two delegates from Berlin and Bremen threatened to obstruct the reelection of the board until businessmen were added to the slate. The dispute was settled when Horwitz made a promise to expand the board and to coopt businessmen.[23]

The chapter leaders won over Horwitz and Fuchs by arguing that the centralized and bureaucratic operation of the Centralverein left the membership passive. Salinger called attention to the way in which membership in the Centralverein was becoming a "substitute Judaism." A large body paid dues but remained inactive in the defense struggle.[24] By paying dues they assumed that they had fulfilled their obligations to the Jewish community. Horwitz and Fuchs became acutely sensitive to this criticism. More and more frequently, they heard Zionists say disdainfully that the Centralverein provided a "substitute Judaism" for assimilated middle-class Jews who did not practice religious observances or wish to become personally involved in community life. They disputed this assertion with a trace of defensiveness, but inwardly they were more troubled than they were willing to admit.[25]

Horwitz and Fuchs responded flexibly to the pressure for change from the young generation. The central board was made socially and geographically more representative by the cooptation of businessmen and persons living in Western and Southern Germany. Steps were taken to broaden the social composition of the delegates to the convention. Reading the biennial report at the meeting in 1911,

Holländer conceded that because the delegates were not given compensation for travel expenses, more affluent men attended the convention than men of modest circumstances. He called this discrepancy a "serious grievance" and expressed regret that "in this way the democratic foundation of the Centralverein is undermined."[26] The governing board pledged to redress this fault as soon as finances increased. In 1913 funds were appropriated for the travel costs of delegates to the convention.

Other actions were undertaken to decentralize the defense movement and to give the chapters more responsibilities. In the provinces of Prussia and in the other states of the empire committees were formed to handle matters on a regional level. The provincial and state committees were encouraged to arrange meetings in small towns and to make contacts with Jewish tradesmen and small retailers. Activists in Frankfurt and Essen were allowed to organize campaigns to contest anti-Semites in Reichstag by-elections in Hesse and Westphalia. Holländer concluded his report for the years 1909 to 1911 with the statement that experience had "shown that only by operating the Centralverein in a democratic way can its work be furthered."[27]

Another reason for the readiness of Horwitz and Fuchs to introduce reforms was their own ambition to have the Centralverein play a larger role in politics. In the past the jurisdictional boundaries between the Centralverein and the Verband were not clear-cut. It was generally assumed that the Centralverein would confine its work to legal defense and the Verband would be the political arm of German Jewry.[28] Rapidly the Centralverein outstripped the Verband. The transactions of the Verband's executive committee suggest that Horwitz used his influence to keep the new pressure group out of party politics and to have all matters concerning elections referred to the Centralverein. In 1911 a proposal that the Verband should engage in campaign activities in the forthcoming Reichstag election was set before the committee. After Horwitz spoke against it, the committee decided to leave election work to the Centralverein.[29] At a November meeting the committee discussed a letter from the Jewish congregation in Cologne seeking advice on whether to accept an offer made by Center party politicians, who promised to defend Jewish interests in religious matters if the Jews supported the

Center's candidate. Horwitz contended that the Verband should not advise the Jews in Cologne and, as a rule, should not get involved in elections.[30]

The growing political ambitions of the Centralverein's leaders were manifest around 1910. On speaking tours Julius Brodnitz and Ludwig Holländer described the organization as the central political union of German Jewry. With pride they observed how increasingly the Jews expected the Centralverein to coordinate all Jewish initiatives in political life and recognized it as the foremost spokesman of their interests in politics.[31]

In January 1912, at the start of a new year, the central board announced a policy to make the Centralverein a democratic mass movement. The message, which Holländer entitled "The Democratic Foundation of the Centralverein," indicated that the changes were contemplated as part of the increasing politicization of the organization. Holländer wrote that if the Centralverein was to achieve its goals, it had to educate the Jews for political life, mold private individuals into activists, and adopt democratic procedures so that the people, not merely an elite, participated in its work.[32] For this task the central board turned to the chapters. Holländer stated that the political indoctrination and mobilization of the Jews could be accomplished only if the defense movement was vital on the local level. The chapters were told to hold meetings frequently and encourage discussion, to establish collegial leadership, and to decide on policies by open discussion rather than by bureaucratic procedures. The Centralverein members were to become activists by working in the chapters.

The influence of the chapters led also to changes in the tactics of the Centralverein. Many regional leaders were personally not so deeply involved in Progressive party politics as Lövinson, Sonnenfeld, and other Berlin notables were. They were not inclined to give priority to party interests and allegiance over the honor of the Jewish religious community. Having observed the Progressives in the Bülow bloc, they were too critical to become ardent party loyalists. On the other hand, boycotting the Progressive parties and forming a separate Jewish bloc did not seem to them a pragmatic alternative. They supported the Progressives as the only political option open to the Jews. Fabius Schach gave expression to the sober realism with which they confronted the political dilemma of the Jewish liberals when he wrote in 1912: "We have often called it an unhealthy situation that the Jews in Germany are forced to belong to the Progressive parties because the others are almost all imbued with anti-Semitism. As circumstances stand today, a change can not be contemplated for the time being."[33]

Also in contrast with the Berlin Jewish Progressives, activists in the chapters of Western Germany wanted the Centralverein to play a more visible role in elections. At meetings of the provincial committees in Prussian Hesse in November 1909 and in the Rhineland in November 1910, the main item on the agenda was election campaigning.[34] In the political addresses that opened the discussion, Rudolf Geiger and Max Mainzer of Frankfurt pointed out that when anti-Semitic candidates had won, it was often because the votes of the Left were split among competing parties. They advised the chapters to start work for the next Reichstag election early and to urge the leaders of the parties on the Left in their districts to negotiate agreements. Both speakers advocated that the chapters support Social Democratic nominees if their chances of beating anti-Semitic candidates were good. These two regional conferences paved the way for the policy adopted by the 1911 convention that any candidate opposing an anti-Semitic reactionary should be supported no matter how far Left his party stood.[35]

The influence of the younger activists can be traced in the Reichstag election of 1912. After Bülow's resignation and the breakup of the bloc in 1909, the Germans expected his successor Bethmann Hollweg to call new elections before the Reichstag's regular term was scheduled to end in 1912. Early in 1911 the central board started collecting campaign funds. The Centralverein's leaders awaited the upcoming election with confidence and expected a defeat for the anti-Semitic parties, which had lost four seats in by-elections.[36] *Im Deutschen Reich* took notice of the Reichstag seats won by the Social Democrats in by-elections and discerned signs that public opinion was swinging to the Left in the parliamentary elections in the states of Baden and Saxony. It hailed the outcome of these elections as the bell tolling for the blue–black bloc, the progovernment coalition of the Conservatives and the Center party.[37]

During the campaign political speakers at chapter meetings agitated for the defeat of the blue–black bloc. Opposition to the Center party was a position taken by the Centralverein reluctantly. In 1910 and in the early months of 1911 its criticism of the Center's coalition with the Conservatives was moderate. *Im Deutschen Reich* lamented that the party no longer championed equality of rights for Germans of all faiths as it had done in the days of Lieber and Windhorst.[38] Criticism of the blue–black bloc was coupled with praise for Center deputies such as Adolf Gröber, who defended in the Reichstag the kosher slaughtering of animals when anti-Semites demanded a legal ban on the practice under the guise of preventing cruelty to animals.[39]

Relations between the two confessions were strained by attacks on the Center party in the left-liberal newspapers, especially the *Berliner Tageblatt* and the *Frankfurter Zeitung*, whose publishers were Jewish. In retaliation, party propagandists vented their wrath on the Jews as a group. Chapters in the Rhineland reported increasing evidence of anti-Semitism in the Center press.[40] The provincial committee discussed the problem in November 1910. Several chapter representatives wanted something done about newspapers, widely identified as Jewish, whose criticism of Church politics provoked Catholic believers.[41] A proposal was made that the Centralverein should release a public statement disclaiming responsibility for the left-liberal press attacks and assuring Catholics that the Jews respected other religions and found the criticism distasteful. The proposal was forwarded to the Berlin headquarters.

Horwitz and Fuchs disapproved of the caustic remarks that the left-liberal dailies made about Clerical politics but decided not to issue any public disavowal.[42] They thought that it would be demeaning as well as politically unwise to make any public apology. Neither the Jews collectively nor the defense movement could be held responsible for what the Mosse and Sonnemann publishing houses printed.[43] A public disclaimer might leave the impression that the Centralverein possessed influence over the Jewish press lords and could intervene to stop the criticism.

Throughout January 1912 the Center press made anti-Jewish remarks and supported the election campaign of the Christian Socials. An estimated 80 percent of the ballots cast for the Christian Social candidates came from Center voters.[44] The Centralverein reacted by sharpening its opposition to the Catholic party. After the runoffs were over, Holländer justified the defense movement's opposition to the Center party. He acknowledged that some Center deputies had defended religious liberty, but he insisted that this help could "not be remunerated with a complete surrender of political convictions on the part of the Jews because the party concluded vote-trading agreements with enemies of the Jews during the election and fraternized with the Agrarians."[45] The Centralverein blamed the Center for the victories of three Christian Socials, Behrens, Mumm, and Vogt.[46]

The Centralverein's support for the Progressives was more conspicuous in the 1912 campaign than it had been in previous elections. Chapter meetings provided party propagandists with a platform for campaign speeches. Hermann Cohn delivered speeches on behalf of the Progressives in December in Chemnitz, Cologne, and other cities. The Centralverein gave substantial sums to the party. Collaboration between the Jewish defense movement and the Progressives was facilitated by the Abwehrverein. Before the election the two organizations agreed to establish a joint campaign fund and to set up a committee to decide on the distribution of the money to electoral districts.[47] The Centralverein gave a public endorsement to the Progressives. After quoting from a speech that Karl Schrader, the party's deputy chairman, had made against the government's foreign policy, *Im Deutschen Reich* stated that "the Progressive deputy has issued a watchword for the coming Reichstag election, which can appeal to all patriotic voters who are no longer inclined to support the power politics of the privileged classes."[48]

In the campaign Horwitz and Fuchs ceased to disguise their political sympathies by professing nonpartisanship and openly aligned the Centralverein with the Progressives. After the Bülow bloc disintegrated in June 1909, relations between the Jewish defense movement and the Progressives improved. When the Progressive People's party held its annual congress in the autumn of 1909, Franz von Liszt and Friedrich von Payer proposed a resolution calling for the merging of the three parties of the liberal Left. The Centralverein encouraged this movement to unite the splintered Progressives.[49] It hailed the fusion of the Progressives in March 1910 and anticipated that, now as a single party, they would contest anti-Semitic candidates more successfully.[50]

No longer restrained by obligations to the Bülow bloc, the Progressives were willing to oppose government anti-Semitism. In 1910 lobbyists representing the Centralverein and the Verband gave to Progressive deputies in the Reichstag material on specific cases of discrimination in the army and asked them to bring up the matter during the reading of the military budget.[51] Müller agreed in February 1910 to discuss the cases privately with Minister of War von Einem, and Gothein consented to call upon him in the Reichstag to end the exclusion of Jewish soldiers from the reserve officer corps.[52] At the end of December Otto Wiemer, the party's chairman, promised Jewish lobbyists that the *Fraktion* would open the issue again when the government presented the military budget in 1911.[53]

The nomination of Jews to run in districts where their prospects of winning were good also led the Centralverein to back the party openly. Cohn prevailed upon the Progressives in Dessau to accept the candidacy of Hugo Preuss. Three other Jewish candidates whom the Progressives selected belonged to the Centralverein, Ludwig Haas in Karlsruhe, Lewis Löwenthal in Briegs-Namslau, and David Waldstein in Schleswig-Eckernförde. The Centralverein's leaders were convinced that party officials acted in good faith in responding to their demands for the nomination of Jewish candidates, and they publicly refuted allegations that the Progressives selected Jews only as "stand-in candidates."[54]

At the same time that the Centralverein's political friendship with the Progressives grew intimate, its leadership adopted a friendlier position toward the Social Democratic party. Jewish activists learned from the Reichstag election of 1907 that the hostility of many liberals to social democracy would have to be softened before they would heed party appeals not to support anti-Semitic reactionaries in runoffs against the Socialists.[55] They saw that Jewish voters too would have to be prepared psychologically to cast ballots for the Social Democratic party instead of abstaining as they had done in many runoffs matching Social Democrats against anti-Semites and Conservatives. In by-elections in 1910 the Centralverein supported Social Democratic candidates who fought anti-Semites and instructed Jewish voters not to abstain.[56]

In its political propaganda the Centralverein impressed upon the Jews that the Social Democrats could be relied upon to oppose discriminatory laws. Speakers at chapter meetings called attention to the party's commitment to the principles of religious toleration and civil equality and discounted the significance of anti-Jewish remarks in the Socialist press as "literary slips," which had no effect on the party's politics in the Reichstag. At one meeting in 1911 the speaker, a left-liberal journalist, made a point of conceding to the Social Democrats that "even if one belongs among their political opponents, one must not deny them the credit of adhering to the principle that religion is a private matter or more correctly a matter of the heart and that in political life no one has the right to ask about religious faith."[57] The Social Democrats were praised for being free of bigotry and for electing Jews such as Paul Singer to the Reichstag and appointing them to prominent party offices.

Working with the Abwehrverein and the Centralverein, the Progressives conducted a wholehearted and intensive campaign against the anti-Semites. The party's united front against the anti-Semites was facilitated, first, by improvements in party organization and discipline. The Progressives entered the 1912 election as a single party. The central committee was connected with the local organizations through 25 district secretaries.[58] It no longer left the local clubs free to negotiate election coalitions with the Right or to follow runoff tactics from which right-wing candidates could profit. Local club officials were directed to make the defeat of the blue–black bloc, not the Social Democrats, their primary goal.[59] Secondly, the Progressives adopted an emphatic stand against anti-Semitic candidates. The central committee issued a manifesto naming the Agrarian League's Economic Union and other anti-Semitic groups among the right-wing parties for which the Progressives should not vote in the runoffs.

Also making the left-liberal campaign against the anti-Semites more effective was the election pact that the Progressives concluded with the Social Democrats. At the start of the campaign the left-liberal press called for a united front of Progressives and Social Democrats to defeat the blue–black bloc. Recalling how liberals in the past had succumbed to instinctive fears of the "red peril" and had voted for right-wing candidates in the runoffs, the *Berliner Tageblatt* urged party leaders to instruct the Progressives to vote for the Social Democrats, if necessary, in order to rout the reactionary Right.[60] Some party notables recognized the tactical necessity of cooperating with the Social Democrats, but they feared that such an alliance would cost the Progressives the support of right-wing voters in those districts where they ran against the Social Democrats. This reservation was set aside when the central committee of the Social Democratic party reduced the conditions that Progressive candidates had to accept in exchange for working-class votes. Representatives of the two parties conferred secretly and negotiated an agreement on January 16. As part of the bargain, the Progressives agreed to endorse 31 Social Democrats in the runoffs and received, in return, Socialist support in districts where Progressive candidates contested the Conservatives and the Center.[61]

Activists in the defense movement saw the Progressives act more honorably in the runoffs than they had done in the 1907 and 1908 elections. In the district of Giessen-Nidda the Progressives announced their support for the Social Democratic candidate challenging the anti-Semitic incumbent Werner.[62] Progressives in Marburg resisted the temptation of settling old scores with the Democratic Union and endorsed Helmut von Gerlach, who was running a close race with Johann Rupp of the German Social party.[63]

In the district of Eschwege-Schmalkalden, where the anti-Semite Raab and the Social Democrat Thöne were locked in battle, Otto Wiemer was put to a hard test but upheld the party's manifesto. The party's local committee issued a declaration that criticized Raab's unscrupulous campaign tactics but stopped short of endorsing his challenger. It left up "to the good sense of our voters to act in whatever way they can reconcile with their consciences."[64] The provincial committee of Hesse issued another directive explicitly endorsing Thöne as well as Social Democrats fighting anti-Semites in runoffs in two other districts.[65] Raab's campaign manager sent to Wiemer a telegram complaining about the support that the Progressives were giving to Thöne. The telegram threatened Wiemer that if he did not endorse Raab, the German Social party would advise its followers to abstain in Nordhausen, where his bid for reelection was being challenged by a Social Democrat.[66] Wiemer refused to endorse Raab and was defeated in Nordhausen. The extent to which his moral stand against the anti-Semites hurt him politically is not known. His integrity won him public praise. The *Berliner Tageblatt* expressed the hope that he would win a Reichstag seat soon in a by-election.[67]

Only in the Kingdom of Saxony did the Progressives barter for votes with the anti-Semites. The state committee in Dresden balked at the directive issued by the central committee in Berlin for the second balloting and contended that party rules left decisions on runoff tactics up to the local organizations. The Progressive incumbent Günther in the district of Plauen was not confident of defeating his Socialist challenger. To ensure his reelection with votes from the Right, the Progressives endorsed the anti-Semite Emil Gräfe in the district of Bautzen and two Conservatives campaigning elsewhere in Saxony.[68]

Hermann Cohn, who headed the Progressive organization in the duchy of Anhalt, was implicated in a second unprincipled election agreement. The Progressive nominee Hugo Preuss was defeated in the first balloting in Dessau. In discussions with the National Liberals Cohn agreed to endorse their candidate North, who was fighting a Social Democrat in the runoff. Opposition to Cohn's decision appeared in left-liberal newspapers in Anhalt. Cohn's critics argued that North had reached the runoff with the help of anti-Semitic and Conservative voters and that North's campaign workers had stressed his Christian faith and had circulated innuendos about the Jewish origins of Preuss.[69] Cohn justified his action in a statement released to the press. He denied that North was an anti-Semitic reactionary and asserted that it was not North's party but "irresponsible supporters of his candidacy" who played up his Christian belief in the campaign against Preuss.[70] He explained his decision to back North on the grounds that the Progressives would have a better chance of regaining the district in the next election if the Social Democrats were beaten. Cohn's action provoked a rebellion among young left liberals in Anhalt. They forced the local committee to convene a special meeting at which Cohn's tactics were rejected, and a motion to endorse the Social Democratic candidate was passed.[71]

The incident, widely publicized in the daily press, was a severe humiliation for Cohn. After the election he felt obliged to give his co-religionists an account of why he had endorsed North. In a statement sent to *Im Deutschen Reich*, he said that he had asked and had received assurances from National Liberal leaders in Anhalt that they did not approve of anti-Semitism. Now he omitted any reference to party interests and tactics and said that his decision to promote

North's election was determined by the ideological differences between the Progressives and the Social Democrats and his "love for and loyalty to the fatherland and the monarchy."[72]

Cohn was a member of the Centralverein's governing board. Unlike the uproar created over Lövinson's endorsement of Mugdan, this incident passed without provoking a challenge to the organization's top leadership. Since 1909 the Berlin bureau had improved communications with the chapters. The disclosure of Cohn's political opportunism did not cast any cloud over the foremost leaders of the defense movement, Horwitz, Fuchs, and Holländer.

The anti-Semites were battered in the 1912 election. Jewish activists hailed the defeat of seven anti-Semitic incumbents and took pride in the effectiveness of their propaganda, which had presented factual evidence of the low moral character of many anti-Semitic candidates and of the impotence and failures of the anti-Semitic *Fraktion* in the Reichstag. From the decline in the anti-Semitic vote, by more than half in Saxony alone, they concluded that the majority of the nation had grown weary of anti-Semitic demagoguery.[73]

Activists in the defense movement rejoiced even more over the election of two Jewish Progressives, Ludwig Haas and David Waldstein. Haas, a lawyer in Karlsruhe, was a member of the executive board of the Centralverein's *Landesverband* in Baden. Jewish left liberals saw the victories of Haas and Waldstein in districts where the population was overwhelmingly Christian as a breakthrough. The *Allgemeine Zeitung des Judentums* declared:

> What is the essential and important point is that neither Waldstein in his almost wholly Protestant constituency in Schleswig nor Haas in a district stirred up by confessional differences complain about serious anti-Semitic attacks. It actually seems that this most hideous tendency is being gradually eliminated from German domestic politics or is at least greatly diminishing, as the striking failure of fanatical, Jew-hating anti-Semitism in the Reichstag election shows as clear as day.[74]

The Centralverein tempered the optimism of Jewish liberals by reminding them how anti-Semitism had waxed and waned over and over again. Cautioning the Jews not to fall into complacency, Holländer wrote in a post-election analysis: "Anti-Semitism has always been popular as an admixture and a tactic by which declining parties put wind back into their sails and shall probably remain so for a long time. The fact of the matter is that after centuries of Jewish persecution there prevails in wide circles of the population the feeling that one can safely vent one's anger on the Jews."[75]

7

JEWISH LOBBYING AND GOVERNMENT SCHOOL POLICIES

Jewish activists who built up the defense movement in the 1890s propagated the idea that, besides being a religious community, the Jews had to act as a particular interest group in German politics. They cast themselves in the dual role of defenders against anti-Semitism and lobbyists representing Jewish interests in the state administration and in parliament. At first the Jews, who had been striving for integration into German society, were reluctant to call attention to their ethnic differentness and to exclusively Jewish interests. They did not easily accept the argument that the Jews had as much a legitimate right to protect their interests as Catholics, Protestants, the Agrarian League, and other pressure groups. After the turn of the century German Jewry finally emerged as a consciously organized interest group. Founding the Verband der deutschen Juden in 1904, Jewish left liberals created a lobby to defend Jewish rights in the Reichstag and state parliaments.

The entrance of Jewish organizations into political life as representatives of particular interests came in the wake of the increasing fragmentation of German society into aggressively articulate economic and ideological blocs. Sooner or later this trend would have affected the Jewish community. What speeded up the development of Jewish lobbying was the enactment and execution of school legislation in Prussia. The school question touched all Jews as no other issue in the Wilhelminian era had done. Jewish teachers mobilized to protect themselves against discriminatory treatment. The Orthodox Jews were roused to ward off threats to the survival of Jewish schools built by the congregations to nurture children in the traditions of Judaism. For assimilated Jews the administration of the school system became another front in the fight for civil equality. They saw in the legislation proposed by the Ministry of Education provisions which treated the Jewish minority as second-class citizens and fostered segregation in the public primary schools.

Party controversies that arose over school policies in Prussia were provoked most frequently by measures affecting the elementary schools. The state took supervisory control over the secondary schools away from the Protestant church in 1787. This step set a trend for making the high schools interdenominational. The primary schools continued to be organized on a Christian confessional basis even though they were state institutions and thus subject to government supervision.[1] Article 24 of the Prussian constitution of 1850 stipulated that confessional circumstances were to be taken into consideration as far as possible in making provisions for primary schools and that religious instruction in the schools was to be left to the care of the Protestant and Catholic churches. Teachers were generally appointed to schools according to the confession of the pupils. Interconfessional schools, called *Simultanschulen*, were opened in areas where the population was confessionally diverse. Children of different faiths attended the schools, and the teachers were appointed regardless of confession. Only for religious instruction were the pupils separated according to faith. In the 1870s the Ministry of Education under Adalbert Falk promoted the establishment of interdenominational schools. Whereas the liberals favored the removal of clerical influence from the schools, the Catholic Center and the Protestant Conservatives protected confessional interests in the school system. The introduction of any new measure affecting the schools was bound to stir up conflicts.

The Law of July 23, 1847, and subsequent decrees regulating school matters did not extend to the Jews the same rights and financial support that the state gave to the Christian confessions. Article 64 of the Law of July 23, 1847, granted the Jewish communities the right to open schools but laid upon the Jews complete responsibility for their upkeep.[2] Article 67 allowed synagogue congregations operating schools to request a subsidy from the *Gemeinden* (the unit of local administration for a city or for several villages or hamlets) that maintained Christian public schools. The communes remained free, however, to grant or deny funds to Jewish schools. Unlike Catholic and Protestant pastors, who exercised the right of inspecting schools for their confession, rabbis were to be assigned the task of inspecting Jewish schools "only in exceptional cases," according to a ministerial decree of 1866.[3]

Religious instruction also reflected differences in the treatment of Jews and Christians. The school curriculum included Christian confessional instruction, which was mandatory for Christian children. The Law of 1847 exempted Jewish pupils attending non-Jewish schools from this requirement and obliged each congregation to make provisions for religious education. Article 62 was loosely phrased and did not state specifically that religious instruction should be given in school and that Jewish pupils should be required to receive it as Catholic and Protestant children were. Although some Jews believed that this was the intent of article 62, the government did not interpret it so.[4]

Furthermore, the Law of 1847 did not obligate the government to appropriate funds for the religious instruction of Jewish children as it did for Christian religious education in school. The congregations had to pay the teacher's salary and other expenses. Explaining this distinction, an explication that accompanied the Law of 1847 stated that the Jews were a tolerated community whereas the Lutheran and Catholic confessions enjoyed government support and other privileges as communities approved by the state.[5]

The Jews bore a double financial burden, supporting non-Jewish public schools as taxpayers and providing religious instruction for their children outside the schools. A ministerial decree of July 8, 1875, attempted to end the inequity by permitting the appointment of Jewish teachers for religion lessons in Christian schools. The decree redressed the injustice slightly because it did not require but merely allowed the communes to make voluntary provisions for Jewish religious instruction.[6]

In Greater Prussia in the early 1890s there were 244 Jewish public schools with an enrollment of 9,502 children. The schools were located mainly in the western half of the state, 82 in Hesse, 48 in Hanover, 22 in the Rhine Province, and 18 in Westphalia.[7] Except for Posen, where there were 57 Jewish schools, few were established in the eastern provinces. Berlin and Frankfurt am Main had, respectively, 3 and 5 Jewish private schools but no Jewish public schools. Most Jewish schools were small, with one or two classrooms. Three-hundred and five teachers were employed for 244 schools. The majority of Jewish children attended non-Jewish schools. They numbered 10,853 in Protestant schools, 4,327 in Catholic schools, and 5,704 in interconfessional schools.[8] In comparison, 95.6 percent of the Protestant and 91.2 percent of the Catholic pupils went to schools to which teachers of the same faith were appointed.

To maintain their schools the Jews accepted a heavy financial burden, and many small congregations strained their resources. The Jewish schools were found more commonly in the small communities than in the wealthy and urban ones.[9] Funds were raised by levying on the members taxes as high as 100–200 percent of the state income tax they paid. The congregation tax paid by the Jews was 10 times more than the church tax paid by the Protestants.[10] The Jewish teachers also made sacrifices. They received lower wages than teachers at the other public schools. A ministerial decree in 1872 declared that there was no legal necessity to put the compensation of teachers at Jewish schools on a par with teachers' salaries at the other schools.[11]

When Count Zedlitz, the minister of education, introduced the draft of a new school law in the Diet on January 15, 1892, the issue that aroused the Jews was the government's policy of phasing out the interconfessional schools and organizing schools on a confessional basis. Ministry officials admitted that a system of separate schools was costly and created difficulties in areas populated by diverse religious groups, but the government did not stop or slow down the trend that increased Protestant schools by 626 and Catholic schools by 93 from 1886 to 1891. The Jews did not benefit from this policy. Their schools were closing; during these five years the number dropped from 318 to 244.[12] By 1892 many Jews had come to identify their interests as a small minority with interdenominational schools.

The controversial feature of the school bill of 1892 was article 14, which provided that, as a rule, children should be instructed by teachers of their confession and that new schools should be established only on a confessional basis.[13] If a school's confessional minority had more than 30 pupils, the *Regierungspräsident*, the chief administrator of the provincial district, could order the building of a separate school for them. Such action was mandatory if the number exceeded 60.

Probably because anti-Semitic deputies and journalists endorsed the school bill, the Jews scrutinized it suspiciously. They noticed ambiguities and loopholes that would allow reactionary officials to interpret the law arbitrarily and to the disadvantage of the Jews.[14] To Jewish liberals the bill was a setback for the development of a progressive educational system. They thought that the confessionalization of the schools prevented children of different faiths from having friendly relations with one another and developing mutual respect.

Underlying this criticism was an anxiety about the segregation of Jewish schoolchildren. The bill did not require the local authorities to consult Jewish community leaders before they decided to establish a separate school for Jewish pupils. The Jews feared that against the wishes of the parents anti-Semitic officials would remove Jewish children from Christian schools, which had good facilities, and send them to one-classroom Jewish schools.[15] In 1892 the Jews bore such suspicions with good reason. Recent events in the Provincial District of Arnsberg gave them a foretaste of what this loophole in the school bill might bring. An administrative order was issued forcing 28 Jewish children in the town of Hörde to leave the interconfessional school by April 1, 1892, and to go to a separate Jewish school. The parents protested this action. The *Regierungspräsident* held firm to the decision until the ministry intervened and countermanded the order.[16]

After the school bill was introduced in the Diet, the *Allgemeine Zeitung des Judentums* summoned the congregations to press demands for amendments to it. When some Jews objected that such agitation would be imprudent, Rabbi Heinemann Vogelstein, who had written the appeal, replied with a bold defense of Jewish political activism. Rabbi Vogelstein argued that the Jews as citizens must be involved in politics whenever questions as vital as the public schools arose. "Whoever advises the Jews to remain passive in the controversy raging over the school bill is asking them to give evidence of spiritual and moral bankruptcy," he remarked.[17] He denied that opposition to the bill would hurt the Jews and insisted, on the contrary, that Christians would have contempt for the Jews if they refrained from political action out of fear of arousing hostility among officials, Conservatives, and Catholics, who backed the measure.

A Jewish campaign to revise the school bill never started. Bowing to the opposition of the National Liberals and the Progressives, the government withdrew the bill, and Count Zedlitz resigned.[18] Nonetheless, this event marked an important step in the development of a Jewish lobby. The Jews began to discuss publicly the role that they should play in the enactment of legislation. The school question was recognized as a political matter on which they could not be neutral spectators.

The determination of the Jews to protect their interests in school affairs appeared more boldly in a crisis the following year in Hesse, where Jewish schools were threatened with a mass shutdown. The Provincial District of Cassel had 80 Jewish public schools, of which 27 were receiving government grants totaling 4,050 marks in 1893. The subsidies were introduced in 1875 by Falk, who allocated the money specifically for the salaries of teachers at Jewish schools in the Provincial District of Cassel. Trouble started with the appointment of a new director for the district's Department of Church and School Affairs. Carl von Altenbockum, the new appointee, was not disposed to treat the Jews fairly and begrudged the state aid given to the Jewish schools. In his brief against the subsidies he asserted that the moral concern which the Jews expressed about providing schoolchildren with an education rich in spiritual values was a pretext. To be thrifty and to reduce expenses, congregations used teachers for religious functions that a rabbi or a cantor should normally perform.[19]

From Altenbockum's reports to the ministry it is apparent that he handled requests for government assistance to the Jewish schools with an anti-Semitic bias and was eager to see financial stringency force small congregations to close their schools. Reporting how difficult it was to assess the financial capability of any community, he wrote:

> [The Jews] are engaged in the cattle and grain trade, acquire property by foreclosing mortgages, loan money, etc. The profit that they may gain from these enterprises is mostly concealed from the government.

He blamed Jewish avarice for the declining economic circumstances of the small-town congregations:

> This is partly explained by the fact that the Jewish usurer does

his mischief in this region, the Jews who become rich move away, and for those who remain in the exploited area not much is to be earned, a situation connected also with political currents. The influence of anti-Semitic agitation has been especially effective in Southern Hesse so that the peasants do business with the Jews no longer so gullibly as before.[20]

On January 31, 1893, Altenbockum's office notified the *Landräte*, the head administrators of the counties, that it intended to raise the salaries of teachers at Christian schools, and that, to acquire the funds for this purpose, it was withdrawing government subsidies for the compensation paid to teachers at Jewish schools.[21] The *Landräte* were ordered to inform the congregations that starting April 1, 1893, they must pay the entire salary of the teachers. If they could not raise the money, their schools would be closed, and the pupils would be transferred to Christian schools. Altenbockum made this decision without consulting the communities or making inquiries about the financial circumstances of the communities affected.

Only in March, following inquiries from the Ministry of Education, did Altenbockum instruct the *Landräte* to submit reports on the financial resources of the congregations and to state whether those congregations losing subsidies had the funds to keep up the schools. The *Landräte* did not confer with the executive boards of the communities. They drew up short perfunctory reports in which personal attitudes toward the Jews determined to a large extent their recommendations.[22] Some officials assured Altenbockum that the communities would suffer no hardships and could be left to shift for themselves. Others advised him not to take away the subsidies because the small congregations remained poor despite the heavy taxes paid by their members.

The communities were stunned by Altenbockum's decision and turned for help to the *Vorsteherämter der Israeliten*, the four councils constituted by government edict in Electoral Hesse in 1813 to supervise Jewish affairs. In March the *Vorsteherämter* petitioned Altenbockum not to cut off the state subsidies. The petitions described the economic hardships of the small congregations in Hesse and claimed that the congregations, without government grants, would have difficulties paying the full salary of qualified teachers and would have no other choice than to close the schools.[23] After conceding that the schools had a low attendance, the *Vorsteherämter* contended that the dissolution of the schools would hurt the spiritual and moral life of the communities. Some small congregations did not have sufficient resources to employ a rabbi, so that the teacher became the center of Jewish religious life for schoolchildren and adults in these small towns and villages.

At the same time the *Vorsteherämter* appealed the case to Minister of Education Bosse. The protests aroused Bosse to intervene by demanding from Altenbockum an explanation for his unauthorized decision. Altenbockum replied that he considered "neither the teachers fully employed nor the schools any longer viable" because the enrollment had fallen.[24] In April Bosse sent a briskly worded letter to Altenbockum rebuking him for acting precipitantly. The minister disagreed with his judgment that the Jewish teachers were not doing a full day's work and said that the low enrollment at the Jewish schools did not warrant such a conclusion.[25] He sternly told Altenbockum that if he thought any Jewish school was not viable, he must consult the Jewish community and act in accordance with the law to close it. In a second letter in July Bosse once again reproved Altenbockum and wrote that it was a wrong interpretation of the law to make the right of a Jewish community to have a school dependent on its capacity to maintain it completely. The minister pronounced the cutoff of the subsidies for Jewish teachers' salaries illegal because the Diet in 1875 had approved an appropriation in the budget expressly for this purpose.[26] The school department was ordered to investigate each case anew and to restore the state grants to congregations in financial need.

In the meantime Altenbockum took steps to liquidate the Jewish schools. He sent to the *Landräte* on June 22 a list of Jewish schools with an enrollment of fewer than 12 children and commanded that they be shut down. He instructed the county officials to send announcements to the local authorities and the executive boards of the congregations and to make arrangements with them to transfer the pupils to other schools in the commune.[27] A six-week deadline was set so that plans for these changes had to be made in haste. The communities, notified in July about the imminent extinction of their schools, brought the news to the *Vorsteherämter*. The *Vorsteherämter* protested Altenbockum's high-handed behavior. They reproachfully reminded him that the law empowered them to supervise Jewish schools and complained that he had not consulted them. Angry at his arrogance, they demanded to know what his reasons were for ordering the closing of Jewish schools.[28]

Finally on July 28 the *Vorsteherämter* were officially informed that proceedings to close Jewish schools with an enrollment of fewer than 12 children would begin soon and were asked to state whatever objections they had. During the summer the *Vorsteherämter* sought to delay the shutdown and pleaded for more time to prepare a report on the projected enrollments of the schools in coming years. Altenbockum's answer was a discourteous and brusque refusal.[29] The congregations sent protests to the *Landräte*. The community leaders contended that Jewish children would be deprived of religious instruction once they were transferred to Christian schools. They pointed out that attendance would increase as children under six years of age entered the schools. Some protests mentioned that the communities had already spent considerable sums to build and equip the schools.[30]

In a desperate attempt to save the schools, the *Vorsteherämter* addressed appeals to Altenbockum on September 19. The *Vorsteherämter* disputed his policies by making references to the law of 1833, which granted the congregations in Hesse the right to open schools and set no condition regarding the number of pupils.[31] They pointed out that the Jewish schools served the interests of the state by cultivating morality in the children and by teaching them to be loyal to the monarchy. The petition from the *Vorsteheramt* in Marburg warned that the decision to close Jewish schools would have bad effects. It came at a time "when, on the one side, atheistic social democracy is making giant strides . . . and, on the other side, a brutal and vulgar anti-Semitism, which would like to see the Jews banned, spreads and shall certainly exploit these measures in a malicious way."[32]

The resoluteness with which the Jews of Hesse fought anti-Semitic elements in the Prussian bureaucracy prevented a full-scale dissolution of the Jewish schools in the provincial district. In August, following Bosse's orders, Altenbockum announced that state subsidies for the stipends of Jewish teachers would be continued. In May 1894 Bosse made another concession to Jewish appeals when he reversed Altenbockum's decision to close three schools.[33]

Altenbockum devised another scheme after the massive protests of the Jews and Bosse's intervention blocked his first attempt to liqui-.date the Jewish schools. His aim this time was to drive the Jews into dismantling the schools by making the expenses of maintaining them burdensome. The school department announced in April 1894 that the salaries of teachers at Jewish schools should be raised.[34] Altenbockum made this decision although he knew that many poor congregations would be hard pressed. Some county officials had no sympathy for the hardships of the communities and anticipated not unhappily the misfortune that would befall the Jewish schools. The *Landrat* of Ziegenhain, for example, expressed his approval of the decision and added that "if the Jews wish to maintain their own schools, they must bear the burdens that come with them even though one or another community may find it hard."[35]

The conduct of administrators in the Provincial District of Cassel reveals how disheartening and frustrating the experiences of the Jewish lobbyists in Germany were. Within the Prussian bureaucracy were many officials hostile to the Jews. In making decisions on Jewish matters they were not objective or neutral.[36] Officials in the Ministry of Education, like Altenbockum, begrudged the appropriation of government money for Jewish educational needs. They showed no scruples about interpreting the law arbitrarily. They acted arrogantly, disdaining to consult the authorized representatives of the Jewish communities or to offer reasons for their actions. Their replies to Jewish complaints were apt to be brusque and cold.

Although the government's school policy was a political issue of deep concern to the Jews, the leaders of organized German Jewry did not depend on the Progressive parties to represent Jewish interests. In the early 1890s Jewish liberals assumed that there existed a natural harmony between Jewish interests and political liberalism because the Progressives stood out as champions of civil equality. In matters of school policy, however, they discovered that the political creed of liberalism did not coincide with the needs and desires of the Jewish community. Two questions forced Jewish activists to decide whether to support the platform of the Progressives or to lobby in-

dependently for school policies that met Jewish needs: Should the
Jews continue to assert, like the Progressives, that the religious
training of children belonged outside the public schools or should
they demand that the Prussian government make the Jewish religion
a required subject for Jewish pupils in school as it did already for
the Protestant and Catholic confessions? Should the Jews defend
the cause of interdenominational schools or should they take into
account the government's policy of confessionalizing the primary
schools and establish separate Jewish schools?

The Progressives disapproved of confessional instruction in public
schools and the regulation obliging Christian children to receive
it.[37] Their basic view was that religion was a matter of the individual's conscience and did not fall within the government's province of action. The teaching of religion was part of worship so
that any application of coercion violated the fundamental rights
of citizens.

A dispute over elective or required religious instruction for Jewish
schoolchildren arose in Berlin in November 1895. Candidates campaigning for election to the community's representative council
charged that more than 10,000 Jewish children in the city were
growing up without religious instruction.[38] Under the pressure of
public outcries, the council took up the issue. At a meeting on
March 15, 1896, one representative introduced a resolution to petition the government to make religion lessons a compulsory part of
the school curriculum for Jewish children. The members of the
council disagreed, and the motion was tabled.[39]

Both sides thrashed over the question at the congress of the
Gemeindebund in Berlin in 1896. Opponents of obligatory religious
instruction invoked the principle of freedom of conscience.[40] They
contended that religion did not properly belong in the school curriculum. The cultivation of piety was not the responsibility of the
state and should be left to the church and to family life. Jewish
liberals who spoke out for required instruction conceded that this
argument was sound in theory. But they insisted that the situation
of the Jews in Germany made such appeals to freedom of conscience hollow.

Demonstrating the boldness with which some Jewish activists
looked at the issue from a Jewish perspective and independent of

the Progressive platform was Martin Philippson, the chairman of the Gemeindebund and an active member of the Progressive Union. Philippson declared that as long as the Jews lived in the ghetto, they needed no requirement for religious instruction, because their entire life was an education in the practices of their faith.[41] With assimilation, the more the Jews appropriated the culture of their surroundings, the more easily were they able to separate themselves from their religious community. He contended that if young Jews studied their religious heritage, they would cope better with the pressures of living as a minority in a Christian cultural environment. Jewish children frequently heard false and hostile views about Judaism, and "a weapon must be given to them in religious instruction."

The Centralverein refrained from taking a public stand at first. Members who belonged to the Progressive parties argued that the defense movement should not lobby for compulsory religious instruction, because such action "would bring countless members into conflict with their political convictions."[42] Sitting on the central board, however, was a Berlin high school teacher whose argument for mandatory religion classes was made persuasive because he accepted, in principle, the Progressives' point of view. Julius Schneider maintained that the Jews would accept any government decision to keep confessional teaching out of the public schools—provided it applied to all faiths. As long as the Protestants and Catholics were required to receive religious instruction in school, the Jews must demand the same regulation for the sake of equal treatment. He pleaded with Jewish Progressives to set aside their personal feelings and opinions and to give priority to the attainment of equal rights and equal treatment: "It is pragmatic to subordinate even justified party principles or other objections to the demand for parity. In reality, the freedom of the Jews in this respect is only evidence of the government's indifference to Jewish concerns, a *privilegium odiosum* in which is contained generally more *odium* than *privilegium*."[43]

Horwitz and Fuchs were persuaded to work with the Gemeindebund in lobbying for a ministry regulation to require religion classes for Jewish schoolchildren. Horwitz defended this decision by declaring that the Jews could not optimistically expect a liberal solution to the problem so long as officials viewed Prussia as a "Christian

state."[44] Fuchs stated that the question of obligatory religious instruction showed that "the commands of liberalism do not always
correspond with the vital interests of Judaism." There were times
when the treatment of the Jewish religion on an equal footing with
the Christian confessions was more important than liberal theories,
and in this matter "Jewish interests can be correctly evaluated and
defended only from the standpoint of Judaism and not from that of
any political party."[45]

The Centralverein and the Gemeindebund appealed to the Ministry
of Education in 1897 to provide elective religious instruction in
school. The two organizations modified their demand for tactical
reasons. In his discussions with ministry officials, Siegmund Meyer,
the chairman of the Berlin community's executive board, found
them unsympathetic to Jewish requests for compulsory lessons.[46]
Rabbi Prager, who was acting for the Rabbinerverband, concluded
from his conversation with Friedrich Althoff that the government
would find excuses to turn down Jewish proposals.[47] Althoff, the
director of the ministry's department for university affairs, enumerated all the difficulties that prevented the government from issuing
a regulation requiring Jewish religious instruction in school. He mentioned that Orthodox and Reform tendencies divided Jewish believers and that the Prussian Jews did not have a central council
which the government could consult. More captious was Althoff's
objection that the ministry did not have complete and reliable information on whether there were enough qualified Jewish teachers and
suitable books.

More complicated was the question of whether the Jews should
establish and secure government funding for separate Jewish schools.
Once again the Jews questioned the practical value of the Progressive
point of view, but they remained deeply divided. The issue of establishing separate schools was probably the most agonizing dilemma
that Jewish left liberals confronted in German politics in the Wilhelminian period.

In the 1890s the Progressives criticized Minister of Education
Zedlitz for introducing a policy of confessionalizing primary schools
and reproached his successor Bosse for allowing interdenominational
schools to be transformed into Christian confessional schools by the
exclusion of Jewish teachers.[48] Despite the fact that interconfes-

sional schools declined in number and stood in official disfavor, the Progressives continued to support them as the best kind of school for a pluralistic society. They praised interdenominational schools for unifying Germans in civic culture and said that, in comparison, confessional schools gave children a sectarian and intolerant outlook and prepared them badly for civic life in which citizens must work together irrespective of differences of faith.[49]

The Progressives impressed upon the Jews the ideas that interconfessional schools promoted toleration and contributed to the improvement of their position in public life.[50] Jewish left liberals supported interconfessional schools as especially suited to erase class and ethnic hostility and resisted the pressure of Orthodox believers to set up Jewish schools.[51] They admitted that some interconfessional schools no longer met the standard of confessional parity and had a Christian character, but they insisted on upholding the principle of interconfessional schools. Felix Coblenz, a teacher in Bielefeld, wrote in the *Allgemeine Zeitung des Judentums:*

> If this principle is administered in an insincere way now in a period of political and religious reaction, this proves nothing against the idea itself but at most speaks against the incompetence, ineptness, or perhaps ill will of those who are appointed here and there by chance to carry it out. If at present interconfessional schools do not *in part* measure up to our conception of schools, this means nothing more than that we cannot yet rise to the heights of absolute parity, which must form the firm foundation of the genuine interconfessional school. To reject the interconfessional school for this reason would be to throw out the baby with the bath water.

Coblenz concluded with the exhortation:

> Just as the liberal politician does not abandon his principles in a time of reaction, just as he does not deviate by a hair's breadth from what is right or does not give up, discouraged and afraid, the fight for his ideals, so in grim times of religious bigotry we should not abandon an idea that is for us the embodiment of tolerance and freedom of conscience in the domain of public

schools. On the contrary, these grave times must strengthen our courage in battle.[52]

Ten years later Jewish left liberals were still entreating the Jews not to lose faith in attaining a confessionally integrated school system. The Centralverein admitted that the present minister of education, Konrad Studt, stood in close rapport with the Conservative and Clerical majority in the Diet and favored confessional schools, but it told the Jews that separate schools were not a remedy for this deplorable political situation.[53] Horwitz and Fuchs thought that, to overcome the argument that public institutions in the Prussian state had to bear a Christian character, the Jews had to uphold uncompromisingly the principle of confessional pluralism in the school system. Deeply disturbing to the leaders of the Jewish defense was the possibility that a segregated school system would emerge and lead eventually to exclusion in other areas of social life. Calling the establishment of separate schools a mistake, *Im Deutschen Reich* argued: "We do not want to segregate ourselves; this is what our enemies wish. . . . The separation of children according to the religion of their parents is inadmissable; for just as it proceeds from a spirit of exclusiveness, if not from hostility and hatred, so it leads to nothing other than segregation and division. The youth should receive their basic education in the same schools."[54]

Another reason for the opposition to the construction of Jewish schools was the likelihood that they would not be fully graded. In many congregations the number of children was too small to warrant the maintenance of a school with several classes. Of the 244 Jewish schools already established in Prussia in 1904, 209 had only a single classroom. Many of the schools had fewer than 30 pupils. Educated middle-class Jewish parents preferred to send children to a fully graded Protestant or Catholic school than to a one-room Jewish school.

After 1900 Jewish teachers questioned the pragmatism of Jewish support for interdenominational schools. Salo Adler of Frankfurt am Main and Moritz Steinhardt of Madgeburg, who had organized the Verband der jüdischen Lehrervereine im Deutschen Reiche (Federation of Jewish Teachers' Associations in the German Empire) in 1895, started to agitate for the establishment of Jewish schools.

Jewish teachers in Prussia were embittered by the increasing practice of discrimination in the 1890s.[55] At regional conferences and in a newssheet that Steinhardt edited, members of the Lehrerverband aired their complaints. They asserted that the interconfessional schools were de facto Christian schools and that Jewish liberals were naive to believe that such schools guaranteed equal treatment.[56] Administrators did not observe the rule of parity in hiring teachers and in making provisions for religious instruction. Singled out as evidence was Breslau, where municipal officials rejected the congregation's request that religious instruction be provided for about 500 Jewish children attending the city's schools.[57]

The Lehrerverband criticized the leaders of organized Jewry, who persisted in advocating interconfessional schools, for lacking hardnosed realism and for hurting Jewish interests unwittingly. Reproaching the notables, Salo Adler wrote: "In making new policies or changes in the school system, the political authorities are thereby relieved of the moral obligation to give some consideration to that part of the population which adheres to the Jewish religion. Not entirely without justification, they can refer to the fact that in the ranks of this minority concern for adhering to the Jewish faith is missing."[58] Bernhard Traubenberg, another activist teacher, advised the Jews not to make the mistake of defending a lost cause and arousing the antagonism of state officials.[59] The Lehrerverband contended that the government's policy of favoring confessional schools would continue for a long time and that it was foolhardy for a minority of idealistic liberals to believe that they could reverse this course. Jewish schools should be established as the only means to guarantee the Jews equality with the Christian confessions.

The Lehrerverband sought to dispel the fear that a system of Jewish schools would be a step back to the ghetto. Steinhardt called the anxiety about Jewish separateness paranoid and observed that Jewish schools in Cologne, Dortmund, and Essen did not prevent the Jews from having cordial relations with the Christian population.[60] Traubenberg stated that the philosophy of life that Judaism taught was "a tried and tested safeguard against degeneration into a persecution complex and exclusiveness. Earlier centuries with so much exclusion and prejudice could not separate the Jews from their surroundings."[61]

At the Lehrerverband's convention in 1904 the delegates drafted a new platform. The program endorsed the interdenominational school in principle and declared that until this ideal could be truly realized, existing Jewish schools should be maintained and new ones opened.[62] The teachers demanded that where there were no Jewish schools the commune should be required to provide religious instruction for Jewish schoolchildren and to appoint Jewish teachers, who would not be barred from teaching subjects other than religion. Knowing that the government planned to propose a school bill, the teachers stated that the new law should be so clearly worded that no doubts would arise concerning the meaning of provisions affecting the Jews.

By the time Minister of Education Studt introduced the school bill in the Prussian parliament in December 1905, several organizations had appeared within the Jewish community ready to lobby for Jewish interests. During the deliberations on the school bill in 1905 and 1906 Jewish activists spoke out more boldly than community leaders had done in the past. They mobilized quickly because they had many reasons to suspect that legislation drafted in the Ministry of Education would contain provisions unfavorable to the Jews. With Studt's blessings, school administrators gave a pronounced Christian confessional character to the primary schools. The minister justified this policy by asserting that the historical development of Prussia's school system had been along confessional lines and that interconfessional schools made teaching and learning difficult because religious differences between teachers and pupils created friction and hostility.[63]

As Jewish activists learned from recent experience, Studt shielded school officials whose discriminatory practices against Jewish teachers were exposed as unconstitutional. In March 1904 the Centralverein's directors protested to the Brandenburg provincial school board that a newspaper advertisement, announcing an opening at a high school in Berlin, specified as a qualification that the teacher be of the Protestant faith.[64] Horwitz's letter stated that this restriction violated the law and requested the school board not to confirm the appointment made on the basis of a hiring policy that barred non-Protestants from the job. Passing the buck, the school board forwarded the protest to the school department of the

Provincial District of Potsdam. The head of the department, von Doemming, rejected the Centralverein's complaint as unjustified and designated the high school as Protestant on the grounds that the Protestant students numbered 76 and the Catholic and Jewish students only 5 and 3.

Horwitz submitted the case to the ministry in October. His letter disputed the legality of von Doemming's policy, which made the confession of the majority of children at a school a factor in determining the qualifications for teachers at the same school. Horwitz pointed out that, in accordance with the Imperial Law of July 3, 1869, religion could not be stipulated as a condition for employment in public offices, and he requested Studt to state officially his disapproval of von Doemming's policy. The reply that Horwitz received was an insolent brush-off. Von Doemming answered brusquely that the minister had instructed him to give the Centralverein a negative reply. Horwitz and Fuchs were angry with Studt and his subordinate, who disregarded the law in so cavalier a manner and disdained to give Jewish citizens an explanation for official actions.[65]

The fact that the chief draftsman of the school bill was Philipp Schwartzkopff, the director of the ministry's bureau for primary school affairs, put the leaders of organized Jewry on the alert. From previous contacts with Schwartzkopff they knew that he did not act with impartiality or good will in matters affecting the Jews. One instance in June 1904, still fresh in their memory, was the ministry's rejection of a plan, proposed by the Gemeindebund, whereby Jewish religious instruction would be given in the Berlin elementary schools at the community's expense. To cover up their prejudice, ministry officials cited the difficulties created by the Jews through their own religious divisiveness.[66] Martin Lövinson expressed the distrust of the state bureaucracy that many Jewish activists felt when he said at a Centralverein meeting in January 1906:

> If in Prussia today a bill appears that deals with Jewish affairs, one has to look at it with a certain suspicion from the outset. In more than 30 years we have not encountered conclusive evidence of generous, liberal or even tolerant policies in this area.

Instead, petty annoyances, increasingly transformed into very effective administrative measures, have aroused in our Jewish population suspicion, bitterness, and a mood of indignation or despair. Today officials, indoctrinated with the idea of the inferiority of the Jews, ... have moved into the highest positions. Must the Jews not then fear that legislative proposals coming from such offices will show signs of the bigotry in which their authors have been raised and educated.[67]

In January 1904 Studt announced in the House of Deputies his intention to introduce a school law draft in the next session. Schwartzkopff arranged with the Conservatives and the National Liberals to sponsor a resolution that recommended guidelines for drafting the school bill. The resolution declared that a new law should implement article 24 of the Prussian constitution so that, as a rule, pupils belonging to the same confession should attend school together and should be instructed by teachers of their faith.[68] Another guideline stated that church representatives should participate in the supervisory school boards. The Progressives opposed the resolution, but it was passed on May 13, 1904, with additional votes from the Center party.

After the house voted for the resolution, the Verband's executive board assigned work on the school bill to its subcommittee on political affairs. In July the subcommittee undertook a study of the conditions of Jewish schools in Prussia and a survey of public opinion in the congregations on school questions. Felix Makower, a Berlin lawyer who headed the subcommittee, wrote to Schwartzkopff on July 1 asking him which parts of earlier school law drafts would be incorporated in the new bill and at what time and to which ministry officials the Verband should communicate the views of the Jews.[69] Schwartzkopff did not welcome the involvement of Jewish lobbyists in the preparation of the bill and declined to release any information. The subcommittee addressed a petition to Studt on August 28. Copies of the petition were forwarded to the deputies who had sponsored the resolution of May 13 and also to Albert Ernst, a member of the Progressive *Fraktion*, who had attacked the government's school policy in the parliamentary debate on May 13.

The petition of August 28 reveals the strategy that the Verband adopted in lobbying on the school bill. The executive board members disapproved of separate schools for Jewish children but did not wish to see the Jews without recourse if the school law brought about the extinction of the interconfessional school.[70] The Verband sought to defend interdenominational schools without undermining the claims that the Jews might make in the future for the establishment of Jewish schools on the grounds of equality. The Verband had to take into account differences of opinion. Orthodox believers favored confessional schools to nurture in the children reverence for Jewish traditions. The Verband's leaders decided to be flexible rather than dogmatic. They withstood pressure from Reform Jews such as Dr. Carl Reich, the head of the Liberal Association of the Breslau Community, who urged the Verband to oppose separate schools.[71]

Makower's subcommittee constructed an argument for interconfessional schools that did not weaken the right of the Jews to have public schools as the Christian confessions had. The petition declared that the Verband desired the maintenance and expansion of the interdenominational schools "from the point of view of state interests, specifically because the power of the state abroad increases the more it stresses solidarity and plays down divisions at home."[72] The Verband declined to say whether the Jewish community had a greater interest in interconfessional or confessional schools "because we acknowledge that on this fundamental question church interests must be subordinated to state interests as long as the equality of all the recognized religious communities is preserved." The subcommittee reinforced this qualifying clause by adding that in localities where confessional schools were built for the majority of the population, the same right should be recognized for the Jewish minority.

Because only 30 of the existing 244 Jewish schools in 1904 had an enrollment of more than 30 pupils, the Verband tried to protect them from being closed by the government on the grounds that attendance was too low. The petition affirmed that the law should have no article making the existence of a confessional school dependent on a fixed number of pupils. The argument justifying this demand suggests the awkward position in which the Verband's lobbyists found themselves as they tried to form a policy acceptable to all segments of the community. The petition declared that Jews living in big cities "put no value on separate Jewish schools" and would accept them only under the force of law. Jews living in small towns "wish only for themselves the maintenance of already established Jewish schools as long as in the commune the confessionalization of the schools for the majority continues in the future."

The petition's defense of Jewish schools was equivocal. The Verband's leaders did not conceal their personal dislike of a school system separating Jewish and Christian children. Without mentioning segregation, the Verband tried to protect Jewish children attending Christian schools from being transferred by administrative order. The petition demanded a provision in the law stating that no child could be denied admission to a public school on account of religion or the existence of a school for the confession to which the parents belonged. As another guarantee against enforced segregation, the petition proposed an article requiring the consent of a religious community before the commune set up a separate school for it.

Addressing the Diet after the school bill was introduced in December 1905, Studt emphasized that the purpose of the now law was to regulate primary school affairs uniformly and to make the communes responsible for building, operating, and funding the schools. Up to this time the burden of maintaining the schools was carried by school associations composed of the heads of households in each locality. The state was not responsible for the costs of running the schools, and in most parts of Prussia there was much confusion about the maintenance of the schools. The new measure was intended to remedy this situation.

Studt discussed his other aim with less candor. The government wanted to organize the school system along confessional lines. Article 18 of the school bill stipulated that schools were to be organized so that, normally, Protestant and Catholic children received instruction from teachers of their own faith.[73] Article 20 made it mandatory for the commune to establish a separate school for Protestant or Catholic children attending an interconfessional school if they numbered more than 60 in an urban commune and more than 120 in a rural one. To facilitate the conversion of interconfessional into confessional schools, article 22 required that in any one school all Catholic or all Protestant teachers were to be appointed.

The school bill dealt with the Jews in a separate article. Article 24 had an anti-Jewish slant, which liberal Christians as well as Jews detected quickly. An allusion to this bias was made in the Diet on December 11, when Carl Funck, a non-Jewish deputy of the Progressive People's party, remarked that "whereas the bill strives so scrupulously to lay down to the last detail the rights of the Christian confessions," there was in article 24 "an arbitrariness, which has a character that I will not describe in detail but in any case is not good."[74]

Jewish activists reacted to the school bill with outcries of injustice. Critics of the draft law attacked article 24 because it left up to the commune to decide whether to keep or to dissolve existing Jewish schools, whether to establish new ones, and how to handle the disposal of the property of the liquidated Jewish schools, which the congregations had built with their own money.[75] They protested that the Jewish communities and parents were denied the right to participate in making these decisions because the bill omitted to require commune officials to consult them or to act with their consent. Arousing the Jews to a consciousness of the dangers lurking in the school bill, Traubenberg wrote:

> An entire network of thorny regulations and traps laid out with cunning will take care that the Jewish school is inevitably caught and choked to death. . . . But far beyond the school domain this legal net of wires for the destruction of the Jewish school is of immense importance. In the constitutional and political sphere it means for the Jews a fatal turning point insofar as the arbitrary administrative practices that are commonly used in the treatment of Jews receive legal sanction. The Jews also stand with their school *de jure* under a special law. This consideration illuminates the full gravity of the bill. If in the past clever legal experts broke their heads pondering how to cut a little snip from a right guaranteed on paper, so in the future on the basis of the law they can give free play to their feelings, without hindrance, without sophistical interpretation tricks, untroubled by doubt and scruple.[76]

Jewish critics of the school bill scored the flagrant discrepancies in the treatment of Jews and Christians. Whereas article 21 compelled the communes to provide religion lessons in school for the Catholic or Protestant minority if the children numbered at least 12, article 24 simply left up to the commune to provide Jewish religious instruction if there were 12 or more pupils and only "in places where this has happened up till now." Jewish critics suspected that this condition, couched in such vague language, was intended to prohibit the introduction of Jewish religious instruction in school. Also discriminatory was article 51. It entitled Catholic and Protestant pastors to a voting seat on the school board, which was entrusted with the administration and the inspection of the local schools. The rabbi, in comparison, was admitted to the board only with the approval of the county school superintendent and if there was a Jewish school in the commune.

Instead of waiting for the Progressives to act, the Verband's executive board met on December 8 and decided to lobby itself for the revision of the school bill.[77] Spokesmen for the Verband called upon deputies in the Diet and persuaded the National Liberal Eugen Schiffer and the Progressive Carl Funck to criticize the bill's unfair treatment of the Jews in the first reading on December 11 and 12. The executive board sent a protest to the Diet and the ministry on December 10. Remembering from past experiences how government officials had exploited the differences between the branches of Judaism to reject Jewish demands, Makower tried to coordinate the activities of the Jewish interest groups. He invited representatives from the Lehrerverband and the Rabbinerverband to attend the meetings of his subcommittee and urged Jewish organizations not to address to the government separate petitions with conflicting views but to endorse the Verband's petition of December 10.[78]

When Makower's subcommittee drafted another petition, this time with specific proposals for amendments to the bill, it debated what the Verband's tactics and priorities should be. The committee members thought that the bill threatened much more than the survival of the Jewish schools. The erosion of the principle of equal rights for the Jewish and Christian communities and the possibility of the segregation of Jewish schoolchildren seemed to them graver dangers.[79] The petition that they drafted focused on the differences in the treatment of Jews and Christians in the draft law. It stressed the point that Jewish citizens, who performed the same duties in civic life as did other Germans, should enjoy equal rights and should receive equal protection under the law and demanded amendments to strike out inequitable clauses and to extend to the Jewish community provisions applying to the Christian confessions.[80]

Makower's subcommittee decided also that the Verband's political activity would give priority to the welfare of Jewish children attending interdenominational and Christian schools. The committee members thought that the interests of Jewish schools could not be the exclusive or primary focus of their work because 71 percent of the Jewish children attended the other schools.[81] As a result, the Verband's lobbyists concentrated on winning amendments that would provide religious instruction for the Jewish minority enrolled in non-Jewish schools and would secure the status of Jewish teachers at these schools. They gave less attention to the desire of the Orthodox Jews to protect separate schools.

The Verband submitted the petition to the Diet on January 7, 1906. When 889 congregations speedily endorsed the petition and sent copies to the Diet, the Verband was confident that it spoke for Prussian Jewry. To prevent the enforced segregation of Jewish schoolchildren, the petition proposed one article which stipulated that no child could be denied admission to any local school on the grounds that there existed a separate school for his confession, and a second article which provided for the approval of the religious community before the commune opened a new confessional school. For article 21 the petition demanded an amendment to require the commune to provide Jewish religion lessons in school if there were 12 or more Jewish pupils and to permit the teacher, hired for this purpose, to give instruction in other subjects. Turning to provisions of the bill that discriminated against the Jews, the petition called for the revision of article 20 so that teachers of all religions, not Catholics and Protestants alone, could be appointed to interconfessional schools. It proposed an amendment to article 51 entitling a representative of any recognized religious community, including the rabbi, to sit on the school board if at least 12 pupils were of that faith.

Besides the Verband, the Centralverein, interest groups representing teachers and rabbis, and congregations all over Prussia mobilized in opposition to the school bill. Opposition was especially strong in the Provincial District of Cassel, where there were 80 Jewish schools. On New Year's Day, more than 70 teachers, community leaders, and

Jewish councilors attended a conference to discuss the school bill. They selected a committee and instructed it to work with the *Vorsteherämter* for the revision of the draft law.[82] The Jews in this region of small towns and villages were afraid that their schools would be dissolved because attendance fell far below the minimum figures specified in the bill for the establishment of a school for children of one confession, more than 60 in urban communes and more than 120 in rural communes. In a petition to the Diet on January 14, the *Vorsteherämter* pleaded for the maintenance of Jewish schools irrespective of the number of pupils.[83]

With single-mindedness and zeal, the Orthodox Jews took up the fight for Jewish schools. Two spokesmen for the Freie Vereinigung für die Interessen des orthodoxen Judentums (Association for the Interests of Orthodox Judaism), Rabbi Moritz Cahn of Fulda and Rabbi Salomon Breuer of Frankfurt am Main, attempted in December to persuade the Verband's lobbyists to strive for the establishment of Jewish schools. The leaders of Orthodox Jewry were incensed when the Verband replied that such efforts had little prospects of success.[84] They surmised that this reason was a pretext to conceal a preference for interconfessional schools. For a long time Orthodox believers had looked upon the Verband's board of directors as assimilationists who could not be relied upon to represent Jewish interests. The petition of January 7 seemed to confirm this suspicion.

Der Israelit, a newspaper voicing Orthodox opinion, assailed the petition for uttering no words in praise or defense of Jewish schools. It charged that the Verband's lobbyists were surrendering Jewish schools "for the sake of a pottage of theoretical equality."[85] The leaders of Orthodoxy thought that it was a mistake to propose amendments aimed at improving the situation of Jewish children attending Christian schools instead of strengthening the legal foundations of the Jewish schools. They believed that Jewish religious instruction, offered in the curriculum of Christian schools, was a poor substitute for Jewish schools and could not cultivate in the children a pious observance of religious traditions. Explaining why the Orthodox Jews disagreed with the Verband's strategy and could not cooperate with it, *Der Israelit* contended that the demand for the equal treatment of the Jewish and Christian religions was "commendable and justified but for us, as for Orthodox Jews in general,

[it] is a secondary consideration, one of the various means by which our striving for an unhindered fulfilment of the obligations set by the Thora is advanced. To us, in contrast with the Verband, more important than complete equality with the other confessions is the maintenance of our Jewish schools as an essential factor in the education of Jewish youth."[86]

Because the Orthodox Jews did not see the political and social position of the Jews in Germany at stake in the school question, they could not understand the unflinching determination of the Jewish activists to fight for the equality of all citizens before the law. The Orthodox leaders thought that the Jewish left liberals had become so obsessed with attaining complete equality of rights that they failed to see that in school matters the interests of the Jews, as a minority, were advanced by special provisions in the law and not by legislation which treated the Jews and the Christian majority in the same way.[87] They were not disturbed by the possibility that the new school law might lead to the segregation of Jewish schoolchildren and were not concerned about the problem of ethnic isolation. *Der Israelit* sneered at the notion that bigotry would end if Christian and Jewish children sat on the same school bench.[88]

The Freie Vereinigung and a group of Orthodox teachers submitted their own petitions to the Diet.[89] The two Orthodox organizations adopted a strategy that differed from the politics of the Verband. Instead of invoking the principle of equal treatment, they sought to gain a sympathetic hearing in official circles by conceding the validity of the views expressed by the ministry. They accepted the government's contention that, according to the Prussian constitution, the communes were not obliged to support Jewish schools and they defended Studt against the criticism of treating the Jews unfairly.[90] The primary aim of the Orthodox petitions was to increase the number of Jewish schools and to exempt these schools from any condition that set a minimum enrollment figure. The petitions proposed an amendment to article 24 whereby existing Jewish schools would be kept open as long as the communities, using state subsidies, provided the salaries and lodgings of the teachers. Another amendment to article 20 would allow congregations to request under these conditions that the commune open a separate school for Jewish children.

As the Orthodox leaders lobbied for the revision of the school bill, they called attention to the discord among the Jews. Their petitions entreated the Diet to add a provision requiring the school board to consult the rabbi before Jewish teachers were hired. Justifying the demand that the views of Orthodox believers be heard, the petition from the Freie Vereinigung declared: "Two fundamentally divided tendencies stand opposed to each other, one standing on the foundation of tradition and one representing so-called Reform Judaism. An Orthodox congregation would take offense if a teacher who lived and worked according to the ways of so-called Reform Judaism was appointed and would categorically reject as wrong his religious instruction for their children."[91] Furthermore, Rabbi Cahn pointed out in his discussions with Schwartzkopff and with deputies in the Diet that the Verband did not speak for the Orthodox branch. He attempted to correct "the damage" which he thought that the Verband's petition had caused, and he argued against introducing Jewish religious instruction into the curriculum of non-Jewish schools.[92] One of the reasons offered by Rabbi Cahn was that Prussian Jewry had no central governing council which was authorized to examine the qualifications of religion teachers and to decide what should be taught.

Among the deputies sitting on the parliamentary committee that reported on the school bill for the plenum debate was Oskar Cassel. Cassel belonged to the Verband's board of directors. He was present when the board met on January 7 and discussed what political actions it should take when the school bill committee started its work on January 11. It was "not opportune," he said, for the Verband to lobby against the draft law.[93] Fuchs disagreed and pressed him to speak for the Verband's proposals before the commission. He declined. Despite Cassel's advice, the board voted to hold talks with officials in the ministry and deputies on the committee. Confessional matters were not taken up in the commission's hearings until February 28. During the interval Felix Makower and Benjamin Hirsch, representing the Verband, spoke with the deputies and Schwartzkopff.[94] Four rabbis working in collaboration with the Verband visited Studt and Schwartzkopff.

The confidential talks that Jewish spokesmen had with Schwartzkopff were not successful. The insinuations that the bill had an anti-Jewish bias irritated him. At the committee's hearings Schwartz-kopff admitted that the "construction" of the bill "could arouse the impression that the Jewish schools come off worse than the Christian schools," but he denied that it treated the Jews unfairly.[95] To justify the different provisions for the Jewish and Christian confessions, he cited Article 14 of the Prussian constitution, which declared that state institutions connected with religious observance should be based on the Christian faith. The conclusion he drew was that the Prussian state did not stand in the same relationship with the Jewish community as it did with the Protestant and Catholic "national churches." He argued that the government would violate article 14 if it made the communes responsible for providing Jewish religious instruction in school and required Jewish pupils to attend the lessons.

There is no detailed record of Makower's conversation with Schwartzkopff. From an article that Makower published in a law journal afterwards, it is clear that he questioned the validity of Schwartzkopff's interpretation of the Prussian constitution. Makower affirmed that article 14 was restricted to religious worship and did not apply to such public institutions as the schools.[96] With references to the historical background of article 14 as well as article 12, which guaranteed the full exercise of civil and political rights to all citizens irrespective of religion, he proved that it was not the intent of the constitution to confer a Christian character upon the state and to oblige the government to treat Christian and Jewish schoolchildren differently.

Before the parliamentary commission Schwartzkopff spoke out against the amendments for which the Verband was lobbying. He took care to offer reasons that appeared objective and would cover up his personal antipathy to the Jews. In a patronizing manner he said that the government respected the autonomy of the Jewish communities and did not interfere in matters relating to their internal afairs.[97] The Jews themselves were blamed for the government's refusal to meet their demands. Schwartzkopff mentioned again and again the dissension among the Jews and repeated Rabbi Cahn's argument. He stressed how difficult it was for the government to consider proposals made by the Jews because the petitions contradicted one another and were not presented by a central authority constituted by law to speak for Prussian Jewry as a corporate body.

It was impossible for school administrators to set qualifications for appointing Jewish religion teachers and to make decisions on what should be taught because they could not judge which one of the branches in Judaism was right.

The rationalizations that Schwartzkopff gave for rejecting the amendments did not deceive the Verband's lobbyists. Writing later about his experiences, Makower related that "for those persons who were inclined to create obstacles to the attainment of full equality, it was a very convenient objection" to say that among the Jews themselves a segment opposed the Verband's proposals. He added:

> It is an old technique, which the Prussian Ministry of Education and Religious Affairs has used repeatedly in the course of the last century, to exploit factional divisions among the Jews in order to block the development of the religious institutions of the Jewish communities. From the conduct of the ministry and its representative in the proceedings on the School Law must arise the plausible suspicion that also this time the same tactics were followed. The ministry did not respond objectively to the demands presented by the Verband. Again and again in the proceedings, the representatives of the ministry opposed the amendments advocated by the Verband, often with reasons that appeared substantively untenable.[98]

Besides speaking with ministry officials, Makower and his collaborators engaged in behind-the-scenes talks with deputies on the school bill committee. They prevailed upon the Progressives to introduce amendments safeguarding Jewish rights and interests. The passage of the amendments was uncertain. From their discussions the lobbyists learned that although many deputies thought that article 24 was unfair, the parties differed on the concessions which they were willing to make to Jewish demands.[99]

The emergence of Cassel and Peltasohn as vigorous spokesmen for the Jews in the deliberations on the school bill was unexpected. The two deputies had no reputation for radical oratory and had always worried that any impression of being the mouthpiece for Jewish pressure groups might compromise their standing in political life. Peltasohn did not speak at all in the first debate on the school bill in December, and Cassel's criticism skipped over article 24. In the course of the proceedings both men ceased to be reserved. In the commission Cassel sponsored amendments that the Verband wanted. During the debates of the full house Peltasohn refuted Schwartz-kopff's objections to the proposed revisions.[100]

Why Cassel worked so hard to revise the bill cannot be answered from any personal testimony. His experience on the commission must have affected him emotionally and, most likely, dispelled his doubts about the advisability of acting as a spokesman for the Jews. At the commission's hearings he heard Schwartzkopff advance an interpretation of the Prussian constitution that amounted to a legal justification of discrimination against the Jews. He found Schwartz-kopff's reasons for opposing amendments desired by the Jews to be inconsistent and specious.[101] He tartly remarked on one occasion that ministry officials exaggerated the difficulties and magnified problems that could readily be solved by administrators with good will toward the Jews. The mutual antipathy that Cassel and Schwartz-kopff felt grew. On the floor of the Diet Cassel, Schwartzkopff, and Studt exchanged sarcastic remarks, and after one incident the minis-ter made a public apology for an offensive reference to Cassel's religious background.[102]

Cassel introduced in the school bill committee amendments spon-sored by the Progressives. One amendment, intended to preserve interdenominational schools and to prevent segregation, stated that the school system was to be organized so that children were in-structed by teachers without any regard for confessional differences, and that no child was to be denied admission to a public school on account of religion.[103] Another amendment to article 24 required the communes to retain the existing Jewish schools and made the liquidation of Jewish schools subject to the condition that the com-munes provide Jewish religious instruction at the schools to which the pupils were transferred.[104] Cassel's revision of article 24 stated unambiguously that the commune was responsible for the upkeep of Jewish schools. The application of provisions for Protestant and Catholic religious instruction was extended to the Jewish faith, and Jewish religion teachers were entitled to give instruction in other subjects.

The Progressive amendments were voted down by the other parties in the committee's sessions on March 2 and 28. Representatives of

the Conservative, Free Conservative, Center, and National Liberal
parties agreed with Schwartzkopff that the Prussian constitution
conferred a privileged status on the Christian confessions and accepted his reasons for rejecting the amendments. They conceded at
the same time that the phrasing of article 24 had aroused "not entirely unjustified fears" that the Jews were treated unfairly in the
school bill.[105]

The four parties and the ministry agreed to an amendment which
would make some concessions to the Jews without undermining the
idea that the public institutions of the Prussian state were imbued
with a Christian character. The compromise amendment to article 24
required the communes to allocate grants toward the expenses of
Jewish schools.[106] The communes were left free to decide whether
to provide religious instruction for Jewish pupils attending Christian
and interconfessional schools. If they decided not to do so, the compromise amendment entitled the congregation to claim a contribution toward the expenses of religion lessons given outside the schools

Another concession made to the Jews was a resolution requesting
the state government to appropriate in the budget a special fund to
assist congregations which made provisions for religious instruction
in communes where the schools did not offer it. Government officials disapproved of this proposal and tried to defeat it. A spokesman
for the Ministry of Finance told the committee that the constitution
did not oblige the state to subsidize Jewish religious instruction and
that, according to the ruling of the High Administrative Court on
May 29, 1896, the government could not make the Jewish religion a
compulsory subject for Jewish schoolchildren.[107] Following the example set by Schwartzkopff, he added that difficulties would arise if
the government did so because of the divisions among the Jews.
These considerations disguised the real motives behind the government's opposition to the resolution. High-level officials were not
willing to help the Jewish communities with state subsidies. They
thought that government funding might confirm the impression
that Jewish religious instruction was part of the school curriculum,
and they did not wish to lend any support to this point of view.[108]

Overriding the government's objections, the commission and later
the full house passed the resolution. Eugen Schiffer defended this
vote on the grounds that it was not fair to impose on the Jews, who

supported local schools as taxpayers, the additional burden of
raising funds for Jewish schools and religious instruction without
the compensation of government grants.[109] A Center party deputy,
Wilhelm Marx, said that the resolution offered a way of achieving
justice and helping the congregations without surrendering the
principle that Prussia was a "Christian state."[110]

The Verband's lobbyists also prevailed upon the Progressives to
strengthen the right of the Jewish community to be represented on
the school board. The Progressives in the commission sponsored an
amendment to article 28 that entitled the rabbi to membership on
the school board if there was a Jewish school or more than 12
Jewish children attending any school in the commune. If there was
no rabbi residing in the locality, the amendment permitted the congregation to designate another person.[111] The Progressives moved to
strike out of article 28 a clause that the Jews regarded as an affront
to the dignity of rabbis—a stipulation that the seating of a rabbi on
the school board had to be approved by the county school superintendent.

The Ministry of Education did not respond sympathetically to the
Verband's demand that the Jews, like the Christian confessions,
were entitled to have someone representing their interests in the
administration of the schools. Schwartzkopff exhorted the deputies
to vote down both revisions of article 28. Defending the difference
in the treatment of pastors and rabbis, he stated that there were no
state regulations on the academic training and qualifications of
rabbis as there were for the Protestant and Catholic clergy, so that
the government had legitimate reasons for examining the credentials
of a rabbi before he was seated on the school board.[112] The only
concession that the Verband could wring out of the commission was
a new provision that admitted the rabbi to the school board if there
were at least 20 Jewish schoolchildren in the commune.

Unwilling to accept defeat, the Verband's board of directors met
on April 3 and decided to continue lobbying for improvements
in the school bill. The Verband submitted another petition to the
Diet on April 9 and asked that provisions for Christian religious instruction be applied also to the Jewish religion.[113] Makower started
another round of talks with friendly deputies. The prospects for
more concessions were not very good and became less promising

when a quarrel broke out between the Orthodox Jews and the Verband.

In the petition of April 9 the Verband sought to impress upon the Diet the idea that Orthodox believers were a minority whose opinions were not representative of Prussian Jewry. The petition provoked the Orthodox Jews by referring to them as a "sect" that had seceded from the main community. The leaders of the Freie Vereinigung and Orthodox congregations in Berlin and Wiesbaden reacted with blind rage by submitting counterpetitions that assailed the Verband.[114] The Orthodox Jews once again made the mistake of supplying state officials with an arsenal of arguments that they could use to rationalize their subjective reasons for rejecting the Verband's demands.

The Freie Vereinigung worked to defeat one of Cassel's amendments to article 24 that the commission had accepted. The revision embodied the Verband's demand that the commune be required to provide religious instruction for Jewish schoolchildren in the same way as article 21 obliged it to do for Christian pupils. Orthodox rabbis persuaded Wilhelm Marx to oppose the amendment before the full house.[115] In the plenary session of May 25 the Center party deputy called attention to the protests made by the Orthodox Jews and said that "among a growing number of our Jewish fellow-citizens there is the fear that if the law is revised according to the Cassel proposal, then they will have deeply troubled consciences insofar as they see themselves compelled to send their children to religious instruction which is provided by the commune and does not accord with their religious convictions—a situation that would cause them deep anguish."[116] Marx proposed that the communes be obliged only to make a contribution toward the costs of religion lessons that the congregations provided outside school.

Cassel attempted to counteract the Orthodox protests, but his speech could not undo the harm. A spokesman for the ministry alluded to the vehement Orthodox attacks against the Verband as a vindication of the government's policy. He argued that religion could not be a required subject for Jewish children in school as it was for Christian children because dissension among the Jews made it difficult for school administrators to select the teachers and a curriculum acceptable to all branches of Judaism.[117]

When the deputies passed the Marx amendment, the Verband's lobbyists fumed and blamed the Orthodox leaders, especially Rabbi Cahn, for their failure to gain for the Jews the same benefits that the school bill guaranteed to the Christian confessions. Makower charged that, by stressing adamantly the schism within Judaism, the Orthodox Jews had played into the hands of Schwartzkopff.[118] Even Salo Adler of the Lehrerverband regretted that, through bad political judgment and zeal, the Orthodox rabbis had given officials antagonistic to the Jews an excuse to reject justified demands.[119]

Both houses of the Prussian parliament passed the school bill, and it was enacted as the Law for the Maintenance of Public Elementary Schools on July 28, 1906. There were gross inequities and ambiguities in article 40, which contained the provisions affecting the Jews in the School Law. Whereas the communes were required to maintain Christian schools and to provide for Christian religious instruction, article 40 left them free to decide whether to allocate funds for Jewish schools and religious instruction. If the authorities of the commune did not do so voluntarily, the School Law entitled a congregation which provided for these needs to apply for a contribution.[120] Article 40 was vague concerning the assessment of the grants and the procedures for handling the applications. Ambiguities opened up the possibility of discrimination against Jewish teachers. The language of article 38 made crystal clear that Christian religion teachers could be assigned to give instruction in other subjects, but article 40 stated vaguely that "existing regulations" were to be followed in the appointment of Jewish teachers for purposes of religious instruction and "concerning other work to which they would be assigned." Uncertainty pervaded the Diet's resolution which requested but did not require the state government to appropriate funds for Jewish religious instruction. The resolution neglected to specify what guidelines officials should use in awarding the subsidies.

Several incidents that occurred in the last days of the proceedings on the school bill left the liberal Jewish activists with distrust and doubts. A National Liberal asked Schwartzkopff in the Diet on May 25 how the government stood on the resolution for state subsidies to the Jewish communities. He replied evasively that the ministry "must reserve for itself the decision on the way it shall take into consideration the wishes that were expressed in the resolution." [121] Cassel was stunned by this answer. According to his recollection, the government had given the school bill committee the impression that it would carry out the resolution if the full house accepted it. He regarded Schwartzkopff's reply as a breach of honor and integrity. [122]

The other jolt came from the upper house on July 7, when an anti-Semitic Junker demanded that the Ministry of Education restrict the employment of Jewish teachers and not assign them to teach subjects other than religion. Coldly and without a trace of scruple, Schwartzkopff replied that the government appointed Jewish teachers only out of absolute necessity and would act in the same manner in the future. [123] The *Allgemeine Zeitung des Judentums* commented bitterly that the answer of Schwartzkopff, "the real father of the School Law," revealed the outlook and the spirit with which Prussia's school administration worked. [124] *Im Deutschen Reich* observed sarcastically that "this episode offers a foretaste of what awaits our teachers under the rule of the new and illustrious School Law." [125]

For the execution of the School Law of July 28, 1906, the Ministry of Education issued a set of instructions on February 25, 1907. [126] The directive did not plug all the loopholes. The procedures for the application and the enforcement of article 40 remained imprecise. The directive ordered local officials and the congregation's executive board to work out an agreement on the commune's subvention. The ministry failed to state what recourse the Jews had if the commune stalled negotiations or offered them unacceptable terms. On the method of computing the grants, the directive stipulated that the sum should be averaged out of two figures: (1) the amount that the Jews contributed to the support of local schools through tax payments, and (2) the money that the commune saved because a congregation maintained its own school. Tax receipts and school budgets made it easy to compute the first figure. It was less easy to estimate the financial savings that accrued to the commune when the congregation provided the money for operating a school. The directive neglected to specify the criteria for making such an estimate.

Before the law went into effect on April 1, 1908, those congregations maintaining schools submitted to the communes requests for grants. The problems that beset them may be observed in the Provincial District of Cassel, which had the heaviest concentration of Jewish schools in Prussia. Reporting on the execution of the law in the district in March 1908, Max Fliedner, who was now the director of the school department, assured the provincial governor that the communes were "fulfilling very promptly the requests of the synagogue congregations" and that "up to now difficulties have not arisen." At the end of 1908 he wrote again that the "communes are very obliging toward the Jews" and that "negotiations shall lead to amicable settlements."[127] Neither the experiences of the communities nor the reports of the *Landräte* to Fliedner bear out his account. He filed false reports to his superiors. His deception was characteristic of the unconscientious way administrators in the district carried out the provisions of the School Law dealing with the Jews.

Early in 1908, when community leaders sought to work out agreements on school grants, they discovered that uniform and systematic procedures had not been set and encountered commune officials who were uncooperative and sometimes hostile.[128] In some communes high-handed magistrates refused to meet with Jewish representatives and made a peremptory decision on the amount of the grant. Elsewhere, they stalled action on the applications so that many congregations were still waiting for decisions in November and December. Commune officials who begrudged giving public funds to the Jewish communities proposed the dissolution of the Jewish schools or rejected the applications. They read erroneous and arbitrary interpretations into article 40 to dodge the obligations that it laid upon the commune. By manipulating or ignoring the guidelines in the ministry's directive, some communes gave the congregations smaller sums than were due to them. In assessing the grants, the stratagem of these officials was to give little or no weight to the factor of local taxes paid by the Jewish population and to argue that the money saved by the commune because the Jews maintained a school especially for their children was little or nothing. By the end of 1908, only 30 out of the 76 communities with schools in the Provincial District of Cassel had reached settlements with the communes.

Disputes arose in many communes. The executive boards of the communities contested the legality of the methods used to compute the grants.[129] To keep their contributions low, the communes estimated the factor of savings according to whether the present school facilities could accommodate Jewish pupils if they were transferred or whether additional classrooms would have to be built and more teachers hired. This measuring rod seemed too elastic and subjective to the Jews. It was easy for the commune to assert that the schools could accommodate the Jewish children. The congregations preferred to use the mathematically exact procedures recommended by Jewish legal experts. Jewish lawyers held the opinion that the money the commune saved should be figured out by multiplying the number of Jewish pupils by the cost of educating a child in the local schools.[130] Another point of contention was the decision of some communes not to give the grants on the grounds that Jewish schools were not needed.

The communities sent complaints to the *Landräte,* and the *Vorsteherämter der Israeliten* appealed to Fliedner to correct wrong interpretations of the School Law and arbitrary methods of handling Jewish claims.[131] Fliedner issued a directive on June 6, 1908, to eliminate the "great confusion among the communes about their obligation to give contributions for the maintenance of Jewish schools."[132] The directive discounted the legality of many reasons that the commune officials offered to deprive the Jews of school funds. However, the dispute over the estimation of the grants was decided to the advantage of the communes. Fliedner rejected the formula that the Jewish legal experts devised and gave his approval to the procedure used by many communes to cut their contributions by as much as one half the amount that the congregations were entitled to receive.

Fliedner would have allowed the communes to shirk even this light obligation, but spokesmen for the congregations persisted in sending protests to the district administration. In one case the Frankenau community complained that the commune computed a small contribution by disregarding the factor of taxes paid by the Jewish townspeople. Fliedner decided the dispute in favor of the commune as he had done earlier in disagreements arising in the communes of Fritzlar and Gilserburg. Instead of resigning themselves to Fliedner's biased judgment, the Jews in Frankenau appealed to Berlin. In August 1909 the Ministry of Education issued a decision validating the legal position of the congregation.[133]

Although the ministry's ruling passed over silently the improper conduct of officials in the Provincial District of Cassel, Fliedner was upset about the judgment against him. He defended his policy in a letter to Berlin on September 24 and pleaded with the ministry again on November 29 to uphold his stand.[134] The ministry yielded and declared in December that in computing their contributions the communes had to consider, besides the two guidelines in the directive of 1907, many other factors, including "the more or less financial capability of the Jewish community."[135] The ministry seemed determined to perpetuate rather than to eliminate the confusion; it declined to set formal and uniform procedures for assessing the grants. In effect, these two decisions gave the communes a green light to make decisions arbitrarily and to the disadvantage of the Jews.

That the policymakers in Berlin knew that the communes would take advantage of the lack of regularized procedures for figuring out school grants is evident from the government's response to a protest from the *Vorsteheramt* in Cassel on December 21, 1909. The ministry chose not to investigate the charges that the communes estimated the contributions for Jewish schools in an illegal manner. It dismissed the protest by replying in March 1910 that the School Law provided no specific regulations for determining uniformly the size of the grants and that, according to the circumstances of the situation, the communes could disregard the criteria mentioned in the directive of 1907.[136]

Jewish leaders found state officials also biased and negligent in carrying out the parliament's request that the government appropriate funds to assist congregations which provided religious instruction in places where there was no Jewish school or where the commune did not hire a religion teacher to give lessons to Jewish children attending Christian confessional schools. Official action on the Diet's resolution was neither efficient nor conscientious. The Jewish communities were not given the compensation the deputies had voted for out of a sense of equity. The experience of the Jews in Hesse reveals the difficulties that arose.

Schwartzkopff announced on July 10, 1907, that the government was prepared to appropriate money to carry out the resolution. His directive ordered the *Regierungspräsidenten* to report on the expenditures of the communities for religious instruction and to estimate the subsidies they needed.[137] Restrictive clauses were laid down for the first time. To qualify for the subsidies, congregations had to be financially distressed, and the schoolchildren had to number at least 12. Thereafter, work on the project came to a halt. The ministry had been discouraged from taking further action by the falsified reports that it had received. Many district administrators made no inquiries about the financial needs of the communities. Despite this negligence, they filed reports saying that the Jews could pay all expenses and did not need government aid.[138]

The ministry did not act again until the Jews whose patience had worn thin applied pressure. In February 1908 the *Vorsteheramt* in Cassel boldly reminded the government that a budget appropriation had already been made and demanded that the money be disbursed promptly. The *Vorsteheramt* in Fulda prodded officials in Berlin with a similar petition.[139] Encouraged by the Gemeindebund, community leaders throughout March flooded the school departments in the Provincial Districts of Cassel and Wiesbaden with requests for the state subsidies.

The Gemeindebund issued a circular containing instructions on how to file applications for state funds. It took the initiative in coordinating this activity because it wanted the congregations to follow uniform procedures in estimating the sums they claimed. Another reason seems to have been the desire of the leaders of organized Jewry to prevent errors and scandals that might subject all Jews to criticism. The circular advised the communities not to demand extravagant sums. Pointing out that in some congregations cantors and rabbis acted as religion teachers, the circular recommended that the wages for the lessons should be scrupulously separated from the salary to be paid for the performance of liturgical functions.[140]

In the February and March 1908 issues, *Im Deutschen Reich* criticized Schwartzkopff's directive and expressed the hope that the ministry would administer the appropriated fund with a greater sense of justice. The Centralverein argued that the directive violated the spirit and the letter of the resolution. In making "financial disability" a condition for receiving the subsidies, the ministry was handling the fund as "a kind of charity, which one gives to the needy." But the deputies on the school bill committee, who drafted and discussed the resolution, "considered it a requirement of compensatory justice that just as Jewish taxpayers have to provide for the expenses of Christian religious instruction so the state must provide in the same way for Jewish religious instruction."[141] The Centralverein objected to the other condition, setting a minimum of 12 schoolchildren. It expressed the hope that administrators would apply this stipulation flexibly and would allow two rural congregations to qualify for a subsidy by joining together to employ one itinerant teacher.

District officials were puzzled over the applications from the congregations because they had received no orders from Berlin. The Cassel office asked the ministry in April how it should handle Jewish requests for the state subsidies. Compelled to take action, Schwartzkopff issued a directive on May 6, 1908, announcing the budget appropriation of 40,000 marks and ordering from the provincial districts reports on the financial needs of the communities and recommendations on the applications for the subsidies.[142] Many Landräte prepared reports in a slipshod manner, without conferring with community leaders. They wrote that the communities were not financially hard-pressed. Poor communities were often disqualified on the grounds that they had fewer than 12 children of school age.[143] Giving an interpretation to this regulation which was unfavorable to the Jews, the government declared that all 12 pupils had to belong to the same congregation. Ineligible for subsidies were small, neighboring congregations that shared the services of an itinerant teacher.

The implementation of the resolution did not bring the benefits expected by the Jews. Many poor communities did not meet the stipulation of 12 schoolchildren. No standards were set for determining the financial capability of communities, and decisions were left up to the Landräte. It was easy for officials who were unsympathetic to the Jews to decide that a congregation needed no financial assistance.

Jewish activists attempted to liberalize the conditions qualifying communities for the subsidies. The Gemeindebund petitioned the ministry in January 1909 to lower the minimum number of pupils to 8. Peltasohn attacked the restrictions attached to the subsidies in the Diet. He reminded the deputies that their resolution contained no restrictions. Pointing out that many Jews lived in scattered and small communities, he argued that the requirement of 12 school-children nullified the promise of government assistance.[144] The ministry refused to revise the rule. Schwartzkopff replied to Martin Philippson, the Gemeindebund's chairman, that any Christan confessional minority in a school was entitled to religious instruction only if it comprised at least 12 pupils and that "a different treatment of the Jewish religious community could not be justified."[145]

After months of striving to overcome the prejudice of officials responsible for executing the School Law, Jewish activists became disheartened and questioned the efficacy of further political lobbying. In a mood of discouragement the Verband's board of directors met on September 19, 1909, to decide whether they should press the ministry to liberalize the regulations under which public funds were granted for the expenses of Jewish religious instruction.[146] Makower and Philippson were convinced that the government would never reform the School Law and advised against any action.

Discontented about the effects of the School Law and more determined to act than the lawyers who headed the Verband were the Jewish teachers. The Jewish teachers were bitter and angry because the new law limited job opportunities by requiring the faith of the teachers to be the same as that of the pupils.[147] They found fewer jobs available in the remaining interdenominational schools because many administrators observed the principle of parity only between the Protestant and Catholic confessions. By 1913, according to the Lehrerverband, only 112 out of 1,568 interconfessional schools in Prussia had both Jews and Christians on the teaching staff.[148]

The Jewish teachers were indignant at the discriminatory clauses of the School Law. Article 37 stated clearly that school administrators could assign other subjects to Protestant and Catholic teachers who were hired to give religious instruction. In comparison, the loose and tortuous phrasing of section 2 of article 40 left uncertain whether Jews too would be entitled to teach subjects besides religion in schools attended by Christian children. The ministry's directive of March 14, 1908, on the execution of the School Law made evident that the provision was designed to deny Jewish teachers the same professional standing as their Christian colleagues. The directive stated that Jewish religion teachers could attain an appointment rank with tenure "under certain circumstances" and may be permitted to teach other subjects, "whose instruction to Christian children by Jewish teachers provokes no objections."[149] The Lehrerverband protested that Jews were treated as second-class teachers and were barred from teaching history and German grammar and literature.[150]

By the time the Lehrerverband held its national convention in December 1910, the teachers were militant. Around 700 persons attended the convention in Frankfurt am Main, and a turbulent debate took place.[151] Fears of unemployment and the loss of social status had radicalized many teachers. They demanded that Jewish schools be established in cities where the Jewish population was heavily concentrated and denounced the community leaders of Berlin for refusing to open Jewish schools. The emotions of the assembly were so inflamed that a proposal offered by moderates to appoint a committee to study the problem was voted down. A large majority passed a motion to request the executive board of the Gemeindebund to place on the agenda of its forthcoming congress the question of whether it should recommend and encourage the establishment of Jewish schools.

Under the leadership of Moritz Steinhardt, its militant and temperamental chairman, the Lehrerverband launched an aggressive propaganda campaign. The Jewish teachers generalized their grievances into a crisis for all Prussian Jewry. They argued that since the enactment of the School Law the authorities had put the school system on a Christian confessional basis. To arouse a consciousness of the dimensions of the crisis, the Lehrerverband called attention to government statistics which showed that ¾ of the Jewish children in Prussia went to interdenominational and Christian schools. In 1911 out of 19,965 Jewish schoolchildren, 9,929 attended Protestant schools; 2,426 attended Catholic schools; and 2,090 attended interconfessional schools. Only 5,555 were enrolled in Jewish schools.[152] The Jewish teachers warned that irreparable psychological harm was done to Jewish pupils "by the extreme Christian character of present-day schools." An inferiority complex, a feeling of alienation, and resentment toward the religion of their parents developed in Jewish children who were exposed to prejudice at a tender age.[153]

Knowing that the upper class of Jewish society and educated liberals favored interconfessional schools and tended to view Jewish schools as "ghetto schools," the Lehrerverband criticized this elite. Sharp-tongued agitators such as Steinhardt attacked the upper classes for whitewashing de facto Christian interdenominational schools with rationalizations and a "misconstrued liberalism."[154] They argued that bigotry in the school system could not be treated as a temporary situation and that it was naive to expect reforms in the foreseeable future. The Lehrerverband urged Jewish left liberals to be pragmatic:

> The opponents of Jewish schools think that the principles of the Progressive People's party must be upheld on the question of establishing Jewish schools. However, they fail to recognize that it is a practical school problem which must be judged and decided not according to theories but according to actual circumstances. We are not shattering the ideal concept of the school toward which we should strive and we are in agreement with all liberal men; but we wish that our Jewish liberal politicians adopt pragmatic policies on Jewish questions as they and everyone else do in other respects in politics.[155]

The executive board of the Gemeindebund refused to place the question on the agenda of the congress. The leaders of the Lehrerverband were furious and berated the Gemeindebund's directors for squelching public debate on an issue so crucial to the Jews.[156] The furor raised by the Jewish teachers compelled the Gemeindebund to take up the issue in 1913. Intent on blocking the establishment of Jewish schools, the executive board resorted to the maneuver of presenting the question before a conference attended by representatives of the state and provincial associations within the Gemeindebund—a body of 11 men instead of the congress as the teachers had proposed.

When the conference convened on June 22, 1913, the executive board publicly professed a policy of neutrality. Beforehand, however, plans were made to guide the deliberations. The Gemeindebund sent out a questionnaire to the governing boards of the congregations. From 1,058 replies it learned that throughout Prussia there were 247 Jewish schools, of which 94 had 10 or fewer pupils. An overwhelming number of communities gave a negative answer to the question of whether their members wanted a Jewish school.[157] Only in the

Rhine Province, where 11 out of 87 congregations gave an affirmative answer, was there any sentiment favoring the opening of Jewish schools.

Siegmund Blaschke, a Berlin high school teacher, was unofficially designated to speak for the executive board at the conference. He refuted the arguments raised for opening Jewish schools and stressed the harm that separate schools would bring to the Jews as a minority still subjected to discrimination.[158] For adoption as a school policy he made three propositions: (1) existing and viable Jewish schools should be maintained; (2) new Jewish schools should be built, if necessary, in small communities; and (3) in large urban communities the Jews should not open new Jewish schools but work to prevent the abolition of existing interconfessional schools and urge the communes to establish new ones. This proposal was accepted by seven to four votes.[159]

Blaschke's speech caused an uproar among the teachers, who saw his proposal as an underhanded blow against Jewish schools. The Lehrerverband knew that Jewish schools had a precarious existence in small towns and could thrive only in big cities. Insisting that the question of Jewish schools "be treated at a forum which makes possible the participation of German Jewry as a whole," the Lehrerverband's leaders decided to introduce a motion to discuss it at the forthcoming congress in December.[160]

The Gemeindebund's board of directors acted to head off such a debate. In order to keep their public posture of neutrality and at the same time to defeat the partisans of separate schools, they encouraged prominent Jews to form a committee. The committee had a membership list of more than 300 names and included 5 deputies, Aronsohn, Cassel, Cohn, and Wolff in the Prussian parliament and Waldstein in the Reichstag. Under the committee's name, leaflets were circulated opposing the establishment of Jewish schools. In a confidential letter the committee urged community leaders to pick delegates to the congress who accepted the executive board's point of view and to prevent the selection of delegates who were Zionists and Orthodox Jews.[161] By the time the congress met on December 7, enough votes were rounded up to block an open debate on the school question.

At the end of December the teachers who assembled at the Lehrerverband's convention were dispirited. Their battle for Jewish schools had been lost. Several teachers blamed Steinhardt's vituperative attacks on the Gemeindebund.[162] Steinhardt's chief mistake was the assumption that the Jews would deal with the teachers' demands as an educational matter. As he said in self-defense, he and other members of the Lehrerverband had "not expected that the school question would be blown up into a partisan question."[163]

The left liberals who headed the Jewish defense and the Gemeindebund knew that the School Law adversely affected the Jews but disagreed with the teachers on how the Jews should react. The left-liberal notables believed that because the Jews had taken the stand that the government's policy of confessionalizing the public schools contradicted liberal principles, the congregations should not build separate Jewish schools and, thereby, hasten the demise of interdenominational schools.[164] Setbacks resulting from the enactment of the School Law did not weaken the conviction of Jewish liberals that the interconfessional schools were the best way to educate Germany's youth. It would be politically inexpedient, wrote an anonymous spokesman for the Gemeindebund, "to give gentiles the false impression that there is a certain group of pessimists among the German Jews who are prepared to compromise with the confessionalization of the state's public schools."[165]

Jewish left liberals exhorted their coreligionists to persevere in fighting for the cause of interconfessional schools. Speaking in the Diet in 1910, Cassel set out to demonstrate that the school policies of Studt and his successor Holle had not caused the commitment of the Jews to the ideal of the interconfessional school to waver. He asked, "And why should we despair in the future of the interconfessional schools if we remember how they had spread and flourished in earlier years?"[166] He expressed confidence that just as Schön, Flottwell, and other outstanding statesmen of nineteenth-century Prussia had recognized that the interests of a confessionally pluralistic state lay in an interdenominational school system, so a new minister of education would revive the liberal policies of Adalbert Falk in the 1870s, and these schools would thrive again.

Activist teachers thought that Jews such as Cassel were not being pragmatic and were deceiving themselves with Pollyannaish illusions. They debunked the optimistic idea of the liberals that interconfessional schools promoted tolerance as "unfortunately only a phantasy, which fades quickly into grim reality."[167] The Lehrerverband's propaganda attributed the objections raised against Jewish schools to upper-class snobbishness and assimilationism and to a doctrinaire adherence to the platform of the Progressive People's party. What the aggrieved teachers did not comprehend was that the activist lawyers in the defense movement aspired to equality of rights for German Jews not as an ethnic minority with its own separate schools but as citizens who were completely integrated into the German nation and educated at the same schools with the rest of society.

The question of Jewish schools was not so simple as Steinhardt thought. Viewing it from different perspectives, the teachers and the liberal leaders of organized Jewry made different judgments. The teachers, who were concerned about jobs, stressed the religious and educational advantages that the pupils would gain at Jewish schools: the study of the Torah and the Talmud in Hebrew and the observance of the Sabbath and other sacred days. Jewish liberal activists, on the other hand, saw the political and social position of the Jews in Germany at stake in the school question. They were convinced that the school question had a direct bearing on the Jewish struggle for equal rights. After conceding that many interconfessional schools were no longer genuinely pluralistic, the *Allgemeine Zeitung des Judentums* declared:

These developments are abuses and setbacks, which we fight and try to change but should not sanction by our resignation or acquiescence. Where should we get the moral authority for our fight for the interconfessional school if we ourselves follow the path of the confessional school? With what right would we oppose the principle of confessional separation if we ourselves pay homage to this principle? . . . If we kept in mind the other spheres of our civic life—and the public school system is a part of civic life—then we would never succumb to defeatist resignation. Subject to involuntary restrictions are our Jewish lawyers, academic teachers, and university instructors, indeed, all aspirants of professions in which the Jews are still kept from entering freely.[168]

The leadership establishment of German Jewry believed that the creation of a system of separate Jewish primary schools would have harmful consequences and would lead to Jewish segregation in higher-level schools and to more extensive discrimination. Once the policy of confessional separation in the public schools was accepted by the Jews and Christian liberals, the government would be emboldened to apply the theory that Prussia was a "Christian state" to legislation in other fields. To activists in the defense movement the opening of Jewish schools conjured up the specter of exclusion and discrimination. They had seen too frequently state administrators use differences between the Jews and the Christian confessions to justify disparities in legal rights and legal protection. They did not believe that the Jews could voluntarily segregate themselves in the school system without undermining the foundation of constitutional rights that they had struggled so long to achieve.

Jewish schools evoked memories of ghetto segregation in the minds of many Jewish liberals. Setting up new separate schools would be tantamount to an open admission that the ethnic differentness of the Jews was a barrier to assimilation into the German nation. Explaining why the executive board of the Berlin community rejected the teachers' demand to open Jewish schools, Dr. Moritz Türk said, "We do not want to shut up our children in a ghetto," and added, "We can not accustom our Christian fellow citizens [to think] that the Jews have no social intercourse with them."[169] Another critic scolded the Lehrerverband for "directing us German Jews to a goal which is apt to lead us a step back into the ghetto era."[170]

The Jewish liberals worried about how other Germans would react to Jewish schools. Blaschke thought that the Germans would regard them as inferior to the other public schools. He warned that Jewish children educated apart from the Christian population would not be accepted as Germans and would be at a disadvantage later in pursuing certain vocations.[171] Such apprehensions were not unfounded. The state authorities expected the primary schools to make good citizens out of the pupils and to develop in them an intensity of feeling for all things German, from the landscape and the social customs of the country to the monarchy. Just as chauvinistic and narrow-minded school administrators and Christian parents did not trust Jewish teachers to give instruction in German history and literature, so they were likely to have little confidence in the capacity of exclusively Jewish schools to cultivate a German consciousness in the children. These misgivings were widely held among the Jews. In October 1913 many regional associations within the Gemeindebund passed resolutions declaring "the establishment of exclusively Jewish confessional schools inadvisable."[172] Addressing the Gemeindebund's congress in December 1913, Rabbi Jakob Guttmann of Breslau admitted that "a large number, the majority of influential [congregations], are opposed in principle to the establishment of Jewish schools. They will not let themselves be coerced."[173]

Since the passage of the School Law, the situation in the school system affected all congregations. The Lehrerverband's secretary justifiably asserted that the opening of Jewish schools was "an eminently Jewish question, which the Gemeindebund cannot avoid."[174] By refusing to place the issue on the agenda of the congress and by employing pressure tactics to block an open debate on it, the Gemeindebund's board of directors found themselves criticized for operating in an overbearing and undemocratic manner.[175] The reason for this undemocratic behavior was the involvement of the Zionists in the controversy.

Starting in 1907, the German Zionist Organization agitated for the establishment of Jewish schools in the press and in the community societies that its members infiltrated. It made contacts with Jewish teachers for recruitment and propaganda purposes.[176] The Zionists attributed the opposition to Jewish schools to assimilationism and egged on Steinhardt and his followers to fight the liberal leaders of organized Jewry.[177] They criticized interdenominational schools because the curriculum was not inspired by a religious and ethnic cultural spirit, and they praised Jewish schools for teaching the pupils from a Jewish point of view.

The Zionist agitation gave the campaign for Jewish schools a political character that it did not have earlier. The anonymous spokesman for the Gemeindebund observed that the Zionists were "among the most fanatical champions of Jewish schools" when he defended the Gemeindebund's refusal to put the issue on the agenda of the congress in 1911. He stated that although the teachers were "not conscious of it, the demand for Jewish schools is a jumping-off point for Zionist strivings, from clubs for girls to a separate state and internationally recognized homeland in Palestine."[178] He took care to distinguish between the exclusiveness of Jewish pressure groups and fraternities, which were organized to combat involuntary segregation, and the "Jewish separatist-nationalism" of the Zionists. Zionist propaganda gave Jewish liberals the impression that Jewish nationalism would infiltrate newly founded Jewish schools and would embroil the schools in controversy because Orthodox, liberal, and Zionist groups disagreed over what Jewishness embodied.[179] Believing that the Zionists were exploiting the discontents of the teachers, prominent Jewish liberals were persuaded to form a committee in 1913 to block the Lehrerverband from using the Gemeindebund's congress as a forum of agitation.[180]

The grievances of the teachers did not go unheard. Their agitation spurred the defense movement to take action against the penetration of anti-Semitism into the schools. When the Jewish teachers grew militant after the enactment of the School Law, they started to work more actively in the Centralverein than they had done previously. The injustices suffered by Jews in the school system were now aired at chapter meetings. Henriette Fürth, one of the first women to join the Centralverein in 1908, gave a speech on "The Fight against Anti-Semitism in the Schools" at a joint meeting of two Berlin chapters in October 1909.[181] She reported on the case of three Berlin teachers whose tenure rank was arbitrarily revoked. After the Centralverein contested this action, the school administration agreed to reinstate the teachers on the condition that they give instruction only in technical subjects and the Jewish religion. Another case Henriette Fürth cited was the dismissal of a teacher in Hanover after objections were raised about the suitability of a Jew teaching German literature and history to Christian pupils.

In January 1909 another Berlin chapter assembly passed a motion calling for a Progressive deputy to interpellate Minister of Education Holle about anti-Semitism in the schools.[182] The sponsors of the motion were not satisfied with the outcome of private protests and were seeking a public confrontation with Holle in the Diet. The Centralverein complained to Holle in March 1908 that a high school principal in a town in Posen had publicly maligned the Jews. It requested that the minister censure him and take measures to prevent such conduct. Holle brushed off this complaint with the reply that the administrators and the teachers under his jurisdiction "have no inclination to make themselves responsible for such an offense."[183]

By 1911 the school system had become a major front in the Jewish struggle for civil equality. Rather than create a wall of separation, the Centralverein wanted the Jews to work for a confessionally integrated and tolerant school system, by lobbying to get appointments for Jewish teachers and by reporting anti-Semitic offenses to the authorities for disciplinary action.

In 1911 the Centralverein launched an intensive drive against gymnastic clubs in schools that excluded Jewish pupils and against schoolbooks that slandered the Jews and their religion. The Berlin bureau instructed the chapters to report on school clubs barring Jewish students from membership, and formal complaints were lodged with the principals.[184] In one case the principal at a Berlin high school made a pretense of reprimanding the club, but he did not put an end to the practice of blacklisting Jewish boys. The Centralverein filed a complaint with the Berlin school administration. The principal was ordered to warn the club that it could not reject students on account of their faith and would be disbanded if the same offense was committed again.[185]

The Berlin office requested the chapters also to examine whether books in local school libraries contained any defamation of the Jewish religion. The chapters were instructed to look for passages in history and geography books that conveyed *völkisch* theories or described Christianity as a prerequisite of German nationality. The Centralverein appealed to the book publishers to emend these passages. If the contents of the books were coarsely anti-Semitic, the principals were asked to remove them from the school libraries.[186]

Concerning the source of the problem of anti-Semitism in the schools, the Centralverein was far from indulging in illusions. In an address delivered at the general convention in 1913, Rabbi David from Bockum commented that "never was anti-Semitism so deeply rooted in the outlook of the teachers as is the case today."[187] He explained that the social milieu from which the teachers generally came, a petty bourgeois or a civil-service family background, instilled in them a distrust of the Jews. He pointed also to the respectability that Germans such as Wagner, Treitschke, and de Lagarde had given to *völkisch* ideas. "And if such thinking acquires a scholarly veneer," he said, "then people believe that anti-Semitism is part of a *Weltanschauung*, a German *Weltanschauung* which no German teacher need be ashamed of."[188]

Rabbi David hinted that there was a difference of opinion over whether the Centralverein should demand that the government take disciplinary action against anti-Semitic teachers. Parents were worried that the defense movement would foment confessional tensions in the schools and that their children would be badgered by vindictive teachers.[189] The delicate issue of a conflict between the Jewish defense and the civil liberties of the teachers was another problem that Rabbi David heard about from events in Dortmund.

In 1910 the Dortmund chapter prevailed upon two city councilmen to protest to the magistrates that several high school teachers were leaders in a local anti-Semitic party organization. The two city councilmen demanded that the school administration issue a directive prohibiting the teachers from conducting anti-Semitic agitation.[190] This incident touched off a commotion. The Centralverein was accused of depriving school teachers of their political rights. Rabbi Benno Jacob, who headed the Dortmund chapter, defended the Centralverein in the local press. In response to the criticism that the Jewish defense was striving to curtail the civil liberties of the teachers, he argued that active involvement in an anti-Semitic party was not analogous to affiliation with any other party.[191] Whereas the other parties opposed ideas and institutions, the anti-Semites attacked the Jews as a people and denied them the rights of citizenship. Their platform, sowing religious and racial hatred in the nation, was politically subversive and immoral. Rabbi Jacob implored the citizens of Dortmund to be fair-minded and to recognize the fact that Jewish pupils could have no confidence in teachers who vilified the Jews outside the classroom.

Complaints about anti-Semitic teachers were sent to the Centralverein's Berlin office, and in 1912 the executive directors decided to press the school authorities to censure the teachers. Charges against teachers who had expressed anti-Semitic views in public were submitted to the school department in the Provincial District of Cassel. Paul Blankenhorn, the department's new director, investigated the allegations and reprimanded the teachers.[192] Another case involved a teacher in Krojanke in the province of Posen. The Centralverein charged that he conducted anti-Semitic agitation in a gymnastics club. The county school superintendent censured the teacher and ordered him to stop his anti-Semitic activity.[193]

In private correspondence and at chapter meetings the Central-verein encouraged community leaders to lobby for the appointment of Jewish teachers. It declared that the employment of Jewish teachers had a bearing on the interests of the entire community and was not merely a matter of the livelihood of those seeking jobs. Typical was the letter that Horwitz sent to the executive board of the Danzig community. He wrote that the appointment of Jewish teachers to the public schools would enable the young to receive religious instruction as part of the regular school curriculum.[194] He contended that, to uphold the principle of equality of opportunity, the Jews must not allow Jewish teachers to be excluded from the public schools or placed in a rank less than equal to the status of their Christian colleagues. Capping his argument, he wrote: "The presence of a Jewish teacher on the teaching staff of a school affords the Jewish pupils better protection against the anti-Semitic attitudes of other teachers and gives the gentile children a view of the Jewish teacher as the peer of gentile teachers in respect to professional office and esteem."

Because the School Law of 1906 limited the opportunities of Jew-ish teachers in the primary schools, the Centralverein aimed at placing them in the secondary schools, where the legislative restric-tions concerning confession did not apply.[195] The executive directors located high schools in Charlottenburg, Cologne, Hamburg, Stettin, and other cities in which there was a sizable number of Jewish students but no Jewish teachers. They urged community notables in these places to lobby for the appointment of Jewish teachers to the high schools in negotiations with city officials and in private talks with city councilmen. In cities such as Frankfurt am Main and Ham-burg the chapters were encouraged to mobilize public support and, through the city councils, to bring pressure on the school authorities to cease discriminatory hiring practices.

Early in 1912 members of the Hamburg chapter persuaded the Pro-gressives in the city parliament to open an attack on the school authorities for refusing to appoint Jewish teachers to the high schools. Two Progressive representatives ended their indictment with the demand that the magistrate instruct school administrators to consider qualified Jewish and Catholic applicants in hiring teachers.[196] The criticism embarrassed city officials, who could not deny the allegation that all Jewish applicants had been turned down. At a meeting of the chapter in October, Holländer came from Berlin to give a speech on discrimination against Jewish teachers. The chapter discussed the problem in the Hamburg school system. A resolution was moved to ask candidates campaigning for election to the city parliament how they stood on the issue of appointing Jewish and Catholic teachers to the high schools. The resolution served notice to political circles in Hamburg that "no Jewish voter can cast his vote for a candidate who does not declare, without any reservation, that no Jewish qualified applicant may be excluded from a high school teaching position on account of his religion."[197]

To stir the Jews in the Berlin suburb of Charlottenburg out of complacency, Horwitz asked Bruno Blau, a Frankfurt lawyer and a dedicated activist in the defense movement, to deliver a speech before the chapter in April 1912. Blau criticized the apathy of the Jews in Charlottenburg and pointed out that the suburb had about 22,500 Jewish residents and many Jewish pupils but not a single Jewish teacher in the primary schools.[198] Adding to the embarrassment of the listeners, Blau mentioned that 20 of the 72 representatives in the city council were Jews. He exhorted the Jewish councilmen to take energetic action in the local Progressive party club and in the city council to abolish the practice of excluding Jewish teachers from the schools. Jewish councilmen attending the meeting were angry at Blau and attempted to defend their inaction by laying the blame on the state authorities rather than on the Charlottenburg officials. Blau sharply dismissed their excuses and retorted that the discrimination could be eliminated easily because a Progressive majority controlled the city council. From Horwitz's remarks at the conclusion of the meeting it is clear that he and Fuchs had planned Blau's confrontation with the Jewish left liberals in Charlottenburg. Blau's criticism emboldened the Jewish councilmen to act, and shortly thereafter a Jew was appointed to be a high school principal.

8

CONCLUSION

The history of the German Jews in the post-Emancipation era has been approached in terms of the themes of political timidity and accommodation for so long that the political activism of the Jewish defense in Imperial Germany is given little notice and is even denied. The notion that the Jewish defense abstained from politics persists. To argue that the Centralverein's leaders believed that "political intervention was unnecessary and possibly harmful" and participated in German politics "with extreme reluctance and for limited periods of time" is to ignore the evidence.[1]

In the decades between the Emancipation and the Holocaust, the most important event in the history of German Jewry was the formation of a politically activist defense against anti-Semitism. The Centralverein started in 1893 with a strategy limited to counter-propaganda and the legal prosecution of defamation in the anti-Semitic press. Its founders disclaimed any ambition to create a Jewish pressure group or a "Jewish Centrum," a political party after the example of the German Catholics. Horwitz and Fuchs, more dynamic and courageous than the other notables on the board of directors, had a vision of a political movement that went beyond these modest steps, and in the years from 1898 to 1914 they politicized the Jewish defense.

Beginning with the 1898 election the Centralverein participated in campaigns for the election of the Reichstag and the Prussian parliament. Opposition to the anti-Semitic parties did not remain the only battleground for long. After the turn of the century the Centralverein and the Verband, a lobbying association whose founding in 1904 was financed by the Centralverein, moved to a second front to fight an insidious and a more powerful foe: government anti-Semitism, the discrimination that the Prussian state authorities practiced from the officer corps and the judiciary to the allocation of government funds in the public school system. Drawing its central and regional leadership from Jews in the law profession, who were prime victims of government anti-Semitism, the Jewish defense became a struggle for equal opportunity and equal treatment.

This achievement was the work of left-liberal Jews in Prussia. Jews living in Baden, Bavaria, and Württemberg, where the Christian majority and the government seemed more tolerant, hesitated to join the Centralverein and to establish the Verband. They were fearful that the agitation of Jewish organizations, directed from Berlin, might disturb the harmonious relations between the Jews and the Christian population in Southern Germany, and they preferred to deal with Jewish matters on a regional level.

The Orthodox Jews made little contribution to the Jewish struggle for civil equality. In Orthodox circles the liberal activists were suspected of assimilationism. Orthodox believers were troubled less about discrimination than about the absorption of the Jews in their Christian surroundings. They were willing patiently to suffer unjust differences in the treatment of the Jews and the Christian majority as long as the Jews retained those separate institutions that allowed them to fulfill the obligations set by the Thora and tradition and to preserve their distinctive identity. Whereas the liberals at the head of organized Jewry saw some manifestations of separateness as exclusion incompatible with their sense of belonging to the German nation, the Orthodox were apprehensive that the liberal activists would surrender the traditions of their forefathers for the sake of equal rights.

The Zionists, with the exception of a few men such as Hantke, Heymann, and Klee, did not appreciate the value or effectiveness of the defense movement. Zionist propaganda ridiculed the activities of the Centralverein as futile and trifling and publicized its setbacks as a vindication of the pessimistic view that on German soil "the Jewish question" would never be solved by striving to realize the ideals of religious tolerance and civil equality. After 1907 Zionist attacks on the Centralverein, whose membership and influence had been rapidly growing, became acrimonious. Militant young Zionists charged that its leaders were too deferential to the Progressive party officials, provided campaign funds without bargaining for a quid pro quo, and gave priority to party allegiance over Jewish interests. They clamored

for a break with the Progressives and the adoption of an opportunistic and consciously Jewish strategy in German party politics. As
Horwitz and Fuchs correctly perceived, the strategy advocated by
the radical Zionists was not a pragmatic course. The Zionist programs calling for "Jewish-national politics" were derived from
poorly drawn analogies between conditions in the province of Posen
and the rest of Germany and from a failure to understand the
limited political choices that the Jews had in Wilhelminian Germany.

Once the leaders of the defense movement decided to lobby in
parliament and the government ministries, they needed party allies.
They ceased to profess nonpartisanship and gave open support to
the Progressive People's party. Much more than their own personal
sympathies dictated this choice. For all their faults, the Progressives
were the most reliable defenders of Jewish rights. The National
Liberals, the party of Jewish voters in the 1860s and 1870s, were a
disappointment to the Jews in the Wilhelminian era. Hobnobbing
with the Pan-Germans and the Agrarians, the National Liberals no
longer spoke out for liberal principles. In elections party officials
collaborated with the anti-Semites. In parliament they gave approval
to practices of discrimination that made a mockery of the principle
of government under the rule of law.

Relations between the Jews and the Center party took an unfavorable turn after 1901. Center deputies no longer stood up to oppose
the violation of the rights of Jewish citizens. Bigoted party members
grumbled about Jewish lawyers swamping the legal profession and
invoked the principle of parity to advocate a numerus clausus in the
appointment of judges and notaries public. The Center *Fraktion* in
the Prussian parliament accepted the government's rationale for distinctions made in the treatment of the Jews and the Christians and,
like the Protestant Conservatives, interpreted the Prussian constitution to validate the idea that public institutions in the state must
have a Christian character. The Catholic party was indifferent to the
rights of the Jewish minority when it supported the government's
policy of placing the primary schools on a Christian confessional
foundation.

The relationship of the German liberals to the Jewish community
was probably more complicated during the Wilhelminian era than at
any other time. As Uriel Tal's book makes clear, Protestant theo-

logians of the liberal school during the Second Empire, Adolf von Harnack, Friedrich Paulsen, and Martin Rade, never understood the double aspirations of the Jews to integrate into German society and to retain their Jewish identity at the same time.[2] Liberal Protestant intellectuals never contemplated the elimination of separate Jewish activities through external compulsion. Instead they thought that the Jews should relinquish voluntarily their distinctiveness as the price of admission to German society. Assimilation was to be the complete absorption of the Jews into their Christian surroundings.

Whereas the liberal Protestant theologians dealt speculatively with the question of Jewish integration in the 1870s and 1880s, the Progressive politicians confronted Jewish left liberals who carried out the principle of social pluralism after 1893 in organizing a defense movement apart from the Abwehrverein, which the Progressives had founded two years earlier. The Progressives showed little appreciation of the need felt by the Jews for an organization that fulfilled the twin tasks of combating discrimination and reviving Jewish pride and loyalty. At the time the Centralverein was founded and later when the Verband was formed, the Progressives raised a hue and cry about Jewish political separatism. They wanted the defense against anti-Semitism to be interconfessional and free of ethnic group concerns. They did not welcome the appearance of Jewish pressure groups, which were likely to assert Jewish interests aggressively and to aspire after influence in party affairs. Knowing how unpopular the Jewish cause was in the public eye, the Progressives were not eager to be identified with a highly visible and activist Jewish fight for equal rights. Nonetheless, after the Jewish defense entered politics the Progressives took up arms in the struggle against government anti-Semitism. They were the most helpful, if not always the most zealous, allies that the Jewish activists found in German party politics.

Disappointments and friction were bound to come. In their response to the strivings of the Jews for equal opportunity in public life, the Progressives' profession of liberal principles was put to a credibility test. Policies followed by party officials sometimes stood in blatant contradiction to liberal ideals. The Progressive politicians and the Jewish activists were not of one mind on what party interests required. The Progressives did not give top priority to opposition to the small, loosely organized anti-Semitic parties, whose deeds in parliament never matched the fury of their oratory. The Progressives were losing ground to the Social Democrats as longtime liberal strongholds fell to their rivals on the far Left. In elections they were more concerned about defeating the Social Democrats than the anti-Semites. Until the Progressives changed their tactics in the 1912 election they declined to endorse Socialists contesting anti-Semites and right-wing candidates in the runoffs. More eager to win seats in parliament than to withstand popular bigotry, district party committees made accommodations to the anti-Jewish sentiments of the voting public and refused to nominate Jewish candidates in safe liberal constituencies or wherever they had to woo votes from the Right to defeat the Social Democrats. In localities where the voting strength of the anti-Semites was great, party officials considered a Jewish background as a negative factor in appraising potential nominees and were unwilling to risk the loss of votes by nominating Jewish candidates.

Jewish left liberals were bitterly disappointed that party leaders took the Jewish vote for granted and treated Jewish interests as a secondary factor in making decisions on runoff tactics. The Jews saw an indifference to the immorality of anti-Semitism and a cynical disregard for liberal ideals in the decisions that the Progressives made from political expediency and from an emotionally detached assessment of the menace of the anti-Semitic parties. The Progressive leaders were not latently anti-Semitic as many critics suspected. Their behavior was so inconsistent because party interests and liberal principles pulled them in opposite directions.

With sound political judgment and a deep sense of responsibility, Horwitz and Fuchs steered the defense movement through the troublesome years of 1907 and 1908, when Jewish disillusionment with the politics of the Progressive People's party ran high. Horwitz and Fuchs did not close their eyes to the opportunistic behavior of the Progressives in the Bülow bloc. Shrewd observers of the political scene, they concluded that tactical considerations, not disguised anti-Semitism, led the party's central committee to remain neutral in the runoffs matching anti-Semites with Social Democrats. As much as they deplored these tactics, they refrained from making grandstand denunciations. They sought to change the party's election strategy through quiet, behind-the-scenes negotiations with the central committee and the *Fraktion*. Knowing that the Jewish lobby needed the good will of the Progressive deputies and that the Jewish struggle against discrimination was tied to the fortunes of liberalism in Germany, they wisely saw no advantage in pillorying the Progressives. They doubted that a separate Jewish political bloc would carry much weight and thought that the defection of the Jews from the party would be a feckless tactic. They withstood Julius Moses and other agitators inflaming Jewish disaffection with the Progressives. When intraparty squabbles divided the Progressives, and Barth's faction formed a new party in 1908 and began to recruit disenchanted Jewish left liberals, Horwitz and Fuchs kept the defense movement out of the thick of partisan battles. They admired Barth's courageous opposition to government anti-Semitism, but they viewed his secession as a foolish mistake and did not switch to his new party.

The Centralverein came out of the period of the Bülow bloc united and unharmed by the divisions and the demoralization in the Progressive camp. It continued to be aligned with the Progressives as the most judicious option for the Jews in German politics. Contrary to the contention in Jacob Toury's book, there is no evidence of any large-scale shift of Jewish liberal voters to the Social Democrats during the crisis of confidence between the Jews and the Progressives.[3] The movement instigated by Julius Moses and a handful of radical Zionists for a Jewish boycott of the Progressives fell flat. The Centralverein was successful in sustaining the affiliation of its membership with the Progressives.

Although the Progressive politicians were insensitive to the changes in the values and the behavior of the Jewish liberals, which a stronger consciousness of Jewish identity produced after the turn of the century, they served the Jewish defense well. Party officials yielded to pressure from the Centralverein and nominated Jewish candidates. Six Progressives of the Jewish faith were elected to the Diet in 1903 and seven in 1908. In private talks with ministry officials, Progressive deputies helped the Verband to lobby for government action to abolish discrimination in the officer corps. They rose on the floor of the Reichstag and the Prussian parliament to hold ministers accountable for policies that violated the rights of the Jews.

The Progressive *Fraktion* introduced amendments to the school bill that the Verband requested. It cooperated with the Verband also to eliminate injustices in the government's treatment of the Jewish religion. In 1909 and 1913, during readings of the budget, the Progressives proposed motions requesting the government to appropriate funds to assist poor synagogue congregations. They brought to public notice the injustice of denying state subsidies to the Jewish community when public funds had been appropriated for years to support the Protestant and Catholic churches.

Both the Centralverein and the Verband were headed by a central board of directors. The Jewish defense produced no charismatic leaders. There was little trace of egotism in the character of Horwitz and Fuchs. Neither one aspired to dominate the Centralverein and to identify it with their personal stature. They acquired an ascendant position in its collegial leadership through their selfless and single-minded dedication to the Jewish struggle for justice. Working at their side was a corps of activist lawyers.

Although this vanguard—Breslauer, Brodnitz, Fuchs, Geiger, Herzfeld, Holländer, Horwitz, Mainzer, Salinger, and others—left behind no memoirs or autobiographies, the proceedings of the biennial convention of delegates and the meetings of the chapters, which *Im Deutschen Reich* reported extensively, reveal much about their character and how their experiences affected their reaction to the frustrations and the humiliations of discrimination. By working in the Centralverein, Jewish lawyers shared as a group instead of bearing alone the strains and the pressures of belonging to a discriminated minority. The emotional conflicts that many Jewish intellectuals of their times experienced did not burden them. Long hours of work, self-sacrifice, and the idealism of their goals gave them a sense of purpose and self-confidence. Proudly they recounted the achievements of the Centralverein and declared that it had given the Jews a strong backbone and militancy and had revived community loyalty and interest in the heritage of Judaism. They boasted that their bold and law-abiding fight earned them respect and that the Jewish defense could "stand up to the test of publicity and the law."[4]

The activist lawyers were neither Orthodox in matters of faith nor Zionist in their definition of Jewish identity, but they did not fit the stereotype of the assimilationist Jew who felt ambivalent about his Jewish background. They did not react to the frustrations of discrimination by directing their resentment at the Jewish community. They had none of the self-hatred of Jews who saw ethnic behavior patterns and traditions through the eyes of unfriendly Germans. In combating agitation to ban the kosher slaughtering of animals, which anti-Semites in the Society for the Prevention of Cruelty to Animals conducted, they were just as dedicated as they were in protesting discrimination in the officer corps and the judiciary. Due to their outspoken criticism, baptism ceased to be among educated Jews a socially tolerated way to cross the barriers to professional advancement and social status as it had been in the decades before 1900.

Practical-minded lawyers, they were not interested in formulating theories on the nature of Jewishness or on the relationship of the Jews to the German nation. The Centralverein was not an ideological movement propagating German nationalism within the Jewish community. The statutes drafted in 1893 stated that among its aims was the purpose of encouraging the Jews "in the preservation of German sentiments and values."[5] After 1893 Horwitz and Fuchs felt no need to clarify what *deutsche Gesinnung* meant because they thought that all Jews in Germany shared it.[6] At the 1909 convention anti-Zionists in the Breslau chapter proposed an amendment to the statutes to emphasize the Centralverein's promotion of German national feeling. The central board opposed the amendment and told the delegates that it did not want to open up a thorny debate on this question.[7]

Only from 1912 on, in response to the agitation of younger Zionists, who stressed more than the first generation had done that the integration of the Jews into the German nation was undesirable and impossible to achieve and that the German citizenship of the Jews did not imply German nationality, did the leaders of the Jewish defense affirm ardently that birth, language and culture, common law and government bound the Jews inseparably to the German nation. Also fervently stated was their decision "to achieve equality on German soil without detriment to our Jewish character, our loyalty, our religious community."[8] There was no flag-waving chauvinism in their affirmations of loyalty to the German nation; they were too conscious of the *völkisch* element in German nationalism to be superheated patriots. They were convinced that the will of the Jews to belong to the German nation was a prerequisite for the fight for civil equality. As Holländer contended, the rights of citizens could not be demanded by those who considered themselves transients or foreigners in Germany.[9]

The activist lawyers in the Jewish defense were sufficiently certain of their Jewish identity and German culture that they felt no need to overemphasize Jewish ethnicity or to parade German patriotism. Fuchs made this point in a speech at the 1913 convention. He said: "I need not become German with self-consciousness because I have that sense in my feelings. My life has been such that I need not talk myself into having a German national consciousness."[10] After noting that his Jewish ancestry and home environment had endowed him with "particular intellectual and physical traits," he declared in 1917, "I do not find it necessary to segregate myself from the society around me in order to continue functioning as a Jew and I do not have to argue myself out of my Jewishness in order to continue living as a man among other men."[11]

Fuchs and his co-workers had no psychological traumas about the duality of identities of the German Jew. Double loyalty posed no problem for them. They saw Germany as a pluralistic society with individual citizens belonging to multiple overlapping groups and thought that the Jews could be loyal to the German nation and the Jewish community without being thrown into a constant state of conflict and uncertainty. In another speech responding to Zionist criticism in 1912, Fuchs proclaimed:

> In the German fatherland, on German soil, we were born, and that entitles us to call ourselves German without baptism and so-called assimilation. We want to belong to the German nation and shall belong to it; at the same time we can and must remain true to our religious community and ethnic heritage. . . . National unity and the formation of groups in society are compatible with each other; our distinctiveness is hardly greater than that of other German groups, ethnic groups and classes, and even if that was so it does not matter.[12]

Precisely because the leaders of the Jewish defense did not bandy slogans about assimilationism, they grappled honestly with the agonizing problems of integration and exclusiveness. As the controversy over school policy revealed, solutions to the problem of how the German Jews could retain and strengthen their Jewish identity without jeopardizing their struggle for civil equality were not easily found. Lobbying for amendments to the school bill, the Verband gave priority to the maintenance of an integrated school system rather than to the establishment of separate Jewish schools. The Centralverein gave encouragement to the university students who founded the Verein jüdischen Studenten in Berlin in 1895 and its branches in Breslau and Leipzig in 1899. *Im Deutschen Reich* defended the organization of exclusively Jewish clubs at the universities on the grounds that the fraternities blackballed Jewish students, and it praised the clubs for accustoming educated Jews to assimilate German culture without denying their Jewish heritage.[13] But wherever social and cultural associations bringing Jews and Christians together were "possible and even desirable," the Centralverein promoted such interconfessional activities. *Im Deutschen Reich* stated in 1903:

> We represent the point of view that German Jews must unite in order to take up the fight for civil equality. Therefore, we consider it right that confidence in our complete equality leads to the formation of organizations wherever we Jews are badly treated in society. . . . On the other hand, striving for the general recognition of our equal rights and our merit requires that we do not separate ourselves unnecessarily from our Christian fellow citizens, that we create no competing confessional associations if in the nonconfessional and public associations the Jew is treated like the Christians.[14]

More emphatically the Centralverein declared:

> We warn our coreligionists against unnecessary separateness where no offenses are to be feared, where the collective cultural endeavors of all German citizens are possible and welcomed. We desire a courageous defense . . . but disapprove of excessive sensitivity in cases where really only our sensitive skin appears to feel something hostile. Even the appearance of voluntary exclusion must be avoided now.[15]

The left-liberal lawyers whose activism was nurtured in the defense movement were different from the Jewish stalwarts of the Progressive

People's party such as Cassel, Cohn, and Sonnenfeld. The corps of lawyers working with Horwitz and Fuchs were not inclined to theorize on how a Jew should act in politics or whether party affiliation or a Jewish point of view should determine the stand that a Jew took on political questions. Believing that the Jewish defense aimed at the realization of the liberal principles professed by the Progressives, they did not at first draw any distinction between party allegiance and loyalty to the Jewish community. When Mugdan's nomination, the 1907 election, and issues such as religious instruction in the public schools opened up a chasm between the party's politics and the interests of the Jewish community, the Centralverein's leaders took their stand as Jews and had no qualms about assigning priority to Jewish interests over the party's platform. Refusing to fraternize with anti-Semites and Agrarians in the 1907 election, the Centralverein did not join the Progressives in rallying to Chancellor Bülow's appeal for a united front of the progovernment *bürgerlich* parties against the Center party and the Social Democrats. It disapproved of the Progressives' strident attacks on the Catholic party during the campaign. The issue of the candidacy of baptized Jews after 1908 showed once again that the Jewish activists were prepared to set priorities independently of the party. Criticism in the Progressive press did not inhibit them from looking at this question from a Jewish point of view.

Jews who sought to fulfill their ambitions in the life of the Progressive People's party compartmentalized their political activity and their membership in the Jewish community. On political issues they never felt obliged to take a stand from the vantage point of the Jewish religion rather than the party. The Jewish politicians rendered valuable service to the Jewish community, but they never overcame the idea that the Centralverein and the Verband were manifestations of Jewish political separatism. In discussions on political matters at the congresses and board meetings of the two organizations, Cassel and Cohn counseled moderation and circumspection. The overcaution of the Jewish deputies chafed the restive spirit of the Centralverein's young activists. Holländer's frustration broke out in the sardonic remark that "a certain type of bourgeoisie, standing at the head of Jewish political life, sermonize day after day: 'don't stir up those who are complacent.' "[16]

The Jewish deputies in the Progressive *Fraktion* did not want their position in public life to be compromised by the impression that they were spokesmen for Jewish pressure groups. Their misgivings were by no means paranoid. They were subjected to harassment in parliament from the Right and the Socialist Left. In a debate on the budget of the Prussian universities in 1913, for example, the Social Democrat Karl Liebknecht attacked the university administrators for barring the admission of Russian students and charged that anti-Semitism motivated their treatment of these foreign students. He sarcastically scolded Cassel for not defending the Russian students "as it would be his duty and obligation as the representative of the Jews whose inspired true prophet he seeks to cast himself here in other respects."[17] In another debate in 1913 the Social Democrat Adolf Hoffmann made crude innuendos about Cassel's connections with the Verband after he had defended a Progressive motion asking the government to appropriate funds for subsidies to poor synagogue congregations. Hoffmann ridiculed Cassel and the Verband for pan-handling money from the state.[18] In an impassioned and indignant reply Cassel assured the deputies that he was not hiding the fact that he sat on the Verband's board of directors and that the proposal was introduced at the Verband's request. Angrily he denied that the Jews were begging, and he argued that justice obliged the state to give financial assistance to the Jewish community as it already did to the Christian churches.[19] Cassel walked out of the chamber and did not hear Hoffmann's rebuttal, which was larded with anti-Semitic invective.

After years of resignation, political docility, and mild protests, European Jewry did not easily mobilize to combat anti-Semitism. In republican France the Jews organized no large-scale defense during the Dreyfus affair.[20] In Imperial Germany the Jews found no sympathetic public for a civil rights movement. The public reaction to the Jewish defense was suspicion and disdain. The anti-Semitic Right taunted the Centralverein with the name "informers league" because it filed complaints with state attorneys to prosecute anti-Semitic journalists for defamation. Doubt was cast on the patriotism of the Jewish activists by accusations that they put exclusively Jewish interests above the nation's welfare. The state authorities viewed the defense movement with distrust. The specter of conspiracy was not far from the report that the Prussian *Polizeipräsident* wrote in 1901. He described disapprovingly the Centralverein's goal of "strengthening Jewish influence by uniting German Jews and exercising the influence of united Jewry on other Germans, legislation, and [government] administration." He concluded: "The organization's strivings are by no means politically unquestionable. They contribute not to the elimination but, on the contrary, to the sharpening of friction between the Jews and the Germans."[21] Government officials resented especially protests that they were not scrupulously complying with the law, and they were often haughty and curt in their correspondence with the executives of the Centralverein and the Verband. Despite these obstacles the Jewish activist lawyers persevered in their struggle against discrimination.

The achievements of the Jewish defense are all the more impressive in view of the circumstances in Wilhelminian Germany so unfavorable to a minority fighting for civil equality. The Centralverein did more than instill pride and self-esteem in German Jewry. It broke down a host of attitudes and habits that had caused the Jews for generations to be noninvolved or to keep a low profile in political life. It accustomed the Jews to act as a collective group in politics and to see the protection of Jewish interests by a lobby as a legitimate civic activity. Above all, it offered the Jews an alternative to despair and resignation. It put up a defense that went beyond propaganda. It developed a political strategy enabling the Jews to combat anti-Semitism in the government and in society actively.

The significance of the Jewish defense in Wilhelminian Germany does not end here. By their character and the political values they represented, the Jewish activist lawyers offered the German nation an example of civic courage and an education in the principles of constitutional government and a pluralistic society. Fundamental to the thinking of Horwitz and Fuchs was the conviction that the fight against anti-Semitism was not a specifically Jewish problem but part of a broader struggle for the civil and legal equality of all German citizens. The Centralverein put the state authorities on notice that a body of citizens would not tolerate, without protest, official practices that violated the principle of equality of rights. It impressed upon the Germans the harm that government anti-Semitism inflicted on the respect for law and the sense of justice in society and it warned that discrimination practiced by state officials "has already led to a degeneration of the concept of justice, which must be courageously stopped lest all political liberty be destroyed."[22] The Germans were reminded that besides the political exigencies of national unity was the valid right of any minority to retain distinctive traits derived from historic and religious heritage. The place of the Jewish defense in the history of Wilhelminian Germany is described so well in the words of Julius Brodnitz, who said at the 1902 assembly: "The daily fight for justice has put questions of the defense of rights in the foreground [of political life]. To the Centralverein is set a task that extends beyond the circle of Jews belonging to it. We represent a civil rights association *[Rechtsverein]* in the most ideal sense of the word. We fight for justice, and in our time this is a momentous ethical mission."[23]

ABBREVIATIONS USED IN THE NOTES

ARCHIVES

BK	Bundesarchiv, Koblenz
CAHJP	Central Archives for the History of the Jewish People, Jerusalem
CZA	Central Zionist Archives, Jerusalem
DZA	Deutsches Zentralarchiv, Merseburg
GSt	Geheimes Staatsarchiv, Berlin
HHst	Hessisches Hauptstaatsarchiv, Wiesbaden
HSt	Hessisches Staatsarchiv, Marburg
NSt	Niedersächsisches Staatsarchiv, Wolfenbüttel

FREQUENTLY CITED PERIODICALS

AZJ	*Allgemeine Zeitung des Judentums*
BT	*Berliner Tageblatt*
GA	*General-Anzeiger für die gesamten Interessen des Judentums*
IDR	*Im Deutschen Reich*
MDIG	*Mitteilungen vom Deutsch-Israelitischen Gemeindebund*
MVAA	*Mitteilungen aus dem Verein zur Abwehr des Antisemitismus*

NOTES

CHAPTER 1

1. For the text of the Prussian Law of July 23, 1847, see Ismar Freund, *Die Emanzipation der Juden in Preussen*, 2: 501 ff.

2. *Statut der Synagogen-Gemeinde Köln*, article 12.

3. Joseph Heimberger, *Die staatskirchenrechtliche Stellung der Israeliten in Bayern*, p. 127.

4. CAHJP, rep. AHW 346, vol. 6, minutes of the meeting of the Hamburg community council on Nov. 5, 1905.

5. *Israelitische Wochenschrift*, Feb. 16, 1900, no. 7, p. 97; July 19, 1901, no. 29, pp. 453–54; Oct. 23, 1903, no. 43, p. 610; *Jüdisches Volksblatt*, June 1, 1906, no. 22, p. 250. For Zionist demands for the introduction of equal suffrage and other democratic reforms in the statutes and administration of the congregations, see Max Kollenscher, *Jüdische Gemeindepolitik*, pp. 13–15.

6. *AZJ*, Oct. 2, 1890, no. 38, Beilage; Apr. 21, 1893, no. 16, p. 183; July 21, 1899, no. 29, Beilage; Dec. 13, 1901, no. 50, p. 593; *Israelitische Wochenschrift*, Feb. 13, 1903, no. 7, pp. 95–96.

7. *AZJ*, Feb. 12, 1891, no. 7, pp. 74–75; Dec. 25, 1891, no. 52, pp. 614 ff.; Aug. 3, 1894, no. 31, p. 366; Dec. 20, 1901, no. 51, p. 606.

8. Ismar Schorsch, *Jewish Reactions to German Anti-Semitism, 1870–1914*, pp. 24 ff.

9. Ibid., p. 42.

10. *AZJ*, Apr. 5, 1895, no. 14, p. 161.

11. For a general survey of the political views of Jews in Germany after 1870, see Peter Pulzer, "Die jüdische Beteiligung an der Politik," pp. 143–239; Jacob Toury, *Die politischen Orientierungen der Juden in Deutschland*, pp. 131 ff.

12. *AZJ*, Nov. 30, 1900, no. 48, p. 568.

13. CAHJP, rep. Kn II A II, no. 5, minutes of the meetings of the executive board of the Verband der deutschen Juden on Oct. 15 and Nov. 9, 1910.

14. CAHJP, rep. HAW 866b, fasc. 3, Max Warburg to Aby Warburg, dated Hamburg, Feb. 28, 1913.

15. *Israelit*, Jan. 18, 1906, no. 3, p. 1; Mar. 1, 1906, no. 9, p. 2.

16. Marjorie Lamberti, "The Attempt to Form a Jewish Bloc: Jewish Notables and Politics in Wilhelmian Germany," p. 76; *Mitteilungen*

der Freien Vereinigung für die Interessen des orthodoxen Judentums,
Mar. 1899, no. 11, pp. 3 ff.; July 1901, no. 13, pp. 11 ff.

17. *AZJ*, Feb. 19, 1897, no. 8, p. 85.

18. *AZJ*, Mar. 13, 1891, no. 11, p. 121.

CHAPTER 2

1. *AZJ*, May 30, 1890, no. 20, p. 279.

2. *AZJ*, May 9, 1890, no. 17, p. 239. On the sensitivity that the Jewish Reichstag deputy Ludwig Bamberger felt about being identified with any "Jewish" political action, see Stanley Zucker, "Ludwig Bamberger and the Rise of Anti-Semitism in Germany, 1848–1893," p. 345.

3. *AZJ*, July 22, 1892, no. 30, p. 349.

4. *AZJ*, Aug. 5, 1892, no. 32, p. 374.

5. *AZJ*, Jan. 13, 1893, no. 2, Beilage.

6. *AZJ*, Dec. 23, 1892, no. 52, pp. 614–15.

7. *AZJ*, Jan. 13, 1893, no. 2, p. 14.

8. Anonymous, *Volks- oder Salonjudentum* (Berlin, 1893), p. 9.

9. *Schutzjudentum oder Staatsbürger?* , pp. 7 ff.

10. *AZJ*, Jan. 27, 1893, no. 4, Beilage.

11. CAHJP, rep. Kn II A II, no. 3, Paul Nathan to Dr. Samuel, dated Berlin, Feb. 16, 1893. Dr. Samuel was the chairman of the Königsberg community board.

12. On the founding of the Centralverein, see Arnold Paucker, "Zur Problematik einer jüdischen Abwehrstrategie in der deutschen Gesellschaft," pp. 484 ff.; Paul Rieger, *Ein Vierteljahrhundert im Kampf um das Recht und die Zukunft der deutschen Juden*, pp. 18 ff.; Ismar Schorsch, *Jewish Reactions to German Anti-Semitism, 1870–1914*, pp. 113 ff.

13. *AZJ*, Mar. 31, 1893, no. 13, p. 148.

14. Anonymous, *Volks- oder Salonjudentum*, pp. 5–6.

15. Lamberti, "The Attempt to Form a Jewish Bloc: Jewish Notables and Politics in Wilhelmian Germany," pp. 88 ff.

16. *AZJ*, Mar. 31, 1893, no. 13, p. 149.

17. *AZJ*, May 26, 1893, no. 21, pp. 241–42; June 9, 1893, no. 23, p. 265.

18. Martin Mendelsohn, *Die Pflicht der Selbstverteidigung*, p. 13.

19. Ibid., pp. 8–9.

20. *AZJ*, May 26, 1893, no. 21, p. 242. See also *IDR*, July 1895, pp. 5–6.

21. *IDR*, Nov. 1895, p. 226.

22. *IDR*, Mar. 1896, p. 170.

23. *AZJ*, Feb. 2, 1894, no. 5, p. 53; *IDR*, Mar. 1896, p. 170.

24. Fritz Auerbach, *Der Antisemitismus und das freisinnige Judentum*, pp. 14–15; anonymous, *Ein Wort an die deutschen Staatsbürger jüdischen Glaubens* (Mainz, 1896), pp. 6–9.

25. *AZJ*, Oct. 29, 1897, no. 44, p. 523.

26. Eugen Fuchs, *Um Deutschtum und Judentum*, pp. 91–92.

27. Ibid., pp. 269–70; see also *IDR*, Apr. 1906, p. 222.

28. CAHJP, rep. INV 124, minutes of the executive board meeting of the Centralverein on June 1, 1896.

29. Ibid., minutes of the board meeting on Mar. 1, 1987.

30. For a biographical portrait of Horwitz, see Fuchs, *Um Deutschtum und Judentum*, pp. 160 ff. A thumbnail sketch of Fuchs was published in *AZJ*, Aug. 2, 1912, no. 31, p. 366.

31. Fuchs, *Um Deutschtum und Judentum*, pp. 165–66.

32. Ibid., pp. 54–55; *IDR*, May 1895, pp. 206 ff.; Apr. 1897, p. 210; June 1897, p. 323; Jan. 1898, p. 14; Sept. 1902, pp. 473–74.

33. Fuchs, *Um Deutschtum und Judentum*, pp. 171 ff.

34. *IDR*, Feb. 1897, p. 118; Apr. 1901, pp. 236–37.

35. *IDR*, Mar. 1896, p. 170.

36. Richard S. Levy, *The Downfall of the Anti-Semitic Political Parties in Imperial Germany*, pp. 166–67.

37. Fuchs, *Um Deutschtum und Judentum*, p. 68.

38. Eugen Fuchs, *Bericht der Rechtsschutz-Commission über ihre bisherige Tätigkeit*, p. 19.

39. Fuchs, *Um Deutschtum und Judentum*, p. 73.

40. Ibid., p. 57; Mendelsohn, *Die Pflicht*, p. 13.

41. *Israelit*, Feb. 8, 1894, no. 12, pp. 193–94; Mar. 5, 1894, no. 19, p. 338; Aug. 12, 1895, no. 64, pp. 1179–80; Mar. 16, 1896, no. 22, pp. 457 ff.; Mar. 23, 1896, no. 24, p. 497.

42. Fuchs, *Um Deutschtum und Judentum*, p. 56; CAHJP, rep. INV 124, minutes of the board meeting on July 1, 1895. At the time Löwenfeld published his appeal for Jewish self-defense, the *Allgemeine Zeitung des Judentums* reproached him for attacking the Orthodox Jews and dissociated efforts to establish a defense organization from passages in his pamphlet that disparaged the Talmud. See *AZJ*, Jan. 13, 1893, no. 2, p. 13; Jan. 20, 1893, no. 3, p. 25.

43. CAHJP, rep. INV 124, minutes of the board meetings on May 5 and June 10, 1897, and Apr. 18, 1898.

44. *AZJ*, July 9, 1897, no. 28, pp. 326 ff.

45. *AZJ*, Feb. 25, 1898, no. 8, p. 89.

46. CAHJP, rep. M2/1, Rabbi Mose Werner to Rabbi Siegmund Maybaum, dated Munich, June 11, 1897.

47. *IDR*, June 1897, p. 338; July/Aug. 1897, p. 380.

48. CAHJP, rep. INV 124, minutes of the board meeting on June 10, 1897.

49. *IDR*, Oct. 1897, pp. 476 ff.

50. Fuchs, *Um Deutschtum und Judentum*, pp. 227 ff.

51. CAHJP, rep. INV 124, minutes of the board meeting on Sept. 6, 1897.

52. *IDR*, Nov. 1897, p. 533. With many reservations, the central board agreed to the publication of Fuld's attack on Zionism in the journal. Alphonse Levy, the editor, was instructed to tone down Fuld's acerbic remarks about a Zionist pamphlet written by Rabbi Rulf of Memel. See the minutes of the board meeting on Nov. 3, 1897.

53. *IDR*, Jan. 1898, p. 54.

54. CZA, rep. A 142, no. 59/2, Arthur Hantke to Alfred Klee, dated Berlin, Oct. 25, 1897.

55. CZA, rep. A 15, no. VII/1, Moritz Levy to Max Bodenheimer, dated Cologne, Apr. 2, 1897.

56. CZA, rep. 15, no. VII/34, pamphlet no. 1: *Der Zionismus*; pamphlet no. 5: *Was erstrebt der Zionismus?*

57. CAHJP, rep. INV 124, minutes of the board meeting on Feb. 8, 1899.

58. *IDR*, Feb. 1903, p. 187.

59. Schorsch, *Jewish Reactions*, p. 119.

60. CAHJP, rep. INV 124, minutes of the board meeting on Apr. 18, 1898.

61. Ibid., minutes of the board meetings on Nov. 5 and Dec. 3, 1900, and Sept. 18, 1905.

62. *IDR*, Jan. 1905, p. 19; Apr. 1905, p. 240; May 1906, pp. 307, 311.

63. *IDR*, Jan. 1905, p. 19.

64. *IDR*, Apr. 1900, p. 179.

65. *IDR*, Dec. 1901, pp. 652 ff.

66. *IDR*, Feb. 1903, pp. 150 ff; Nov. 1904, p. 629.

67. *IDR*, Nov. 1909, pp. 617 ff.

68. *IDR*, Feb. 1905, p. 112; June 1906, pp. 396 ff.; Sept. 1909, pp. 520 ff.

CHAPTER 3

1. CAHJP, rep. INV 124, minutes of the board meeting on Sept. 6, 1897.

2. *AZJ*, Feb. 11, 1898, no. 6, pp. 61–62.

3. CAHJP, rep. INV 124, minutes of the board meeting on Apr. 18, 1898.

4. *IDR*, Apr. 1898, p. 205.

5. *IDR*, May 1898, p. 235.

6. Ibid., p. 236.

7. Ibid., p. 239.

8. *IDR*, Nov. 1898, p. 572.

9. *AZJ*, Feb. 11, 1898, no. 6, p. 61; *IDR*, May 1898, p. 238.

10. *AZJ*, Apr. 3, 1891, no. 14, pp. 157–58; *IDR*, Aug. 1898, p. 395.

11. *AZJ*, Feb. 25, 1898, no. 8, p. 87; see also *IDR*, Apr. 1899, p. 212.

12. Fuchs, *Um Deutschtum und Judentum*, p. 74; *IDR*, Sept. 1898, p. 424.

13. *IDR*, Sept. 1898, p. 424; Oct. 1898, p. 529.

14. CAHJP, rep. INV 124, minutes of the board meetings on May 11 and June 8, 1898.

15. Ibid., minutes of the board meeting on Sept. 14, 1898.

16. *IDR*, Apr. 1898, p. 206; May 1898, pp. 240, 255.

17. *IDR*, Aug. 1898, p 410.

18. Fuchs, *Um Deutschtum und Judentum*, pp. 66–67.

19. Ibid., pp. 70–71.

20. Ibid , p. 74.

21. Ibid., p. 73.

22. Ibid., pp. 70–71.

23. Ibid., pp. 74 ff.

24. Ibid., p. 67.

25. Ibid., p. 82

26. *Verhandlungen des preussischen Abgeordnetenhauses*, Jan. 31, 1901, p. 927.

27. Ibid., pp. 928–29.

28. Ibid., pp. 933 ff.

29. *BT*, Feb. 2, 1901, nos. 59, 60.

30. *AZJ*, Feb. 1, 1901, no. 5, Beilage.

31. CAHJP, rep. INV 124, minutes of the board meeting on Feb. 4, 1901.

32. *BT*, Feb. 7, 1901, no. 69.

33. *BT*, Feb. 11, 1901, no. 76; *IDR*, Feb. 1901, pp. 91 ff.

34. *Verhandlungen des preuss. Abgeordnetenhauses*, Feb. 8, 1901, p. 1224.

35. Ibid., p. 1227.

36. Ibid., p. 1237.

37. *AZJ*, Feb. 15, 1901, no. 7, p. 78; *IDR*, Feb. 1901, pp. 84, 122.

38. *BT*, Feb. 11, 1901, no. 76.

39. CAHJP, rep. INV 124, minutes of the board meeting on Nov. 4, 1901.

40. Ibid., minutes of the board meeting on Mar. 3, 1902.

41. *AZJ*, Nov. 15, 1901, no. 46, p. 543.

42. *IDR*, Dec. 1901, pp. 652 ff.

43. *IDR*, Jan. 1902, p. 7.

44. CAHJP, rep. INV 124, minutes of the board meeting on Feb. 9, 1903.

45. Ibid., minutes of the board meeting on Apr. 6, 1903.

46. Ibid.

47. *IDR*, May 1903, p. 363.

48. *AZJ*, June 26, 1903, no. 26, p. 302.

49. Konstanze Wegner, *Theodor Barth und die freisinnige Vereinigung,* pp. 64–65.

50. Ibid., pp. 95–96.

51. Thomas Nipperdey, *Die Organisation der deutschen Parteien vor 1918*, pp. 179, 193 ff.

52. *Israelitische Wochenschrift*, Oct. 23, 1903, no. 43, p. 604.

53. *AZJ*, July 3, 1903, no. 27, p. 318.

54. *BT*, June 17, 1903, no. 301; *AZJ*, June 26, 1903, no. 26, p. 301.

55. On Julius Moses' election agitation for the Social Democrats, see *Israelitisches Familienblatt*, Apr. 16, 1903, no. 16, p. 1.

56. *AZJ*, June 26, 1903, no. 26, p. 301.

57. *BT*, June 20, 1903, no. 308.

58. Wegner, *Theodor Barth*, pp. 115 ff.

59. *IDR*, Aug. 1903, p. 459.

60. *BT*, June 17, 1903, no. 301; June 20, 1903, no. 307; July 3, 1903, no. 332.

61. *Israelitisches Familienblatt*, Apr. 16, 1903, no. 16, p. 1.

62. *AZJ*, June 26, 1903, no. 26, p. 301.

63. *IDR*, Aug. 1903, p. 459.

64. CAHJP, rep. INV 124, minutes of the board meeting on Sept. 10, 1903.

65. *IDR*, Dec. 1903, p. 709.

66. CAHJP, rep. INV 124, minutes of the board meeting on Nov. 2, 1903.

67. Ibid., minutes of the board meeting on Dec. 7, 1903.

68. *AZJ*, Sept. 11, 1903, no. 37, p. 436.

69. *BT*, Sept. 27, 1903, no. 491.

70. *BT*, Oct. 7, 1903, no. 509.

71. Ibid., no. 510.

72. *BT*, Oct. 8, 1903, no. 512.

73. *AZJ*, Oct. 16, 1903, no. 42, p. 494.

74. Ibid., p. 494.

75. For reports on the campaigning of the National Socials in Prussian Hesse, see *Hessische Landeszeitung*, May 10, 1903, no. 109; May 12, 1903, no. 110; May 24, 1903, no. 120; June 16, 1903, no. 138.

76. Ibid., June 23, 1903, no. 144; June 24, 1903, no. 145.

77. *IDR*, Aug. 1903, p. 507.

78. *IDR*, Nov. 1903, pp. 639 ff.

79. Ibid., p. 623.

80. Ibid., pp. 627–28.

81. Ibid., pp. 629–31.

82. Ibid., pp. 636–38.

83. Ibid., p. 633.

84. Ibid., p. 634.

85. *Israelitische Wochenschrift*, Oct. 23, 1903, no. 43, p. 604.

86. Of the various reports on the debate following Sonnenfeld's speech, the most complete appears in the *AZJ*, Oct. 23, 1903, no. 43, p. 510.

87. Ibid., p. 510.

88. CAHJP, rep. INV 124, minutes of the board meeting on Mar. 7, 1904, at which Horwitz gave a report on the runoff election.

89. *Die Nation*, Feb. 20, 1904, no. 21, p. 322.

90. *AZJ*, Feb. 26, 1904, no. 9, Beilage.

91. *BT*, Feb. 25, 1904, no. 102.

92. *BT*, Mar. 2, 1904, no. 113; *MVAA*, Mar. 3, 1904, no. 9, p. 67.

93. *MVAA*, Mar. 3, 1904, no. 9, p. 67.

94. *BT*, Mar. 2, 1904, no. 113.

95. *BT*, Mar. 5, 1904, no. 119; Mar. 12, 1904, no. 132.

96. *Die Nation*, Mar. 5, 1904, no. 25, p. 354.

97. *AZJ*, Mar. 11, 1904, no. 11, p. 123.

98. *GA*, Feb. 29, 1904, no. 9.

99. CAHJP, rep. INV 124, minutes of the board meeting on Mar. 7, 1904.

100. *IDR*, Mar. 1904, pp. 126 ff.

101. Ibid., p. 246.

102. Ibid., pp. 246–47.

103. Ibid., p. 247.

104. For an evaluation of the performance of the anti-Semites in the Reichstag, see Richard S. Levy, *The Downfall of the Anti-Semitic Political Parties in Imperial Germany*, pp. 166 ff.

105. *IDR*, Mar. 1901, pp. 126–27, 176.

106. Ibid., pp. 132–33.

107. *IDR*, Dec. 1903, pp. 709–10.

108. Ibid., pp. 709–10.

109. BK, Nachlass Richard Roesicke, no. 5, stenciled confidential memorandum to the Progressive Union deputies in the Reichstag and Prussian parliament.

110. *BT*, Aug. 6, 1903, no. 394.

111. *BT*, Nov. 13, 1903, no. 578.

112. *BT*, Nov. 17, 1903, no. 586; Oct. 12, 1903, no. 591.

113. *BT*, Oct. 12, 1903, nos. 518, 519.

114. *IDR*, Jan. 1904, p. 2.

115. *IDR*, Apr. 1905, p. 204.

116. CAHJP, rep. INV 124, minutes of the board's meeting on Feb. 1, 1904.

117. *Verhandlungen des Reichstages*, Mar. 5, 1904, pp. 1577 ff.

118. *Verhandlungen des preuss. Abgeordnetenhauses*, Jan. 30, 1905, pp. 9235 ff.; Mar. 18, 1905, pp. 11892 ff.

119. *IDR*, Apr. 1905, pp. 200, 214.

120. *IDR*, Feb. 1905, p. 73.

121. Lamberti, "The Attempt to Form a Jewish Bloc: Jewish Notables and Politics in Wilhelmian Germany," p. 84.

122. CAJHP, rep. Kn II A II, no. 4, minutes of the meeting of the Verband's executive committee on May 29, 1904. See also the minutes of the Centralverein's board meetings on June 8, 1903, and Jan. 4, 1904.

CHAPTER 4

1. George Dunlap Crothers, *The German Elections of 1907*, pp. 53, 97.

2. *BT*, Dec. 18, 1906, no. 641; Dec. 22, 1906, no. 649.

3. Crothers, *German Elections*, pp. 156 ff.; Ludwig Elm, *Zwischen Fortschritt und Reaktion: Geschichte der Parteien der liberalen Bourgeoisie in Deutschland 1893–1918*, pp. 176, 180.

4. Crothers, *German Elections*, p. 112; Konstanze Wegner, *Theodor Barth und die freisinnige Vereinigung*, pp. 128–29.

5. Crothers, *German Elections*, p. 161; Elm, *Zwischen Fortschritt und Reaktion*, p. 178.

6. *AZJ*, Dec. 14, 1906, no. 50, p. 589.

7. Crothers, *German Elections*, pp. 249 ff.

8. *BT*, Jan. 7, 1907, no. 10.

9. *BT*, Jan. 19, 1907, no. 34; Jan. 23, 1907, no. 41.

10. *IDR*, Feb. 1907, p. 108.

11. Ibid., p. 154.

12. *AZJ*, Jan. 4, 1907, no. 1, p. 1.

13. *IDR*, Jan. 1907, p. 1; see also Feb. 1907, p. 103.

14. *AZJ*, Jan. 4, 1907, no. 1, p. 1; *IDR*, Jan. 1907, pp. 1–2.

14. Crothers, *German Elections,* pp. 121 ff.

16. *IDR*, Feb. 1907, p. 106.

17. Ibid., p. 105.

18. *IDR*, Mar. 1907, p. 146.

19. Ibid., pp. 175–76.

20. CZA, rep. A 11, no. 32/20/3, Carl Kassel to Arthur Hantke, three letters. Two are dated Posen, Dec. 4, 1906, and one is dated Posen, Dec. 31, 1906.

21. See Kassel's article, "Die Stellung der deutschen Juden in Politik," *Die Welt,* Oct. 12, 1906, no. 41, pp. 10–12. For Kassel's views on the disadvantages of the Jewish alignment with the Progressives in Posen, see his article in *GA*, Jan. 5, 1908, no. 1.

22. *Die Welt,* Oct. 19, 1906, no. 42, pp. 9 ff.

23. *IDR*, Apr. 1901, pp. 188 ff.; *AZJ*, Apr. 29, 1898, no. 17, p. 196; Dec. 8, 1899, no. 49, p. 580. On the activities of the Deutscher Ostmark Verein, see Piotr S. Wandycz, *The Lands of Partitioned Poland, 1795–1918,* pp. 284–85.

24. *IDR*, Feb. 1901, pp. 86–87; Feb. 1908, pp. 73 ff.

25. *IDR*, Oct. 1903, pp. 577–78; Jan. 1905, p. 27; Nov. 1905, p. 618.

26. CZA, rep. A 11, no. 32/20/3, Carl Kassel to Arthur Hantke, dated Posen, Dec. 31, 1906.

27. Jacob Toury's account of Kassel's negotiations with the Centralverein's agents is not discerning. He accepts Kassel's one-sided explanation for the failure of the talks and does not explore other possible reasons for the unwillingness of Horwitz and Fuchs to promote Kassel's project. See Toury, *Die politischen Orientierungen der Juden in Deutschland,* pp. 292–93.

28. *IDR*, Feb. 1907, p. 129.

29. *IDR*, Apr. 1907, pp. 236–37; Fuchs, *Um Deutschtum und Judentum,* p. 132; *Israelitisches Familienblatt,* June 14, 1906, no. 24, p. 2.

30. *IDR*, Dec. 1903, p. 710; July/Aug. 1908, p. 456.

31. *Israelitisches Familienblatt,* June 21, 1906, no. 25, p. 2; *AZJ*, Oct. 5, 1906, no. 40, p. 471; CZA, rep. A 15, no. VII/47, Max Bodenheimer to Adolf Friedemann, dated Cologne, Nov. 3, 1906.

32. CZA, rep. A 8, no. 92/1, Arthur Hantke to Adolf Friedemann, dated Berlin, Nov. 5, 1906.

33. *Die Welt,* Oct. 26, 1906, no. 43, pp. 6–7.

34. CZA, rep. A 8, no. 59/2, Nahum Sokolow to Adolf Friedemann, dated Cologne, Nov. 14, 1906.
35. CZA, rep. A 15, no. VII/47, Max Bodenheimer to Hermann
Jonas, dated Cologne, Jan. 12, 1907, copy.
36. *Jüdische Rundschau*, Mar. 17, 1905, no. 11, pp. 115, 119; Mar.
31, 1905, no. 13, p. 137.
37. *IDR*, Mar. 1907, p. 176.
38. Ibid., p. 145.
39. Crothers, *German Elections*, p. 174.
40. Ibid., pp. 173-74; *Hessische Landeszeitung*, Jan. 30, 1907, no.
25.
41. NSt, Nachlass Karl Schrader, no. 3, Disposition für Wahlreden.
42. *IDR*, Mar. 1907, p. 145.
43. Ibid., pp. 143-44.
44. *Hessische Landeszeitung*, Feb. 10, 1907, no. 35.
45. *MVAA*, Feb. 27, 1907, no. 9, p. 68.
46. *MVAA*, Feb. 6, 1907, no. 6, p. 41.
47. *MVAA*, Mar. 6, 1907, no. 10, p. 74. The two committee members, Weiss and Winter, were asked by Barth to resign. On the voting
of the Progressives in the election, see also *MVAA*, Jan. 23, 1907,
no. 4, pp. 25-26; Feb. 27, 1907, no. 9, pp. 67 ff.
48. Quoted from the *Weser-Zeitung*, a Progressive newspaper in
Bremen, in *Schulthess' Europäischer Geschichtskalender*, 1907, p. 17.
49. *IDR*, Mar. 1907, p. 142.
50. Ibid., p. 143.
51. Ibid., pp. 145-46.
52. *IDR*, Apr. 1907, p. 211.
53. Ibid., p. 212.
54. Ibid., p. 213.
55. *IDR*, Mar. 1907, p. 142.
56. GSt, rep. 6 B, *Landkreis* Meseritz, no. 39, the *Landrat*'s report
to the *Regierungspräsident* in Posen, dated Meseritz, Feb. 21, 1907.
He reported that the Progressive voters made "no attempt to disrupt
the solidarity of the German elements" and estimated that about 98
Jewish voters supported the Conservative party nominee to victory
over the Polish Catholic candidate.
57. *IDR*, Apr. 1907, p. 212.
58. Ibid., p. 214.
59. Ibid., p. 184.
60. Ibid., p. 213. For an extensive discussion of the School Law of
1906, see chap. 7.
61. Ibid., pp. 211-12.

62. *GA*, Feb. 24, 1907, no. 8; Mar. 3, 1907, no. 9; Mar. 17, 1907, no. 11; *Israelitisches Familienblatt*, Apr. 11, 1907, no. 15, p. 1.

63. *Die Welt*, Feb. 8, 1907, no. 6, p. 4.

64. *IDR*, Apr. 1907, pp. 236–37, 256; July/Aug. 1907, pp. 432–33; *AZJ*, Apr. 5, 1907, no. 14, p. 162.

65. CZA, rep. A 11, no. 32/14, two letters, Berthold Feiwel to Arthur Hantke, both dated Cologne, Mar. 10, 1907. Feiwel made specific references to the content of Hantke's letter.

66. *Die Welt*, Feb. 22, 1907, no. 8, p. 10.

67. *IDR*, Apr. 1907, p. 211.

68. Ibid., pp. 234–36.

69. *BT*, Dec. 16, 1906, no. 638; Dec. 20, 1906, no. 645.

70. *IDR*, May 1907, pp. 313–14. See also Cohn's article in *AZJ*, Apr. 5, 1907, no. 14, pp. 162 ff.

71. *IDR*, Apr. 1907, pp. 250, 254; June 1907, p. 356; July/Aug. 1907, p. 399.

72. *IDR*, Apr. 1907, p. 233.

73. Ibid., pp. 229–30.

74. *Der siebente Parteitag der Freisinnigen Volkspartei Berlin, 12.- 16. September 1907* (Berlin, 1907), p. 105.

75. *IDR*, Oct. 1907, pp. 570–71.

76. Crothers, *German Elections*, pp. 229 ff.; Elm, *Zwischen Fortschritt und Reaktion*, pp. 191 ff.; Beverly Heckart, *From Bassermann to Bebel: The Grand Bloc's Quest for Reform in the Kaiserreich*, pp. 53 ff.

77. *Verhandlungen des preussischen Abgeordnetenhauses*, Feb. 19, 1907, pp. 993, 1019.

78. *IDR*, June 1907, p. 354.

79. *IDR*, Nov. 1907, pp. 628–29.

80. Ibid., p. 635.

81. *IDR*, Jan. 1908, p. 23.

82. *IDR*, Feb. 1908, p. 93.

83. *Verhandlungen des preuss. Abgeordnetenhauses*, Feb. 13, 1908, p. 2099.

84. *IDR*, Mar. 1908, p. 161; Dec. 1908, pp. 694–97.

85. *MVAA*, Jan. 29, 1908, no. 5, p. 33.

86. *MVAA*, Mar. 11, 1908, no. 11, pp. 81 ff.; Mar. 18, 1908, no. 12, p. 94; May 13, 1908, no. 20, p. 153.

87. *GA*, Jan. 26, 1908, no. 4; Feb. 2, 1908, no. 5; Feb. 9, 1908, no. 6.

88. *AZJ*, Jan. 31, 1908, no. 5, p. 51.

89. For an affirmation of confidence in the Progressives during

their participation in the Bülow bloc, see *AZJ*, Dec. 13, 1907, no. 50, p. 589; Dec. 27, 1907, no. 52, p. 613.

90. *IDR*, June 1907, p. 354.

91. *AZJ*, Mar. 20, 1908, no. 12, p. 137.

92. Ibid., p. 137.

CHAPTER 5

1. Ludwig Elm, *Zwischen Fortschritt und Reaktion*, pp. 197–98; Beverly Heckart, *From Bassermann to Bebel*, pp. 65 ff.

2. Elm, *Zwischen Fortschritt und Reaktion*, p. 205; Konstanze Wegner, *Theodor Barth*, p. 134.

3. *IDR*, Apr. 1908, p. 201.

4. *IDR*, May 1908, p. 349.

5. Ibid., p. 351.

6. *BT*, May 29, 1908, no. 271.

7. *BT*, Feb. 4, 1907, no. 62.

8. *BT*, Jan. 10, 1907, no. 17; Jan. 18, 1907, no. 32.

9. *BT*, Jan. 23, 1907, no. 41.

10. *BT*, Jan. 25, 1907, no. 45.

11. *IDR*, Oct. 1906, p. 561.

12. *IDR*, June 1908, p. 350.

13. *Die Welt*, Apr. 10, 1908, no. 15, pp. 2–3.

14. Ibid., May 29, 1908, no. 21, p. 5.

15. Ibid., p. 5.

16. *GA*, May 3, 1908, no. 18.

17. CZA, rep. A 102, no. 12/2.

18. *IDR*, Apr. 1908, pp. 290 ff.

19. Ibid., p. 292; July/Aug. 1908, p. 440.

20. *GA*, Apr. 26, 1908, no. 17.

21. NSt, Nachlass Karl Schrader, rep. 240 N, III, no. 2, stenciled minutes of the meeting of the executive committee of the Progressive Union, 1905. Nathan pledged a contribution of 3,000 marks.

22. Ibid., no. 3, stenciled minutes of the meeting of the executive committee of the Progressive Union on Oct. 8, 1906.

23. Ibid., no. 6, stenciled minutes of the meeting of the executive committee of the Progressive Union on Jan. 13, 1908.

24. Ibid., no. 6, Paul Nathan to Karl Schrader, dated Berlin, Mar. 20, 1908.

25. Bernfeld's article was reprinted in the *GA*, Mar. 17, 1907, no. 11.

26. Reprinted from the *Israelitisches Gemeindeblatt* in the *GA*, Jan. 13, 1907, no. 2.

27. Reprinted in the *GA*, Mar. 22, 1908, no. 12.

28. For a report of the party's third congress in Frankfurt, see *BT*, Apr. 22, 1908, no. 203.

29. *BT*, May 18, 1908, no. 251.

30. *BT*, May 7, 1908, no. 231; May 18, 1908, no. 251.

31. *BT*, May 4, 1908, no. 226.

32. *BT*, Apr. 23, 1908, no. 205; Apr. 24, 1908, no. 207.

33. Werner T. Angress, "Prussia's Army and the Jewish Reserve Officer Controversy before World War I," pp. 32 ff. For the Verband's documentary evidence, see *Wie wird im preussischen Herr die Beförderung von Juden zu Reserveoffizieren vereitelt? Beispielfälle, gesammelt vom Verband der deutschen Juden* (Berlin, 1911).

34. *Verhandlungen des Reichstages*, Mar. 30, 1908, pp. 4430 ff.

35. Ibid., p. 4442.

36. *IDR*, May 1908, pp. 266-67.

37. *IDR*, Mar. 1908, p. 156.

38. NSt, Nachlass Karl Schrader, rep. 240 N, IV, no. 5, Martin Philippson to Schrader, dated Berlin, June 12, 1909.

39. *Jüdische Rundschau*, Apr. 10, 1908, no. 15, p. 127.

40. *Die Welt*, June 5, 1908, no. 22, pp. 7-8.

41. *BT*, May 6, 1908, no. 230.

42. *BT*, May 29, 1908, no. 271.

43. *BT*, June 27, 1908, nos. 322, 323; Peter Pistorius, *Rudolf Breitscheid 1874-1944. Ein biographischer Beitrag zur deutschen Parteigeschichte*, pp. 60-63.

44. *BT*, June 12, 1908, no. 294.

45. *BT*, June 16, 1908, no. 301.

46. *GA*, June 14, 1908, no. 24.

47. *BT*, May 2, 1908, no. 223; May 6, 1908, no. 229.

48. *BT*, May 25, 1908, no. 264; May 29, 1908, no. 271.

49. *GA*, May 17, 1908, no. 20.

50. *BT*, June 19, 1908, no. 308; June 20, 1908, no. 309.

51. *BT*, June 26, 1908, no. 320.

52. *IDR*, July/Aug. 1908, p. 439.

53. Ibid., pp. 440-41, 455.

54. Heckart, *From Bassermann to Bebel*, p. 55; Wegner, *Theodor Barth*, pp. 64-66, 129-30.

55. *AZJ*, May 15, 1908, no. 20, p. 229.

56. *AZJ*, July 3, 1908, no. 27, p. 313.

57. *AZJ*, Feb. 4, 1910, no. 5, pp. 49-50.

58. *AZJ*, Dec. 11, 1908, no. 50, p. 592; *IDR*, Jan. 1909, pp. 1 ff.

59. *BT*, Oct. 20, 1908, no. 535; *GA*, Oct. 4, 1908, no. 40.

60. *BT*, Nov. 7, 1908, no. 570.

61. *BT*, Nov. 14, 1908, no. 583; Nov. 30, 1908, no. 609; Dec. 3, 1908, no. 615.

62. *IDR*, Jan. 1909, pp. 2-3.

63. CZA, rep. A 11, no. 25, Paul Nathan to Arthur Hantke, dated Berlin, Sept. 25, 1908. Heymann had informed Nathan of Zionist plans to protest Mugdan's nomination at a public demonstration to be held in October. Nathan was asked to speak and declined. He did not think that such a demonstration would be beneficial and predicted that agitation against Mugdan would backfire and prompt Christians to vote for him.

64. *GA*, Dec. 13, 1908, no. 50.

65. *GA*, Sept. 13, 1908, no. 37; Sept. 20, 1908, no. 38; Oct. 18, 1908, no. 42.

66. *GA*, Dec. 13, 1908, no. 50; Dec. 27, 1908, no. 52.

67. CAHJP, rep. INV 124, minutes of the board meeting on Jan. 4, 1904.

68. *GA*, Dec. 13, 1908, no. 50.

69. *Jüdisches Volksblatt*, Dec. 18, 1908, no. 51, p. 496. The *Jüdisches Volksblatt*, which was by no means a mouthpiece of the Centralverein, reported that Jews in the Democratic Union and the Zionist movement, led by Julius Moses, wanted to create dissension in the defense organization. They were demanding that the central board call a special assembly at which they intended to agitate for Lövinson's dismissal. If they were defeated, they intended to split the Centralverein by leading a mass secession out of it.

70. *GA*, Nov. 29, 1908, no. 48; Dec. 13, 1908, no. 50.

71. *GA*, Mar. 7, 1909, no. 10. See L. Stein's letter. Stein wrote that Fuchs and Wreschner, another member of the central board, expressed disapproval of Lövinson's conduct in private discussions.

72. *Israelitisches Familienblatt*, Mar. 11, 1909, no. 10, p. 1. See Horwitz's letter to the editor.

73. *IDR*, Jan. 1909, pp. 2-3.

74. *IDR*, Apr. 1906, pp. 233 ff.; June 1906, pp. 394 ff.; Apr. 1907, pp. 221 ff.; May 1907, pp. 270 ff.; July/Aug. 1908, pp. 395 ff.

75. *IDR*, July/Aug. 1908, p. 396; *AZJ*, Dec. 11, 1908, no. 50, p. 592.

76. *IDR*, Jan. 1909, p. 5.

77. Ibid., p. 46; Feb. 1909, pp. 123 ff.

78. *IDR*, Jan. 1909, p. 47.

79. *GA*, Feb. 28, 1909, no. 9; *IDR*, Mar./Apr. 1909, p. 237.

80. *IDR*, Mar./Apr. 1909, p. 136.

81. Ibid., p. 201.

82. Ibid., p. 137.

83. Ibid., p. 212.

84. Ibid., p. 138.

85. Ibid., p. 219.

86. Ibid., pp. 207–08.

87. Ibid., pp. 214–15.

88. Ibid., p. 255.

89. *GA*, Feb. 28, 1909, no. 9.

90. *GA*, Feb. 21, 1909, no. 8. Rabbi Goldmann's entire speech was published in this issue.

91. *IDR*, Mar./Apr. 1909, p. 202.

92. Ibid., p. 261.

93. Ibid., pp. 215–16.

94. *IDR*, Dec. 1910, p. 813.

95. *IDR*, Apr. 1911, p. 183.

96. *AZJ*, June 12, 1908, no. 24, p. 278.

97. *Israelitisches Wochenblatt*, Apr. 14, 1911, no. 16, pp. 36, 41.

98. *IDR*, Mar. 1911, p. 130.

99. *IDR*, May 1911, p. 253. The article in the *Weser-Zeitung* was quoted in this issue.

100. Ibid., p. 255.

101. *IDR*, Oct. 1912, p. 466.

102. *IDR*, Dec. 1912, p. 576.

103. *Israelitisches Gemeindeblatt*, Oct. 25, 1912, no. 43, p. 455.

104. *BT*, Oct. 3, 1912, no. 504.

105. CZA, rep. A 15, no. VII/25, minutes of the meeting of the executive committee of the German Zionist Organization in Berlin on Oct. 1, 1912.

106. *Israelitisches Gemeindeblatt*, Apr. 21, 1911, no. 16, p. 180; *Israelitisches Wochenblatt*, Apr. 14, 1911, no. 16, p. 36; *Jüdisches Volksblatt*, July 28, 1911, no. 30, p. 302.

107. CZA, rep. A 15, no. VII/25, minutes of the meeting of the Zionist executive committee on Oct. 1, 1912.

108. *Jüdische Rundschau*, Nov. 1, 1912, no. 44, p. 419; Nov. 8, 1912, no. 45, p. 431; Nov. 22, 1912, no. 47, p. 455.

109. *Jüdische Rundschau*, Oct. 11, 1912, no. 41, p. 390.

110. *IDR*, Dec. 1911, pp. 679–80.

111. CZA, rep. A 15, no. VII/25, minutes of the conference of the Zionist executive committee with Fuchs, Horwitz, and Holländer on Dec. 18, 1912.

112. Gerhard Masur, *Imperial Berlin*, p. 108.

113. On the attitudes of liberal Protestants on the question of Jew-

ish integration into German society, see Uriel Tal, *Christians and Jews in Germany: Politics and Ideology in the Second Reich, 1870–1914*.

CHAPTER 6

1. *MVAA*, Apr. 24, 1897, no. 17, p. 136; *IDR*, Sept. 1900, pp. 438 ff.; *AZJ*, Oct. 18, 1901, no. 42, pp. 496–97.

2. *IDR*, June/July 1902, pp. 352 ff.; June 1909, pp. 341 ff.; Oct. 1910, pp. 714 ff.; Adolph Asch and Johanna Philippson, "Self-Defence at the Turn of the Century: the Emergence of the K.C."

3. *IDR*, Sept. 1900, pp. 439 ff.; Mar. 1907, pp. 148 ff.

4. *K.C. Blätter*, Feb. 1, 1911, no. 5, p. 70.

5. *IDR*, Jan. 1907, p. 65; *AZJ*, Nov. 23, 1900, no. 47, pp. 559–60.

6. *IDR*, Mar. 1907, p. 148; *K.C. Blätter*, Oct. 1, 1911, no. 1, p. 4.

7. *IDR*, Aug. 1900, p. 382; see also Mar. 1900, p. 161.

8. *IDR*, Mar./Apr. 1909, p. 229. For an account of Holländer's defense activities in Bavaria, see *IDR*, Apr. 1905, pp. 239–40. Holländer, who had studied with the economist Lujo Brentano in Munich, wrote in 1907 a penetrating sociological analysis of anti-Semitism in Germany. Unlike contemporaries who idealized the history of the Jewish Emancipation, Holländer had an acute critical insight into the failure of the emancipation movement of 1815–48 and grasped the hesitant and ambivalent behavior and inconsistent policies of this generation of German liberals on the question of civil equality for the Jews. See Holländer's "Die sozialen Voraussetzungen der antisemitischen Bewegung in Deutschland," *IDR*, Sept. 1907, pp. 479ff.

9. *IDR*, Oct. 1909, pp. 546–47; Dec. 1910, pp. 772–73.

10. *IDR*, July/Aug. 1911, p. 377; *K.C. Blätter*, June 1, 1913, no. 9, p. 188.

11. *IDR*, Dec. 1910, p. 775; see also Oct. 1909, p. 546.

12. CAHJP, rep. Da 749, Horwitz to Philipp Simson, dated Berlin, Dec. 1, 1906; Simson's reply, dated Danzig, Dec. 14, 1906; Alphonse Levy to Simson, dated Berlin, Dec. 18, 1906.

13. CAHJP, rep. INV 124, minutes of the board meeting on Sept. 18, 1905.

14. *IDR*, Apr. 1907, pp. 207 ff.; Mar./Apr. 1909, pp. 152 ff.

15. CAHJP, rep. Da 749, statutes of the Centralverein chapters.

16. *IDR*, Mar./Apr. 1909, pp. 196 ff.

17. *IDR*, Apr. 1911, pp. 185 ff.

18. *Jüdisches Volksblatt*, Jan. 6, 1906, no. 1, p. 3.

19. Ibid., p. 3; Jan. 26, 1906, no. 4, p. 40.

20. Schach's article was reprinted in *GA*, Oct. 18, 1908, no. 42; see also *Israelitisches Wochenblatt*, Oct. 20, 1911, no. 43, p. 473; November 17, 1911, no. 47, p. 533.

21. *IDR*, Jan. 1912, p. 3; see also Mar. 1911, p. 119.

22. *IDR*, Mar./Apr. 1909, p. 159.

23. *AZJ*, Mar. 3, 1911. no. 9, Beilage.

24. *IDR*, Dec. 1910, p. 773.

25. *IDR*, Jan. 1912, pp. 8–9.

26. *IDR*, June 1911, p. 314.

27. Ibid., p. 322.

28. CAHJP, rep. Kn II A II, no. 5, minutes of the Verband's executive committee meetings on May 29 and Dec. 27, 1904, at which the question of the division of the jurisdictional areas of the two interest groups was discussed.

29. Ibid., no. 6, minutes of the meeting of the Verband's executive committee on Apr. 22, 1911.

30. Ibid., minutes of the meeting of the Verband's executive committee on Nov. 25, 1911.

31. *IDR*, June 1909, p. 384; Jan. 1910, pp. 10, 15; Dec. 1911, p. 696.

32. *IDR*, Jan. 1912, pp. 1 ff.

33. *Israelitisches Wochenblatt*, Oct. 25, 1912, no. 43.

34. *IDR*, Jan. 1910, p. 13; Jan. 1911, pp. 12–13.

35. *IDR*, Apr. 1911, p. 183.

36. *IDR*, Mar. 1910, pp. 143–44; Nov. 1910, p. 732.

37. *IDR*, Jan. 1910, p. 23; Jan. 1911, p. 24.

38. *IDR*, Mar. 1910, p. 151. See also Jan. 1910, pp. 18–19; Jan. 1911, pp. 29–30.

39. *IDR*, Feb. 1911, p. 90.

40. *IDR*, Mar. 1912, p. 150; Apr. 1912, p. 165.

41. *IDR*, Jan. 1911, p. 14.

42. *IDR*, Feb. 1911, p. 97.

43. *IDR*, Apr. 1912, p. 176.

44. Richard S. Levy, *The Downfall of the Anti-Semitic Parties in Imperial Germany*, p. 247.

45. *IDR*, Apr. 1911, p. 177.

46. *IDR*, Feb. 1912, p. 84.

47. *IDR*, Apr. 1911, p. 215.

48. *IDR*, Jan. 1912, p. 30.

49. *IDR*, Nov. 1909, p. 636.

50. *IDR*, Feb. 1910, pp. 90–91.

51. CAHJP, rep. Kn II A II, no. 5, minutes of the meetings of the

Verband's executive committee on Jan. 27, 1909, and Jan. 23 and Feb. 12, 1910.

52. *Verhandlungen des Reichstages*, Feb. 10, 1910, pp. 1103 ff.

53. CAHJP, rep. Kn II A II, no. 5, minutes of the meeting of the Verband's executive committee on Dec. 21, 1910.

54. *IDR*, Nov. 1911, p. 643.

55. *IDR*, Jan. 1910, p. 13; *Jüdisches Volksblatt*, Nov. 18, 1910, no. 46, p. 449; *Israelitisches Gemeindeblatt*, Apr. 7, 1911, no. 14, p. 153.

56. *IDR*, Mar. 1910, pp. 143-44; Oct. 1910, p. 675.

57. *IDR*, Mar. 1911, p. 155.

58. Jürgen Bertram, *Die Wahlen zum Deutschen Reichstag vom Jahre 1912*, pp. 67-68.

59. See Otto Wiemer's report on the election in *Der zweite Parteitag der Fortschrittlichen Volkspartei zu Mannheim, 5.-7. Oktober 1912* (Berlin, 1912), pp. 13-14.

60. *BT*, Jan. 4, 1912, no. 6.

61. Bertram, *Die Wahlen zum Deutschen Reichstag*, pp. 224 ff.

62. *BT*, Jan. 22, 1912, no. 38.

63. *Hessische Landeszeitung*, Jan. 11, 1912, no. 8; Jan. 17, 1912, no. 13.

64. *BT*, Jan. 16, 1912, no. 28.

65. *BT*, Jan. 17, 1912, no. 29.

66. *BT*, Jan. 20, 1912, no. 35.

67. *BT*, Jan. 26, 1912, no. 46.

68. *BT*, Jan. 16, 1912, no. 28; Jan. 18, 1912, no. 31.

69. *BT*, Jan. 17, 1912, no. 29.

70. *BT*, Jan. 17, 1912, no. 30.

71. *BT*, Jan. 23, 1912, no. 41.

72. *IDR*, Mar. 1912, p. 133.

73. *IDR*, Feb. 1912, p. 84.

74. *AZJ*, Mar. 22, 1912, no. 12, p. 138.

75. *IDR*, Mar. 1912, p. 122.

CHAPTER 7

1. Richard H. Samuel and R. Hinton Thomas, *Education and Society in Modern Germany*, pp. 91-92.

2. Ismar Freund, *Die Rechtsstellung der Juden im preussischen Volksschulrecht*, pp. 11 ff.

3. Ibid., pp. 194 ff.

4. Ibid., pp. 221 ff.

5. Ibid., p. 225.

6. Ibid., p. 228.

7. Karl Schneider and Alwin Petersilie, *Die öffentlichen Volksschulen des preussischen Staates im Jahre 1891*, appendix 4.

8. Ibid., p. 157; Arthur Ruppin and Jakob Thon, *Das Anteil der Juden am Unterrichtswesen in Preussen*, p. 29.

9. Jakob Thon, *Die jüdischen Gemeinden und Vereine in Deutschland*, p. 5.

10. Jakob Thon, "Besteuerungs- und Finanzverhältnisse der jüdischen Gemeinden in Deutschland," *Zeitschrift für Demographie und Statistik der Juden* 3 (1907): 19, 22–23.

11. Freund, *Die Rechtsstellung der Juden*, p. 183.

12. Schneider and Petersilie, *Die öffentlichen Volksschulen*, p. 157.

13. For the school bill of 1892, see the *Anlagen* to the *Verhandlungen des preuss. Abgeordnetenhauses* (1892), pp. 882–83.

14. *AZJ*, Jan. 22, 1892, no. 4, p. 37; Jan. 29, 1892, no. 5, pp. 50–51; Feb. 5, 1892, no. 6, pp. 61–63.

15. *AZJ*, Jan. 29, 1892, no. 5, p. 51.

16. *Verhandlungen des preuss. Abgeordnetenhauses*, Mar. 7, 1892, pp. 706–07.

17. *AZJ*, Feb. 26, 1892, no. 9, pp. 98–100.

18. Kurt Richter, *Der Kampf um den Schulgesetzentwurf des Grafen Zedlitz-Trützschler vom Jahre 1892*, pp. 36 ff., 93.

19. HSt, rep. 166b, no. 4012, Department of School Affairs to Minister of Education, dated Cassel, May 24, 1893.

20. Ibid.

21. Ibid., stenciled circular of the Department of School Affairs to the *Landräte*, dated Cassel, Jan. 31, 1893.

22. Ibid., reports submitted by the *Landräte* in Apr. 1893.

23. Ibid., petition of the *Vorsteheramt der Israeliten* to Department of School Affairs, dated Fulda, Mar. 19, 1893.

24. Ibid., Department of School Affairs to Minister of Education, dated Cassel, Mar. 27, 1893, copy.

25. Ibid., Minister of Education to Department of School Affairs, dated Berlin, Apr. 26, 1893.

26. Ibid., Minister of Education to Department of School Affairs, dated Berlin, July 18, 1893.

27. Ibid., Department of School Affairs to *Landräte*, dated Cassel, June 22, 1893.

28. Ibid., *Vorsteheramt der Israeliten* to Department of School Affairs, dated Marburg, July 18, 1893.

29. Ibid., *Vorsteheramt der Israeliten* to Department of School Affairs, dated Marburg, Aug. 26, 1893; the department's reply, dated Cassel, Sept. 4, 1893.

30. Ibid., petitions from the congregations to the *Landräte* in the counties of Hofgeismar, Rinteln, and Ziegenhain.

31. Ibid., *Vorsteheramt der Israeliten* to Department of School Affairs, dated Marburg, Sept. 19, 1893.

32. Ibid.

33. Ibid., Minister of Education to Department of School Affairs, dated Berlin, May 2, 1894.

34. Ibid., Department of School Affairs to *Landräte*, dated Cassel, Apr. 16, 1894.

35. Ibid., *Landrat* to Department of School Affairs, dated Ziegenhain, Apr. 24, 1894.

36. Marjorie Lamberti, "The Prussian Government and the Jews—Official Behaviour and Policy-Making in the Wilhelminian Era," pp. 5 ff.

37. *Verhandlungen des preuss. Abgeordnetenhauses*, Jan. 26, 1892, pp. 125–26; *Die Nation*, Jan. 16, 1892, no. 16, p. 237; Feb. 6, 1892, no. 19, p. 285.

38. *AZJ*, Nov. 15, 1895, no. 46, p. 541.

39. *AZJ*, Mar. 20, 1896, no. 12, p. 133.

40. *MDIG*, Oct. 1896, no. 44, pp. 11 ff.; *AZJ*, Feb. 7, 1896, no. 6, p. 62; Feb. 19, 1897, no. 8, p. 89; *Mitteilungen des Liberalen Vereins für die Angelegenheiten der jüdischen Gemeinde zu Berlin*, May 1898, no. 4, pp. 3 ff.

41. *MDIG*, Oct. 1896, no. 44, p. 16.

42. *IDR*, Nov. 1896, p. 586.

43. *IDR*, May 1895, pp. 232–33; June 1895, p. 291.

44. *IDR*, Nov. 1896, p. 587.

45. Fuchs, *Um Deutschtum und Judentum*, p. 57.

46. *MDIG*, Oct. 1896, no. 44, p. 11.

47. CAHJP, rep. M 4/1, minutes of the meeting of the executive board of the Rabbinerverband on Dec. 28, 1898, with Rabbi Prager's report of his meeting with Althoff.

48. *Verhandlungen des preuss. Abgeordnetenhauses*, Jan. 26, 1892, pp. 131–33; Jan. 21, 1899, p. 38.

49. *Die Nation*, Jan. 23, 1892, pp. 252 ff.; Jan. 30, 1892, p. 269.

50. *MVAA*, Oct. 26, 1904, no. 43, p. 340.

51. *AZJ*, May 2, 1890, no. 16, p. 227; June 19, 1891, no. 25, pp. 290–91.

52. *AZJ*, June 19, 1891, no. 25, p. 291.

53. *IDR*, June/July 1901, pp. 326 ff.; *Mitteilungen des Liberalen Vereins*, Jan. 1897, no. 1, p. 9.

54. *IDR*, June/July 1901, p. 329.

55. *AZJ*, Feb. 26, 1897, no. 9, pp. 99 ff.; *IDR*, May 1895, p. 246; Dec. 1898, pp. 636 ff.

56. *Israelitisches Familienblatt*, May 7, 1903, no. 19, p. 11; *AZJ*, Feb. 17, 1905, no. 7, pp. 77. The newssheet that Steinhardt edited was called *Blätter für Erzeihung und Unterricht* and appeared in the weekly issues of the *Israelitisches Familienblatt*, published in Hamburg.

57. *AZJ*, Feb. 17, 1905, no. 7, p. 78.

58. Salo Adler, *Das Schulunterhaltungsgesetz und die preussischen Bürger jüdischen Glaubens*, p. 13.

59. *AZJ*, Feb. 17, 1905, no. 7, p. 78.

60. *Israelitisches Familienblatt*, Oct. 27, 1904, no. 43, p. 9.

61. *AZJ*, Feb. 17, 1905, no. 7, p. 78.

62. Adler, *Das Schulunterhaltungsgesetz*, pp. 30 ff.

63. *Verhandlungen des preuss. Abgeordnetenhauses*, Mar. 9, 1901, p. 3044.

64. *IDR*, Feb. 1905, pp. 63 ff.

65. Ibid., p. 66.

66. DZA, rep. 76 III, sec. I, Abt. XIIIa, no. 23, vol. IX, Minister of Education to the provincial school board of Brandenburg, dated Berlin, June 21, 1904.

67. *IDR*, Feb. 1906, pp. 66–67.

68. *Verhandlungen des preuss. Abgeordnetenhauses*, May 13, 1904, pp. 5342 ff.

69. Felix Makower, *Bericht über die Tätigkeit des Verbandes der deutschen Juden bei der Vorbereitung des preussischen Volksschulunterhaltungsgesetzes von 1906*, p. 3.

70. CAHJP, rep. Kn II A II, no. 4, memorandum of Rabbi Vogelstein to the chairman of the Königsberg community's executive board, dated Königsberg, Aug. 25, 1904.

71. Ibid., minutes of the meeting of the Verband's executive committee on Dec. 27, 1904.

72. Ibid., petition of the Verband to the Minister of Education, dated Aug. 1904.

73. For the text of the school bill, see *Sammlung der Drucksachen des preussischen Hauses der Abgeordneten (1905–1906)*, 2, no. 11.

74. *Verhandlungen des preuss. Abgeordnetenhauses*, Dec. 11, 1905, p. 186.

75. *AZJ*, Dec. 8, 1905, no. 49, p. 578; Dec. 15, 1905, no. 50, pp.

589 ff.; *IDR*, Feb. 1906, pp. 66 ff.; *MVAA*, Dec. 13, 1905, pp. 394 ff.

76. *AZJ*, Feb. 2, 1906, no. 5, p. 53.

77. Makower, *Bericht*, pp. 5 ff.

78. Ibid.

79. Makower was elected in 1896 to the executive committee of the Liberal Association, a grouping of Reform Jews in the Berlin community. At that time he expressed the opinion that congregations would unwittingly segregate Jewish schoolchildren if they established their own confessional public schools. See *AZJ*, Dec. 11, 1896, no. 50, Beilage.

80. For the text of the petitions of Dec. 10, 1905, and Jan. 7, 1906, see Makower, *Bericht*, appendixes 3 and 4.

81. Ibid., p. 7; Felix Makower, "Die Separatisten und der V.d.J.," *Korrespondenz-Blatt des Verbandes der deutschen Juden*, Oct. 1912, no. 12, p. 14.

82. *Israelitisches Familienblatt*, Apr. 5, 1906, no. 14, pp. 9–10.

83. HSt, rep. 166b, no.4013, copy of the petition that the *Vorsteheramter der Israeliten* addressed to the Diet on Jan. 14, 1906.

84. *Israelit*, Jan. 18, 1906, no. 3, p. 1.

85. Ibid.

86. Ibid.

87. *Israelit*, Mar. 1, 1906, no. 9, p. 2.

88. *Israelit*, Feb. 1, 1906, no. 5, p. 4.

89. For the text of the petitions of the Orthodox Jews, see Makower, *Bericht*, appendixes 9 and 10.

90. *Israelit*, Dec. 28, 1905, no. 104, p. 2149; Jan. 18, 1906, no. 3, p. 2.

91. Makower, *Bericht*, appendix 9.

92. Articles in the *Israelit*, Jan. 18, 1906, and Mar. 1, 1906, indicate the arguments that Rabbi Cahn made.

93. CAHJP, rep. Kn II A II, no. 4, minutes of the meeting of the Verband's executive committee on Jan. 7, 1906.

94. Makower, *Bericht*, p. 9.

95. "Bericht der XII. Kommission über den Gesetzentwurf, betreffend die Unterhaltung der öffentlichen Volksschulen," *Sammlung der Drucksachen (1905–1906)*, 7: 3838.

96. Makower, *Bericht*, p. 12; Felix Makower, "Ist Art. 14 der preussischen Verfassung anwendbar auf die im Schulgesetzentwurf geregelten Fragen? "

97. "Bericht der XII. Kommission," p. 3841.

98. Makower, *Bericht*, p. 9.

99. Ibid., p. 10.

100. *Verhandlungen des preuss. Abgeordnetenhauses*, May 23, 1906, pp. 5178 ff.

101. Ibid., p. 5139; May 25, 1906, pp. 5189–91; "Bericht der XII. Kommission," p. 3841.

102. *Verhandlungen des preuss. Abgeordnetenhauses*, May 23, 1906, pp. 5145, 5172.

103. *Sammlung der Drucksachen (1905–1906)*, 9, no. 364.

104. Ibid., no. 370.

105. "Bericht der XII. Kommission," p. 3838.

106. Ibid., pp. 3836–37.

107. Ibid., p. 3839.

108. Ibid., p. 3839.

109. Ibid., p. 3838.

110. Ibid., p. 3838.

111. Ibid., p. 3863.

112. Ibid., p. 3865.

113. Makower, *Bericht*, p. 13.

114. For the text of the petitions of the Orthodox Jews, see Makower, *Bericht*, appendixes 14–16.

115. Ibid., pp. 17–19; Makower, "Die Separatisten und der V.d.J.," pp. 10 ff.

116. *Verhandlungen des preuss. Abgeordnetenhauses*, May 25, 1905, p. 5193.

117. Ibid., p. 5192.

118. Makower, *Bericht*, pp. 9–10.

119. *Israelitisches Familienblatt*, July 5, 1906, no. 27, p. 10.

120. For the text of the School Law of July 28, 1906, see *Zentralblatt für die gesamte Unterrichtsverwaltung in Preussen*, Sept. 1906, pp. 622–55.

121. *Verhandlungen des preuss. Abgeordnetenhauses*, May 25, 1906, p. 5188.

122. Ibid., p. 5188.

123. *IDR*, July/Aug. 1906, p. 459.

124. *AZJ*, July 20, 1906, no. 29, p. 339; July 27, 1906, no. 30, p. 350.

125. *IDR*, July/Aug. 1906, p. 459.

126. For the ministry's directive of Feb. 25, 1907, on the execution of the School Law, see *Zentralblatt für die gesamte Unterrichtsverwaltung in Preussen*, Apr. 1907, pp. 305–12.

127. HSt, rep. 150, no. 1130, Department of School Affairs to the Oberpräsident of Hesse, dated Cassel, Mar. 7, 1908; rep. 166b, no.

3595, Department of School Affairs to the *Oberpräsident* of Hesse, dated Cassel, Dec. 9, 1908, copy.

128. HSt, rep. 166b, no. 3595, reports of the *Landräte* to the school department, which had requested on Oct. 26, 1908, data on contributions that the communes were making toward the maintenance expenses of the Jewish schools; rep. 166, no. 5248, report of the *Landrat* of the county of Gelnhausen, dated Nov. 13, 1908.

129. HSt, rep. 166b, no. 3595. The report of the *Landrat* in Hofgeismar on Oct. 31, 1908, mentioned the dissatisfaction of two congregations with the sums that the communes had offered them. The *Landrat* of Kirchhain related in his letter of Oct. 30, 1908, that Jewish communities had asked him to arbitrate disagreements with the communes and that he was negotiating with Rabbi Munk, a member of the *Vorsteheramt* in Marburg, to resolve the disputes. In his report on Nov. 6, 1908, the *Landrat* of Melsungen made note of two congregations that had contested the method that the communes had used to assess their contributions. He wrote that one congregation had already appealed to the *Vorsteheramt* for help in arriving at an equitable agreement

130. *Das neue Volksschulunterhaltungsgesetz: Materialen und Ratschläge für die jüdischen Gemeinden Preussens* (Frankfurt, 1907), pp. 31 ff.; Freund, *Die Rechtsstellung der Juden*, pp. 53 ff.

131. HSt, rep. 166b, no. 4013, *Vorsteheramt der Israeliten* to Department of School Affairs, dated Cassel, May 19, 1908; rep. 166b, no. 3595, *Landrat* to Department of School Affairs, dated Kirchhain, Oct. 30, 1908; *Landrat* to Department of School Affairs, dated Rosenberg, Nov. 12, 1908.

132. HSt, rep. 166, no. 5248, stenciled directive of the Department of School Affairs to the *Landräte*, dated Cassel, June 6, 1908.

133. HSt, rep. 166, no. 5247, Minister of Education to Department of School Affairs, dated Berlin, Aug. 9, 1909.

134. Ibid., two letters of the Department of School Affairs to Minister of Education, dated Cassel, Sept. 24 and Nov. 29, 1909, copies.

135. Ibid., Minister of Education to Department of School Affairs, dated Berlin, Dec. 24, 1909.

136. Ibid., Minister of Education to *Vorsteheramt der Israeliten* in Cassel, dated Berlin, Mar. 3, 1910, copy.

137. HSt, rep. 166b, no. 4011, stenciled directive of the Minister of Education to school departments in the provincial districts, dated Berlin, July 10, 1907.

138. HSt, rep. 166b, no. 4011, reports of the *Landräte* in the Provincial District of Cassel. GSt, rep. 30 II, no. 2722, reports of the

Landräte in the Provincial District of Bromberg; rep. 6 B XIII, no. 7, report of the *Landrat* of the county of Westhavelland to the school department for the Provincial District of Potsdam, dated Rathenau, Aug. 30, 1907.

139. HSt, rep. 166b, no. 4011, petitions of the *Vorsteherämter der Israeliten* in Cassel and Fulda to Minister of Education, respectively, dated Feb. 11 and Mar. 30, 1908, copies; petitions of the executive boards of the synagogue congregations to the school department for the Provincial District of Cassel in March 1908. HHst, rep. 405, no. 17707, petitions of the executive boards of the synagogue congregations to the school department for the Provincial District of Wiesbaden in May 1908.

140. *IDR*, Mar. 1908, pp. 228-29.

141. *IDR*, Feb. 1908, p. 97.

142. HSt, rep. 166b, no. 4011, stenciled directive of the Minister of Education to the school departments in the provincial districts, dated Berlin, May 6, 1908.

143. Ibid., reports of the *Landräte*.

144. *Verhandlungen des preuss. Abgeordnetenhauses*, May 8, 1909, pp. 6067-68.

145. HHst, rep. 425, no. 889, Philipp Schwartzkopff to Martin Philippson, dated Berlin, June 23, 1909, copy.

146. CAHJP, rep. Kn II A II, no. 5, minutes of the meeting of the Verband's executive committee on Sept. 19, 1909.

147. *AZJ*, Oct. 4, 1907, no. 40, p. 470; *Israelitisches Familienblatt*, Sept. 1, 1910, no. 35, p. 9; Sept. 8, 1910, no. 36, p. 9.

148. *Jüdisches Volksblatt*, Aug. 8, 1913, no. 32.

149. *Zentralblatt für die gesamte Unterrichtsverwaltung in Preussen*, Apr. 1908, pp. 469-70.

150. *Israelitisches Familienblatt*, Nov. 3, 1910, no. 44, p. 15; Oct. 17, 1911, no. 42, p. 9.

151. "Protokoll des 5. Verbandstages der jüdischen Lehrervereine am 27. und 28. Dezember 1910," printed in serial form in the *Israelitisches Familienblatt*, Mar. 2, 1911, no. 9 and the following issues.

152. *Israelitisches Familienblatt*, Apr. 10, 1913, no. 15, p. 11; Erich Simon, "Das Lernbedürfnis der preussischen Juden im Lichte der Statistik," *Zeitschrift für Demographie und Statistik der Juden* 10 (1914): 83-84.

153. *Israelitisches Familienblatt*, Sept. 8, 1910, no. 36, p. 9; Sept. 15, 1910, no. 37, p. 9; Sept. 22, 1910, no. 38, p. 11.

154. *Israelitisches Familienblatt*, Sept. 8, 1910, no. 36, p. 9.

155. CAHJP, rep. Kn II A III, no. 3, Peritz to the executive board

of the Königsberg community, dated Königsberg, Oct. 30, 1913. Peritz was the executive secretary of the Lehrerverband.

156. "Protokoll des 5. Verbandstages," *Israelitisches Familienblatt,* Apr. 13, 1911, no. 15, p. 9; "Protokoll der Vorstandssitzung des Verbandes der jüdischen Lehrervereine am 24. und 25. Dezember 1912," *Israelitisches Familienblatt,* Feb. 6, 1913, no. 6, p. 11.

157. *MDIG,* Sept. 1913, no. 84, pp. 120 ff. The Jews living in Bavaria shared the reluctance of their coreligionists in Prussia to open Jewish public schools. Of the 311 congregations in Bavaria in 1907, only 85 made use of the legal right to establish their own confessional school. As in Prussia it was the small congregations, not the large communities such as Munich and Nürnberg, that maintained separate schools. See "Die Verhältnisse der israelitischen Kultusgemeinden in Bayern nach dem Stande des Jahres 1907," *Zeitschrift des Bayerischen Statistischen Landesamts,* 1910, no. 3.

158. *MDIG,* Sept. 1913, no. 84, pp. 25 ff.

159. Ibid., p. 48.

160. "Protokoll der ausserordentlichen Vorstandssitzung des Verbandes der jüdischen Lehrervereine am 7. September 1913," *Israelitisches Familienblatt,* Sept. 25, 1913, no. 39, p. 10; see also July 3, 1913, no. 27, p. 9.

161. CAHJP, rep. Kn II A III, no. 3, circular entitled "Zur gefälligen besonderen Beachtung!"

162. *Protokoll des 6. Verbandstages des Verbandes der jüdischen Lehrervereine am 29. und 30. Dezember 1913,* pp. 40, 51, 59.

163. *MDIG,* May/June 1914, no. 86, p. 49.

164. *AZJ,* July 21, 1911, no. 29, p. 337; *MDIG,* Sept. 1913, no. 84, p. 27.

165. *AZJ,* July 21, 1911, no. 29, pp. 337-38.

166. *Verhandlungen des preuss. Abgeordnetenhauses,* Apr. 18, 1910, p. 4162.

167. Salo Adler, *Für und wider die jüdische Volksschule in Preussen,* p. 16.

168. *AZJ,* July 21, 1911, no. 29, p. 337.

169. *AZJ,* Nov. 4, 1910, no. 44, p. 525.

170. *AZJ,* July 21, 1911, no. 29, p. 338.

171. *MDIG,* Sept. 1913, no. 84, p. 28.

172. *MDIG,* Nov. 1913, no. 85, pp. 2-3.

173. *MDIG,* May/June 1914, no. 86, p. 48.

174. Ibid., p. 53.

175. *Jüdisches Volksblatt,* July 14, 1911, no. 28; July 25, 1913, no. 30.

176. CZA, rep. A 15, no. VII/25, stenciled minutes of the meeting

of the central committee of the German Zionist Organization on Nov. 3, 1912.

177. *Jüdische Rundschau*, Oct. 15, 1913, no. 42, p. 447; Nov. 14, 1913, no. 46, p. 494.

178. *AZJ*, July 21, 1911, no. 29, p. 338.

179. Ibid., p. 338.

180. CAHJP, rep. K Ge 2, no. 64, circular sent out by the provisional committee of the "Friends of the Gemeindebund."

181. *IDR*, Dec. 1909, pp. 703 ff. Before the enactment of an imperial law on political associations on May 15, 1908, Prussian state legislation prohibited women from participation in political organizations. Soon after the Reichstag passed the new law, removing this restriction, the Centralverein encouraged Jewish women to make use of their new right and to join the defense movement. See *IDR*, May 1908, pp. 288–89; June 1908, p. 331.

182. *IDR*, Feb. 1909, p. 112.

183. *IDR*, July/Aug. 1908, p. 460.

184. *IDR*, June 1911, pp. 223 ff.

185. Ibid., p. 326; Dec. 1911, pp. 661–62.

186. *IDR*, Mar. 1911, p. 147; June 1911, pp. 315–16, 323.

187. *IDR*, May/June 1913, p. 256.

188. Ibid., p. 257.

189. Ibid., p. 258.

190. *IDR*, Mar. 1911, p. 123.

191. Ibid., p. 121.

192. *IDR*, Sept. 1913, pp. 409 ff.

193. Ibid., p. 411.

194. CAHJP, rep. Da 42, Horwitz to the executive board of the Danzig community, dated Berlin, Nov. 6, 1912. See also *IDR*, June 1911, p. 317.

195. Horwitz's letter cited above.

196. *IDR*, June 1912, pp. 289 ff.

197. *IDR*, Jan. 1913, p. 29.

198. *IDR*, June 1912, pp. 292–93.

CHAPTER 8

1. Jehuda Reinharz, *Fatherland or Promised Land: The Dilemma of the German Jew, 1893–1914*, p. 66.

2. Uriel Tal, *Christians and Jews in Germany*, pp. 78–79.

3. Jacob Toury, *Die politischen Orientierungen der Juden in Deutschland*, pp. 203, 212.

4. *IDR*, July/Aug. 1911, p. 380. See also *IDR*, Feb. 1897, p. 118,

and the history of the Centralverein that Alphonse Levy wrote on the twentieth anniversary of its founding in *IDR*, Feb. 1913, pp. 51 ff.

5. For the Centralverein's statutes, see *IDR*, Mar./Apr. 1909, pp. 213 ff.

6. *IDR*, May/June 1913, p. 196. On German-Jewish self-perception during the Wilhelminian Empire, see Peter Gay's "Encounter with Modernism: German Jews in German Culture, 1888-1914," pp. 23 ff.

7. *IDR*, Mar./Apr. 1909, pp. 160-61.

8. *IDR*, June 1912, p. 269.

9. *IDR*, May/June 1913, p. 196.

10. Ibid., p. 220.

11. Fuchs, *Um Deutschtum und Judentum*, p. 252.

12. *IDR*, June 1912, p. 268.

13. *IDR*, Aug. 1900, pp. 382-83.

14. *IDR*, Oct. 1903, p. 606.

15. Ibid., p. 581.

16. *IDR*, Jan. 1912, p. 4.

17. *Verhandlungen des preuss. Abgeordnetenhauses*, Apr. 5, 1913, p. 13465.

18. Ibid., Apr. 2, 1913, pp. 13183 ff.

19. Ibid., p. 13224.

20. André Chouraqui, *Cents An d'Histoire: L'Alliance Israélite Universelle et la Renaissance juive contemporaine*, pp. 140-41; Michael R. Marrus, *The Politics of Assimilation: A Study of the Jewish Community at the Time of the Dreyfus Affair*, pp. 221 ff.

21. DZA, rep. 76 III, sec. 1, Abt. XIIIa, no. 23, vol. IX, *Polizeipräsident* to Minister of Religious Affairs and Education, dated Berlin, Apr. 7, 1901.

22. *IDR*, Apr. 1905, p. 214.

23. *IDR*, Apr. 1902, p. 201.

BIBLIOGRAPHY

UNPUBLISHED SOURCES

Bundesarchiv Koblenz
Nachlass Georg Gothein
Nachlass Richard Roesicke
Central Archives for the History of the Jewish People, Jerusalem
INV 124 Protokolle des Centralvereins 1895–1905
INV 751/3 Rundschreiben des Centralvereins
Kn II A II, nos. 4, 5, and 6 Verband der deutschen Juden. Protokolle des Ausschusses 1904–20
Acta der Synagogen-Gemeinde zu Danzig
Acta der Synagogen-Gemeinde zu Hamburg
Acta der Synagogen-Gemeinde zu Königsberg
M 4/1 Rabbinerverband in Deutschland. Protokolle und Correspondenz 1896–99.
Central Zionist Archives, Jerusalem
A 15 Files of Max Bodenheimer
A 8 Files of Adolf Friedemann
A 11 Files of Arthur Hantke
A 142 Files of Alfred Klee
A 102 Files of Hugo Schachtel
Deutsches Zentralarchiv, Merseburg
Rep. 76 III Sect. I, Abt. XIIIa, no. 51 Acta betreffend die gesetzliche Regelung des Judenwesens
Rep. 76 III Sect. I, Abt. XIIIa, no. 23 Acta betreffend die Ausführung der Allerhöchsten Beordnung von 23. Juli 1847 über die Verhältnisse der Juden in den Königlichen Preussischen Staaten
Geheimes Staatsarchiv, Berlin-Dahlem
Rep. 30 II, no. 2722 Regierung Bromberg. Einrichtung des jüdischen Elementar-Schulwesens und Erteilung des jüdischen Religionsunterrichts 1890–1913
Rep. 180, no. 16063 Regierung Danzig. Bestimmungen über den Religionsunterricht für die Kinder konfessioneller Minderheiten 1876–1910
Rep. 6 B, no. XIII/7 Landratsamt Westhavelland. Jüdisches Kultus- und Schulwesen 1843–1929
Hessisches Hauptstaatsarchiv, Wiesbaden

Rep. 405, no. 12748 Akten betreffend den israelitischen Unterricht
Rep. 405, no. 17707 Akten der Königlichen Regierung zu Wiesbaden betreffend die Nachweisung der den leistungsschwachen Synagogengemeinden behufs des Religionsunterrichts zu gewährenden Staatsbeihilfe 1908–09
Rep. 425, no. 889 Jüdischer Religionsunterricht und jüdische Religionslehrer 1863–1924
Hessisches Staatsarchiv, Marburg
Rep. 150, no. 1130 Oberpräsidium der Provinz Hessen-Nassau. Ausführung des Gesetzes von 28. Juli 1906 betreffend die Unterhaltung der öffentlichen Volksschulen 1907–09
Rep. 166 Preussische Regierung Kassel, Abteilung für Kirchen und Schulen:
No. 3595 Beitragspflicht des Staates und der Gemeinden zur Unterhaltung israelitischen Schulen 1903–08
No. 4011 Israelitischer Religionsunterricht, auch Staatsbeihilfe 1892–1908
No. 4012 Israelitische Elementar-Volksschulen des Regierungsbezirks, Vol 1, 1893–1900; no. 4013, vol. 2, 1901–08; no. 5247, vol. 3, 1909–37
No. 5248 Israelitisches Volksschulwesen 1909–33
Rep. 180, no. 4118 Landratsamt Gelnhausen. Judensachen im Allgemeinen 1859–1933
Rep. 180, no. 2876 Landratsamt Ziegenhain. Israelitisches Schulwesen 1826–1912
Niedersächsisches Staatsarchiv, Wolfenbüttel
Nachlass Karl Schrader

PUBLISHED SOURCES

Periodicals

Allgemeine Zeitung des Judentums, Berlin
Berliner Tageblatt, Berlin
General-Anzeiger für die gesamten Interessen des Judentums, Berlin
Hessische Landeszeitung, Marburg
Im Deutschen Reich, Berlin
Der Israelit, Mainz
Israelitisches Familienblatt, Hamburg
Israelitisches Gemeindeblatt, Cologne
Israelitisches Wochenblatt, Berlin
Israelitische Wochenschrift, Berlin

Jüdische Rundschau, Berlin
Jüdisches Volksblatt, Breslau
K. C. Blätter: Monatsschrift der im Kartell-Konvent vereinigten Korporationen, Berlin
Mitteilungen vom Deutsch-Israelitischen Gemeindebund, Berlin
Mitteilungen der Freien Vereinigung für die Interessen des orthodoxen Judentums, Mainz
Mitteilungen des Liberalen Vereins für die Angelegenheiten der jüdischen Gemeinde zu Berlin, Berlin
Mitteilungen aus dem Verein zur Abwehr des Antisemitismus, Berlin
Die Nation, Berlin
Die Welt, Cologne and Berlin
Zeitschrift für Demographie und Statistik der Juden, Berlin

Other Primary Sources

Adler, S. *Assimilation oder Nationaljudentum?* Berlin, 1894
Adler, Salo. *Für und wider die jüdische Volksschule in Preussen.* Frankfurt, 1913.
——. *Das Schulunterhaltungsgesetz und die preussischen Bürger jüdischen Glaubens.* Frankfurt, 1906.
Auerbach, Fritz. *Der Antisemitismus und das freisinnige Judentum.* Frankfurt, 1893.
"Bericht der XII. Kommission über den Gesetzentwurf betreffend die Unterhaltung der öffentlichen Volksschulen." *Sammlung der Drucksachen des Preussischen Hauses der Abgeordneten* (1905–1906), vol. 7.
Breslauer, Bernhard. *Die Abwanderung der Juden aus der Provinz Posen.* Berlin, 1909.
——. *Die Zurücksetzung der Juden an den Universitäten Deutschlands.* Berlin, 1911.
——. *Die Zurücksetzung der Juden im Justizdienst.* Berlin, 1907.
Centralverein deutscher Staatsbürger jüdischen Glaubens. *An die deutschen Staatsbürger jüdischen Glaubens.* Berlin, 1893.
——. *Die Gutachten der Sachverständigen über den Konitzer Mord.* Berlin, 1903.
——. *Mitglieder-Verzeichnis.* Berlin, 1893; 1895; 1896; 1897; 1902; 1905; 1908; 1912.
Ein Wort an die Deutschen Staatsbürger jüdischen Glaubens. Mainz, 1896.
Freund, Ismar. *Die Rechtsstellung der Juden im preussischen Volksschulrecht.* Berlin, 1908.

Fuchs, Eugen. *Bericht der Rechtsschutz-Commission über ihre bisherige Tätigkeit.* Berlin, 1894.

———. *Um Deutschtum und Judentum. Gesammelte Reden und Aufsätze.* Frankfurt, 1919.

Goldstein, Moritz, "Deutsch-jüdischer Parnass." *Der Kunstwart* 15 (1912): 281–94.

———. "German Jewry's Dilemma before 1914." *Leo Baeck Institute Yearbook* 2 (1957): 236–54.

Holländer, Ludwig. *Die sozialen Voraussetzungen der antisemitischen Bewegung in Deutschland.* Berlin, 1909.

Huber, Ernst Rudolf. *Dokumente zur Deutschen Verfassungsgeschichte.* 2 vols. Stuttgart, 1961.

Kollenscher, Max. *Jüdische Gemeindepolitik.* Berlin, 1909.

Landsberger, Artur, ed. *Judentaufen.* Munich, 1912.

Lehmann, Emil. *Gesammelte Schriften.* Berlin, 1899.

[Löwenfeld, Raphael]. *Schutzjudentum oder Staatsbürger?* Berlin, 1893.

Makower, Felix. *Bericht über die Tätigkeit des Verbandes der deutschen Juden bei der Vorbereitung des preussischen Volksschulunterhaltungsgesetzes von 1906.* Berlin, 1907.

———. "Ist Art. 14 der preussischen Verfassung anwendbar auf die im Schulgesetzentwurf geregelten Fragen?" *Deutsche Juristen-Zeitung,* February 1, 1906, no. 3, pp. 195–97.

Mendelsohn, Martin. *Die Pflicht der Selbstverteidigung: Jahresbericht des Vorsitzenden des Centralvereins.* Berlin, 1894.

Moses, Julius, ed. *Die Lösung der Judenfrage.* Berlin, 1907.

Nathan, Paul. *Xanten-Cleve: Betrachtungen zum Prozess Buschhoff.* Berlin, 1892.

Das neue Volksschulunterhaltungsgesetz: Materialien und Ratschläge für die Gemeinden Preussens. Frankfurt, 1907.

Ostwald, Hans, ed. *Die Assimilation der Juden.* Berlin, 1913.

Parmod, Maximilian. *Antisemitismus und Strafrechtspflege.* Berlin, 1894.

Der dritte Parteitag der Freisinnigen Volkspartei. Berlin, 1897.

Der siebente Parteitag der Freisinnigen Volkspartei. Berlin, 1907.

Der zweite Parteitag der Fortschrittlichen Volkspartei. Berlin, 1912.

Protokoll des Verbandstages des Verbandes der jüdischen Lehrervereine im Deutschen Reiche am 27. und 28. Dezember 1910. Hamburg, 1911.

Protokoll des Verbandstages des Verbandes der jüdischen Lehrervereine am 29. und 30. Dezember 1913. Hamburg, 1914.

Revidirtes Statut für die Jüdische Gemeinde zu Berlin. Berlin, 1896.

Ruppin, Arthur, and Thon, Jacob. *Das Anteil der Juden am Urichtswesen in Preussen.* Berlin, 1905.

Satzung der Synagogengemeinde zu Königsberg in Preussen. Königsberg, 1903.

Segall, Jacob. *Die beruflichen und sozialen Verhältnisse der Juden in Deutschland.* Berlin, 1912.

Simon, J. *Wehrt Euch! Ein Mahnwort an die Juden.* Berlin, 1893.

Sonnenfeld, Hugo. *Zum Meineidsprozess gegen Moritz Lewy in Konitz.* Berlin, 1901.

Statistisches Jahrbuch des Deutsch-Israelitischen Gemeindebund. Berlin, 1899, 1901, 1903, 1905, 1907.

Statut der israelitischen Cultusgemeinde in München. Munich, 1892.

Statut der Synagogen-Gemeinde Köln. Cologne, 1896.

Stenographische Berichte über die Verhandlungen des preussischen Abgeordnetenhauses. Berlin, 1892–1914.

Stenographische Berichte über die Verhandlungen des Reichstages. Berlin, 1892–1914.

Theilhaber, Felix. *Der Untergang der deutschen Juden.* Munich, 1911.

Thon, Jacob. *Die jüdischen Gemeinden und Vereine in Deutschland.* Berlin, 1906.

Verband der deutschen Juden. *Korrespondenz-Blatt.*

———. *Stenographischer Bericht über die erste Hauptversammlung, den 30. Oktober 1905.* Berlin, 1905.

———. *Stenographischer Bericht über die zweite Hauptversammlung, den 13. Oktober 1907.* Berlin, 1907.

———. *Stenographischer Bericht über die dritte Hauptversammlung, den 17. Oktober 1909.* Berlin, 1909.

———. *Stenographischer Bericht über die vierte Hauptversammlung, den 5. November 1911.* Berlin, 1911.

———. *Stenographischer Bericht über die fünfte Hauptversammlung, den 9. November 1913.* Berlin, 1914.

———. *Wie wird im preussischen Heer die Beförderung von Juden zu Reserveoffizieren vereitelt? Beispielfälle.* Berlin, 1911.

Verfassung der Hamburger Deutsch-Israelitischen Gemeinde. Hamburg, 1908.

"Die Verhältnisse der israelitischen Kultusgemeinden in Bayern nach dem Stande des Jahres 1907." *Zeitschrift des Bayerischen Statistischen Landesamt* (1910), no. 3.

Volks- oder Salonjudentum? Berlin, 1893.

Zentralblatt für Unterrichtsverwaltung in Preussen.

Selected Secondary Sources

Adler, Hans Günther. *Die Juden in Deutschland.* Munich, 1960.

Alexander, Thomas. *The Prussian Elementary Schools.* New York, 1918.

Anderson, Eugene. "The Prussian Volksschule in the Nineteenth Century." In *Entstehung und Wandel der modernen Gesellschaft. Festschrift für Hans Rosenberg,* edited by Gerhard Ritter. Berlin, 1970.

Angress, Werner. "Prussia's Army and the Jewish Reserve Officer Controversy before World War I." *Leo Baeck Institute Yearbook* 17 (1972): 19–42.

Asch, Adolph, and Philippson, Johanna. "Self-Defense at the Turn of the Century: the Emergence of the K.C." *Leo Baeck Institute Yearbook* 3 (1958): 122–38.

Bertram, Jürgen. *Die Wahlen zum Deutschen Reichstag vom Jahre 1912.* Düsseldorf, 1964.

Bolkosky, Sidney M. *The Distorted Image: German-Jewish Perceptions of Germans and Germany, 1918–1935.* New York, 1975.

Born, Karl Erich. *Staat und Sozialpolitik seit Bismarcks Sturz.* Wiesbaden, 1957.

Brecht, Arnold, and Glaser, Comstock. *The Art and Technique of Administration in German Ministries.* Cambridge, Mass., 1940.

Cecil, Lamar. "Jew and Junker in Imperial Berlin." *Leo Baeck Institute Yearbook* 20 (1975): 47–58.

Chouraqui, André. *Cents An d'Histoire: L'Alliance Israélite Universelle et la Renaissance juive contemporaine.* Paris, 1965.

Crothers, George Dunlop. *The German Elections of 1907.* New York, 1941.

Demandt, Karl. *Geschichte des Landes Hessen.* Cassel, 1959.

Düding, Dieter. *Der Nationalsoziale Verein 1896–1903.* Munich, 1972.

Ebers, Godehard J. "Staatskirchenrecht." In *Handwörterbuch der Rechtswissenschaft,* edited by Fritz Stier-Somlo and Alexander Elster, vol. 5. Berlin, 1928.

Elm, Ludwig. *Zwischen Fortschritt und Reaktion: Geschichte der Parteien der liberalen Bourgeoisie in Deutschland, 1893–1918.* Berlin, 1968.

Feder, Ernst. *Paul Nathan: Politik und Humanität.* Berlin, 1929.

Foerster, Erich. *Adalbert Falk: Sein Leben und Wirken.* Gotha, 1927.

Freund, Ismar. *Die Emanzipation der Juden in Preussen.* Berlin, 1912.

Fricke, Dieter, ed. *Die bürgerlichen Parteien in Deutschland. Handbuch der Geschichte der bürgerlichen Parteien und anderer bürgerlicher Interessenorganisationen vom Vormärz bis zum Jahre 1945.* 2 vols. Berlin, 1968–70.

Gay, Peter. "Encounter with Modernism: German Jews in German Culture, 1888–1914," *Midstream* 21 (1975): 23–65.

Gerlach, Helmut von. *Von Rechts nach Links.* Zurich, 1937.

Gräter, Carlheinz. *Theodor Barths politische Gedankenwelt.* Würzburg, 1963.

Hamburger, Ernest. *Juden im öffentlichen Leben Deutschlands. Regierungsmitglieder, Beamte und Parlamentarier in der monarchischen Zeit, 1848–1918.* Tübingen, 1968.

Harris, James. "Eduard Lasker: The Jew as National German Politician." *Leo Baeck Institute Yearbook* 20 (1975): 151–77.

Heckart, Beverly, *From Bassermann to Bebel: The Grand Bloc's Quest for Reform in the Kaiserreich.* New Haven, 1974.

Heimberger, Joseph. *Die Staatskirchenrechtliche Stellung der Israeliten in Bayern.* 2nd ed. Tübingen, 1912.

Heuss, Theodor. *Friedrich Naumann.* Stuttgart, 1937.

Hirschberg, Alfred. "Ludwig Holländer, Director of the C.V." *Leo Baeck Institute Yearbook* 7 (1962): 39–74.

Huber, Ernst Rudolf. *Deutsche Verfassungsgeschichte seit 1789.* 4 vols. Stuttgart, 1957–63.

Institute of Social Research. "Analysis of Central-Verein Policy in Germany," New York, 1945. Mimeographed.

Jacob, Herbert. *German Administration since Bismarck.* New Haven, 1963.

Katz, Jacob. *Out of the Ghetto: The Social Background of Jewish Emancipation.* Cambridge, Mass., 1973.

Katz, Leopold. *Die rechtliche Stellung der Israeliten nach dem Staatskirchenrecht des Grossherzogtums Hessen.* Giessen, 1906.

Koszyk, Kurt. *Deutsche Presse im 19. Jahrhundert.* Berlin, 1966.

Lamberti, Marjorie. "The Attempt to Form a Jewish Bloc: Jewish Notables and Politics in Wilhelmian Germany." *Central European History* 3 (1970): 73–93.

——— . "The Prussian Government and the Jews—Official Behaviour and Policy-Making in the Wilhelminian Era." *Leo Baeck Institute Yearbook* 17 (1972): 5–17.

Leschnitzer, Adolf. *Saul und David: Die Problematik der deutschjüdischen Lebensgemeinschaft.* Heidelberg, 1954.

Lestschinsky, Jakob. *Das wirtschaftliche Schicksal des deutschen Judentums*. Berlin, 1932.

Levy, Richard S. *The Downfall of the Anti-Semitic Political Parties in Imperial Germany*. New Haven, 1975.

Lichtheim, Richard. *Die Geschichte des deutschen Zionismus*. Jerusalem, 1954.

Löb, Abraham. *Die Rechtsverhältnisse der Juden im ehemaligen Königsreiche und der jetzigen Provinz Hannover*. Frankfurt, 1908.

Marrus, Michael. "European Jewry and the Politics of Assimilation: Assessment and Reassessment." *Journal of Modern History* 49 (1977): 89–109.

———. *The Politics of Assimilation: A Study of the French Jewish Community at the Time of the Dreyfus Affair*. London, 1971.

Massing, Paul W. *Rehearsal for Destruction: A Study of Anti-Semitism in Imperial Germany*. New York, 1949.

Masur, Gerhard. *Imperial Berlin*. New York, 1970.

Mosse, George L. *The Crisis of German Ideology*. New York, 1964.

Mosse, Werner E., and Paucker, Arnold, ed. *Deutsches Judentum in Krieg und Revolution 1916–1923*. Tübingen, 1971.

———. *Juden im Wilhelminischen Deutschland 1890–1914*. Tübingen, 1976.

Nipperdey, Thomas. *Die Organisation der deutschen Parteien vor 1918*. Düsseldorf, 1961.

Paucker, Arnold. *Der Jüdische Abwehrkampf gegen Antisemitismus und Nationalsozialismus in den letzten Jahren der Weimarer Republik*. Hamburg, 1966.

———. "Zur Problematik einer jüdischen Abwehrstrategie in der deutschen Gesellschaft." In *Judentum im Wilhelminischen Deutschland 1890–1914*, edited by Werner E. Mosse and Arnold Paucker. Tübingen, 1976.

Pistorius, Peter. *Rudolf Breitscheid 1874–1944. Ein biographischer Beitrag zur deutschen Parteigeschichte*. Nürnberg, 1970.

Pulzer, Peter. "Die jüdische Beteiligung an der Politik." In *Judentum im Wilhelminischen Deutschland 1890–1914*, edited by Werner E. Mosse and Arnold Paucker. Tübingen, 1976.

———. *The Rise of Political Anti-Semitism in Germany and Austria*. New York, 1964.

Rathje, Johannes. *Die Welt des Freien Protestantismus: Ein Beitrag zur Deutsch-Evangelischen Geistesgeschichte*. Stuttgart, 1952.

Reinharz, Jehuda. *Fatherland or Promised Land: The Dilemma of the German Jew, 1893–1914*. Ann Arbor, 1975.

Richter, Kurt. *Der Kampf um den Schulgesetzentwurf des Grafen Zedlitz-Trütschler vom Jahre 1892*. Halle, 1934.

Rieger, Paul. *Ein Vierteljahrhundert im Kampf um das Recht und die Zukunft der deutschen Juden. Ein Rückblick auf die Geschichte des Centralvereins deutscher Staatsbürger jüdischen Glaubens in den Jahren 1893-1918*. Berlin, 1918.

Röhl, John C. G. *Germany without Bismarck: The Crisis of Government in the Second Reich, 1890-1900*. Berkeley, 1967.

———. "Higher Civil Servants in Germany, 1890-1900." *Journal of Contemporary History* 2 (1967): 101-21.

Ruppin, Arthur. *Soziologie der Juden*. 2 vols. Berlin, 1930.

Rürup, Reinhard. "German Liberalism and the Emancipation of the Jews." *Leo Baeck Institute Yearbook* 20 (1975): 59-68.

Samuel, Richard, and Thomas, R. Hinton. *Education and Society in Modern Germany*. London, 1949.

Schneider, Karl and Petersilie, Alwin. *Die öffentlichen Volksschulen des preussischen Staates im Jahre 1891*. Berlin, 1893.

Scholem, Gershom. "Jews and Germans." *Commentary* 42 (1966): 31-38.

Schorsch, Ismar. *Jewish Reactions to Anti-Semitism, 1870-1914*. New York, 1972.

———. *On the History of the Political Judgment of the Jew*. Leo Baeck Memorial Lecture no. 20. New York, 1976.

Schwarz, Gotthart. *Theodor Wolff und das "Berliner Tageblatt."* Tübingen, 1968.

Silberner, Edmund. "German Social Democracy and the Jewish Problem Prior to World War I." *Historia Judaica* 15 (1953): 3-48.

Stegmann, Dirk. *Die Erben Bismarcks: Parteien und Verbände in der Spätphase des Wilhelminischen Deutschlands*. Cologne, 1970.

Stern, Fritz. *Gold and Iron: Bismarck, Bleichröder, and the Building of the German Empire*. New York, 1977.

———. *The Politics of Cultural Despair*. New York, 1965.

Stürmer, Michael, ed. *Das kaiserlichen Deutschland: Politik und Gesellschaft, 1870-1918*. Düsseldorf, 1970.

Tal, Uriel. *Christians and Jews in Germany. Politics and Ideology in the Second Reich, 1870-1914*. Ithaca, 1975.

Tews, Johannes. *Ein Jahrhundert preussischer Schulgeschichte: Volksschule und Volksschullehrerstand in Preussen im 19. und 20. Jahrhundert*. Leipzig, 1914.

Toury, Jacob. *Die politischen Orientierungen der Juden in Deutschland*. Tübingen, 1966.

Wandycz, Piotr S. *The Lands of Partitioned Poland, 1795-1918.* Seattle, 1974.

Wegner, Konstanze. *Theodor Barth und die freisinnige Vereinigung.* Tübingen, 1968.

Wilhelm, Kurt. "The Jewish Community in the Post-Emancipation Period." *Leo Baeck Institute Yearbook* 2 (1957): 47-75.

Wolff, Siegfried. *Das Recht der israelitischen Religionsgemeinschaft des Grossherzogtums Baden.* Karlsruhe, 1913.

Zucker, Stanley. "Ludwig Bamberger and the Rise of Anti-Semitism in Germany, 1848-1893." *Central European History* 3 (1970): 332-52.

INDEX